Wisconsin &
Minnesota
Trout Streams

Wisconsin & Minnesota Trout Streams

A Fly-Angler's Guide

Jim Humphrey and Bill Shogren

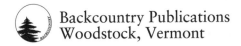

Backcountry Publications
Woodstock, Vermont

An Invitation to the Reader
With time, access points may change, and road numbers, signs, and landmarks
referred to in this book may be altered. If you find that such changes have
occurred near streams described in this book, please let the author and publisher
know, so that corrections can be made in future editions. Other comments and
suggestions are also welcome. Address all correspondence to: Fishing Editor,
Backcountry Publications, PO Box 175, Woodstock, VT 05091-0175.

Library of Congress Cataloging-in-Publication Data
Humphrey, Jim, 1921—
    Wisconsin and Minnesota trout streams : a fly-angler's guide / Jim
Humphrey and Bill Shogren.
      p. cm.
    Includes index.
    ISBN 0-88150-307-X
    1. Trout fishing—Wisconsin—Guidebooks. 2. Trout fishing—Minne-
sota—Guidebooks. 3.Fly fishing—Wisconsin—Guidebooks. 4. Fly fishing—
Minnesota—Guidebooks. 5. Rivers—Wisconsin—Guidebooks. 6. Rivers—
Minnesota—Guidebooks. 7. Wisconsin—Guidebooks. 8. Minnesota—
Guidebooks. I. Shogren, Bill, 1938–. II. Title.
SH688.U6H85   1995
799.1'755—dc20   95-18382
                                                      CIP

Some of the material in this book has appeared in different form in *Fly Fisherman,
Minnesota Sportsman, Outdoor News, Fins and Feathers, Minnesota Trout,* and
Mainstream (the newsletter of the Twin Cities Chapter of Trout Unlimited).

Published by Backcountry Publications
A division of The Countryman Press, Inc.
PO Box 175
Woodstock, Vermont 05091-0175

Cover design by Sally Sherman
Text design by Rachel Kahn
Cover photograph by Joyce Humphrey
Interior photographs by the authors unless otherwise credited
Stream improvement drawings in chapter 1 courtesy Wisconsin Department of
    Natural Resources
Hook removal drawing in chapter 1 provided by O. Mustad and Son (USA), Inc.
Mayfly drawing by Tammy Hiner
Maps by Mapping Specialists, Ltd., Madison, Wisconsin © 1995 The Countryman
    Press, Inc.

Printed in the United States of America

10 9 8 7 6 5 4 3 2

ACKNOWLEDGMENTS

Cheerful and honest thanks are accorded to the many friends who have generously or accidentally contributed to this work, especially the late Dick Frantes, the Acerbic Angler, who fished more Minnesota and Wisconsin streams—and who was skunked on more, by his own admission—than any other fly-fisher. He probably also caught and released more trout than any other fly-fisher. Dick shared his triumphs and failures of more than 35 years. Al Farmes is another fishing partner, an environmental champion, and a better fisherman than either of us.

Bob and Ginnie Adams, Mike Alwin, Jack Ambuhl, Joe and Jim Balestrieri, Mark Beilke, Judge Robert Bowen, Gale Brooks, Jay Bunke, Dan Callahan, Jason Carpenter, Ellen Clark, Royce Dam, Curt Dary, Ron Erlandson, Dave Ewart, Tim Faricy, Dave Fass, Jim Franczyk, DuWayne Fries, Chuck Goossen, John and Vicki Goplin, John Gosz, Forrest Grulke, Pat Hager, Dick Hanousek, Ken Hanson, Bill Haugen, Tom Helgeson, Dr. Mary Henry, Vern Imgrund, Jon Jacobs, Paul Jaeger, Skip James, Louis Jirikowic, Mickey Johnson, Dr. Art Kaemmer, Mike Klimoski, Dr. Will Koukkari, Andy Lamberson, Dan Larson, Ron Manz, Craig Mason, Joe Michl, Pete Mitchell, Ray Newman, Jay Paulson, Shawn Perich, Dave Peterson, Robert Pils, Bob Reynolds, George Rogers, Sandy Rolstad, John Rowell, Mike and Connie Schad, Dick Shira, the late Dr. Ivan Schloff, John and Marilyn Schorn, Dorothy Bergmann Schramm, Bill Schuessler, Dick Schwartz, Gary Sobotta, Bob Talasek, Dick Wachowski—all have contributed wittingly or unwittingly to our education. Others of equal skill and acumen have demonstrated on stream for our benefit. If we have failed to mention your name, forgive us.

Bob and Jean Mitchell of Bob Mitchell's Fly Shop at Lake Elmo, Minnesota, have given professional counsel. We have also gleaned much from the writings of Gary Borger, W. Patrick McCafferty, Caucci and Nastasi, Ernest Schwiebert, Drs. Edmunds, Jensen, and Berner,

Dr. W.L. Hilsenhoff, Swisher and Richards, and Dr. Tom Waters.

The professional fish managers and researchers of the Minnesota and Wisconsin Departments of Natural Resources who have patiently answered our sometimes naive questions are legion, but on some of them we have leaned most heavily: Bill Thorn, Mark Ebbers, Dick Hassinger, Bruce Gilbertson, and Jack Wingate of the Minnesota DNR; Bob Hunt, Ed Avery, Scot Stewart, Marty Engel, Max Johnson, Frank Pratt, and Larry Claggett of the Wisconsin DNR. To them, thanks and admiration for their devotion to the future of trout fishing.

Others of the Wisconsin and Minnesota DNRs are Deserae Bushong, Jim Cox, Peter Eikeland, Paul Eiler, Dennis Ernst, Chris Frieburger, Russ Heiser, James Holzer, Tom Jones, Lee Kerner, Lee Meyers, Rick Nelson, Jeff Roth, Don Schliep, Jim Talley, Ron Theis, Dick Thompson, Tom Thuemler, Dale Togson, and Gene VanDyck.

There are other friends, too numerous to salute, who have worked on legislative matters to ensure scientific trout management that will benefit future generations.

Not least, to our good friend, fellow trout fisher, member of Trout Unlimited, writer, and agent Bob Linsenman, who told us to write this book and who found us a publisher.

DEDICATIONS

For Joyce Eloise Reed Humphrey,
best friend, partner, photographer, and wife,
who made me do it.

—Jim Humphrey

To the late Orrin Stanwick of Henry's Sport Shop,
Eau Claire, Wisconsin, who gave thousands of dollars
to youth fishing programs.

—Bill Shogren

GOOD COMPANY

To the list of distinguished Presidents-fishermen cited in our profile of the Brule River of Wisconsin we can add the name of that good and gentle man, Jimmy Carter, a committed fly-fisher for trout.

We may also go back to the roots of our collective history for an endorsement of the noble sport. George Washington, our greatest President, during a break in the Constitutional Convention on Monday, July 30, 1787, fished for trout near Valley Forge on the evening stream. Later, he noted in his diary that he went fishing for perch near Trenton "with more success." So be cheered. If the trout don't rise for you, know that you are in good company.

Contents

Preface: The Drift of This Book

This is not a scientific treatise, although inevitably some arcane terminology must be employed because trout fishing is part science, even if mostly art. The neophyte, the occasional trout fisher, and the expert will all find something useful. It is a handbook for fly-fishers who want to expand their horizons while they explore the graceful trout streams of Wisconsin and Minnesota. We know these streams, have parked at the bridges and in the Department of Natural Resources parking lots, have waded long into the interiors, have planted trout, and have electro-fished and helped to debrush several. We have fished most of them; on a few we have only walked the banks. Sometimes we have caught trout, too.

The streams that we have chosen to showcase are personal choices. Some sections of streams are so beautiful that the catching of trout is less important than the sound of moving waters and the play of light and shadow among the trees. In truth, this book is not for meat hunters. We have not included any super-productive streams that happen to meander through the town dump.

Several of our rivers are big and brawling, requiring cautious exploration in belted waders and with the support of a staff. Others may be fished in hip boots with short, delicate rods and gossamer leaders. A few should be fished in prayerful attitude from the banks.

It is not difficult to obtain county maps or U.S. Geological Survey maps that reveal those thin blue threads of streams that run through unfamiliar country. The Wisconsin and Minnesota Departments of Natural Resources produce excellent maps of most designated trout waters, but the peripatetic fisher on vacation in strange territory is traveling blindly if he or she relies solely on those publications, as good as they are. That stream that appears so inviting on the map and in the imagination may be only a trickle during the heat of August. Or the stream may be posted against trespass, or that fire trail is meant for four-wheel-drive vehicles only. Many headwaters creeks are too narrow or brushy to allow for even the most accurate of presentations. And sometimes the hike in from the road is too exhausting or too long for the day fisher.

We have had help and advice from countless friends from Trout Unlimited, from the Federation of Fly Fishers, and from the dedicated professionals of the states' Departments of Natural Resources. Additional information has been gleaned by watching, or reading the works of, more accomplished anglers. While help was always welcome, we have not always accepted the advice. Egregious mistakes are our own.

Reasonable people will aver that one stream is better than another. We've had fishers tell us that a stretch of river is dead. Others have enjoyed the best fishing of their lives there a week later. One experienced angler insisted there were no Hex or brown drakes on his river; a second expert gave us time frames for both emergences. Taxonomists may disagree over the classification of a mayfly. Many of us have a decided preference for best length and weight of rod for use on our midwestern streams. Everybody has his secret "meat fly" that is better than all others.

We have tried to report factually on the character and fishability of these fine streams, but conditions change from year to year—flash floods may alter watercourses or scour aquatic life, dams may be removed and improve the habitat for trout, beavers may impound free-flowing streams, drought can reduce flows to a trickle. Streams may alter their character by reason of logging, farming, development, or neglect along their corridors. Certain species of aquatic insects may decrease in number or disappear. Fishing regulations will change as the fisheries researchers acquire new knowledge. A dozen other factors can affect trout fishing in a stream between the time of research and publication of the information.

We may have missed a notable hatch of mayflies because we weren't there at the right time, or our superb experience on a stream may have been the result of happenstance—sheer luck, if you will.

Inevitably, some errors have crept into our maps or travel directions. Roads and bridges can be rerouted between the times of our surveys and publication. Road names may be changed by fiat of county commissioners. When you find a grievous error, please write to the fishing editor of Countryman Press. We'll try to do better next time.

Sometimes the "I" used in our reports is Bill telling the story, sometimes Jim. The "we" may be a composite of overlapping experiences. We don't care for the "Me and Joe" stories any more than you do—tales of how me and Joe caught big fish—but often we must use the personal pronouns to give you the "feel" of a stream or sense of place.

In the course of our far-flung explorations, we have gone headfirst down a steep bank on the Root River, snared by barbed wire. We have stepped off a bank cover to submerge ourselves and a new microcassette recorder. We have braved snow and sleet and the doldrums of midsummer. All for you!

We've been confronted by a surly badger in southwestern Wisconsin, and Paddy or Beverly Beaver has put down our trout on numerous occasions. Too often we've had to pull stakes before the possibilities of a grand stream were exhausted. But someone has to do the grub work, you will say.

We have encountered a young barred owl crying for its mother, and the mother replying with her seven hoots from the vastness of the woods. We've had a bear and her cub cross our path, and had wild turkeys run from us. We've seen moose, the rare "cross fox," a fisher, and coyotes, and have heard the howlings of a wolf pack on spectral nights.

We've had otter kits, paws on a log and peeping over, watching us while we watched them. We've seen sandhill cranes, and white flies patrolling at dusk, trailing their banners.

We've had triumphs and failures, from the secret streams of southeastern Minnesota, through the green and gentle lands of west central Wisconsin, to the primitive tangles of northeastern Wisconsin and the North Shore of Minnesota. Alas, we have not yet encountered a mountain lion. And we missed by a week or so the chance to fly-fish for a hippopotamus in the Mecan River.

We've dined on superb but inexpensive fare in many friendly supper clubs, and have lunched alfresco at streamside on mushrooms and magnificent Wisconsin cheese, with a split of chenin blanc to wash them down—even while trout were rising.

The air is pure, the folks are friendly, and the landowners are cooperative (mostly). The scenery is often spectacular, and the trout will test your acumen and skill. Paradise!

Wisconsin and Minnesota may be unsung in the fly-fishing annals, but if you like the thought of 3000 trout streams and more than 12,000 miles of designated trout waters, come fish with us.

PHOTO BY DON BRENEMAN

The trout lily, whose leaf markings resemble the skin of a brook trout, welcomes spring anglers to the woods of northern Minnesota.

1

Introduction to Wisconsin and Minnesota Trout Fishing

THE LAND AND THE SEASONS

This is an immense land of more than 135,000 square miles—a ragged square some 400 miles north to south and another 400 east to west. Its population of 9 million is spread thinly through the vast conifer forests, bogs, and lakelands of the north and along the major waterways, but is more heavily concentrated where the land is intensively farmed in the southern half. From the spate rivers of the Arrowhead country along the North Shore of Lake Superior to the spring creeks of southwestern Wisconsin, there is a spectrum of waters and scenic delights for every fisherman, even a couple of "mountains" rising to 2000 feet. The topography is generally flat or rolling, except for the pitches from the escarpment of the North Shore and the drop through hardwood forests in the coulee country of the lower Mississippi River.

In the north are huge state forests, national forests, wildlife areas, Native American reservations, the wilds of the Boundary Waters canoe country, and, in the northwest corner of Minnesota, the shallow valley of the Red River of the North. A surveyor's anomaly produced the Northwest Angle, which intrudes into Canada to include a piece of the Lake of the Woods. This is the most northerly point in the Lower 48.

There is perhaps more fresh water at the surface here than on any comparably sized area on earth. In surface area, Lake Superior is the largest body of fresh water in the world; Lake Michigan is not far behind. Some 25,000 lakes and countless ponds attract hordes of fishers for warm-water species. Among those lakes are more than 300 that are managed for stream trout on a "put-grow-take" basis.

To the south are the cornlands of Iowa and Illinois. The western third of Minnesota is part of the Great Plains region. To the east is the Upper Peninsula of Michigan, which should logically be part of Wisconsin, and the long southward thrust of Lake Michigan into the heartland of the Midwest. Two waterways dominate both history and topography—the Mississippi, which originates in Minnesota, and the Wisconsin River, the hardest-working river in the United States, which bisects much of the state of Wisconsin north to south, and then fishhooks into the Mississippi close to the Illinois border. Curiously, rainfall can flow north into Hudson Bay, east into the Great Lakes, the St. Lawrence, and finally the Atlantic Ocean, or south into the Gulf of Mexico.

More than 600 Minnesota trout streams are concentrated along the North Shore of Lake Superior and in that great shaggy southeast triangle between the Mississippi and the Iowa border. Wisconsin has 2500 trout streams spread generously, some flowing north into Superior, some east into Green Bay on Lake Michigan. Many others are tributaries of the St. Croix and the Mississippi, or of the Wisconsin River in the coulee country. A surprising number of streams meander through state forests or wildlife management areas. At least two rivers have been designated Wild and Scenic Rivers by act of Congress. Thousands of miles of streams are under easement to the states' Departments of Natural Resources, offering easy access and the illusion that one is fishing through the original wilderness.

Temperatures in the upper Midwest run to extremes, from 90 degrees Fahrenheit in August to 30 below during the winter. There is no distinct rainy season; of the approximately 30 inches of annual precipitation, a somewhat larger proportion falls in June and July. Sudden spring snowmelt may discourage fly-fishers for weeks at a time in the northern streams, but the southern streams are usually in good shape on opening weekends in mid-April in Minnesota and the first week of May in Wisconsin.

Although far from the Atlantic seaboard, this interior country was opened early to exploitation by explorers, traders, and priests. In 1634, a mere 27 years after the settlement of Jamestown in Virginia and only 14 years after the Pilgrims foundered near Plymouth Rock, Jean

The Pine River and one of southwestern Wisconsin's limestone castles near Yuba, Wisconsin

Nicolet canoed into Green Bay on Lake Michigan, paddled up the Fox River, and, legend has it, reached the Mississippi over the portage to the Wisconsin River. Twenty years later, Medard Chouart and Pierre-Esprit Radisson coasted along northern Wisconsin to the western end of Lake Superior. On May 17, 1673, Father Marquette and Louis Joliet left civilization at the Mackinac Straits to follow Nicolet's water trail into the Mississippi as far south as the Arkansas River. In 1680 Father Louis Hennepin reached St. Anthony's Falls in what is now downtown Minneapolis. That same year Daniel Greysolon, the Sieur du Lhut, labored up the Misakota and traversed the portage into the St. Croix, a major tributary of the Mississippi. The Ojibways' Misakota was the Dakotas' Nemetsakouat, which the English called Burntwood and the French Bois Brûlé; now it is known as the Brule, a premier trout and steelhead stream in northwestern Wisconsin. With our usual American practice of modifying difficult names or words for ease of pronunciation, or sometimes as a cartographer's misspelling, du Lhut became Duluth, now Minnesota's gateway to the North Shore.

There is a trout stream for every traveler. A few, like the Wolf, are wide and wild. Some pitch down in fury through channels carved in stone; some wind softly through groves of sighing trees. Many open into green pastures where the air is sweet and jewelweed adorns the banks.

THE FISHES

Any attempt to delineate fully the complicated life histories or biological diversity of the salmonids now present in midwestern waters is beyond the scope of this book. In prehistoric times, only two species of char inhabited the area now known as Wisconsin and Minnesota. They were the lake trout, *Salvelinus namaycush*, and the brook trout, *S. fontinalis*. You see the problem already—taxonomically these are not even trout! Because fish biologists were rare during the early days of the exploitation of the continent, the original ranges of native salmonids remain subject to conjecture. It is generally agreed that lake trout occupied all the Great Lakes except Lake Erie, and a few large, deep, northern inland lakes left behind by the retreating glaciers some 10,000 to 15,000 years ago. The brook trout, also called speckled trout, or "specs" in midwestern parlance, are thought to be indigenous to the northern Great Lakes and many of their tributaries, to Ontario's Lake Nipigon, to the spring-fed streams of the St. Croix watershed of Wisconsin, and to a few spring creeks of southeastern Minnesota, northern Iowa, and possibly southwestern Wisconsin. The Nipigon brook trout, which are still carefully segregated from the Lake Superior population, are considered a separate race or population.

During the late 1800s, European brown trout, *Salmo trutta*, and rainbow trout, *Oncorhynchus mykiss*, were introduced into the waters. Within the past 25 years, several popular species of Pacific salmon have been imported, together with the Atlantic salmon, *Salmo salar*, and planted in tributaries of the Great Lakes.

In the spring of 1884, brown trout eggs from Germany were reared in the Northville, Michigan, hatchery and viable fry were deposited into the Baldwin River, a tributary of the Père Marquette. Eggs of Loch Leven brown trout arrived in the United States from Scotland in 1885; additional shipments from Germany, Scotland, and England followed. Progeny of the various shipments were soon inextricably mixed and distributed widely. Even that first German shipment of eggs may have included two subspecies or races of brown trout—one a lake resident, the other a riverine inhabitant.

In 1887 Wisconsin imported 1000 European brown trout eggs and raised them in the Bayfield hatchery. That was only the beginning of a multitude of plantings from various sources, most often from mixed hatchery strains. A few were planted in Lakes Michigan and Superior, where they have reproduced and contribute to the fishery. Hatchery-raised browns were distributed widely in inland rivers. Hundreds of first-class Wisconsin streams now provide superb fly-fishing for naturally reproducing browns; marginal streams must be stocked. Introduced into Minnesota's Root River system in 1888, browns have since established "wild" populations in many streams, although some marginal streams still require supplementary stocking to maintain a quality fishery. Brown trout have become the salmonid quarry of choice for legions of midwestern fly-fishers.

The history of the rainbow is even more richly obscure. Rainbow trout were imported from the Pacific coast before the turn of the century. As early as 1872 they were stocked in private ponds in Wisconsin. In 1883 they were introduced into Lake Superior by the Province of Ontario. In 1885–1886, 600,000 were distributed throughout the state of Wisconsin. By 1887 they had been planted in tributaries of the Root River in southeastern Minnesota. Subsequently, they were planted extensively in rivers and lakes throughout the region. Rainbows have become a successful fixture in the Great Lakes and many of their tributaries, where they are known as "steelhead," but in inland streams they have rarely developed reproducing populations. Anecdotal evidence asserts that rainbows in inland streams tend to drift downstream in response to instinct. Another case can be made that rainbows disappear because they are easier than browns to catch and keep.

The populations, races, or strains of rainbows imported into the Midwest were innumerable. Since then they have been bred and cross-bred to the point that their histories and separate genetic characteristics have become diffused.

And that leads us inexorably to the consideration of the proper taxonomic identification of our several species of trout. We tiptoe with trepidation through the minefield of subgenera, subspecies, populations, stocks, strains, races, and even "nations." Most ichthyologists agree, somewhat reluctantly, that all American brown trout are one species, *Salmo trutta,* composed of many different races, populations, or strains. Some brown trout, however, are anadromous, going to sea, or in this case to a large lake, such as Lake Superior or

Lake Michigan; others spend their entire lives in the stream. Are they different subspecies, strains, or races?

The rainbow provokes similar speculation. At one time we traced the origin of the Irwin strain of rainbow trout, discovering after some effort that it was named for a hatchery. The Irwin strain supposedly has lost its anadromous behavior. Dr. Lauren R. Donaldson of the University of Washington, creator of that popular strain of rainbow that bears his name, is reported to have said, "We like to think our results compare with the poultrymen's development of the broad-breasted turkey."

It appears after close reading of the literature that the term "strain" is most often applied to domesticated trout, namely hatchery stock. "Population" is a useful term to describe a group of trout within a species that has marginally distinctive characteristics. Probably none of our browns or rainbows are wild trout in the sense that they are direct descendants of an originally imported discrete population. So when we refer to wild trout in the pages that follow, take it to mean trout and char that have successfully reproduced over several decades or seasons without a continuous infusion of hatchery strains. Fortunately, both the Wisconsin and Minnesota Departments of Natural Resources have raised the protection and propagation of wild trout to the top of their priority lists.

Most fly-fishers, we suspect, will be satisfied to know that they are fishing brooks, browns, or rainbows without questioning the particular lineage of their quarry.

THE STREAMS AND RIVERS

In this book we profile more than 100 trout streams, from pristine brooks to potent rivers, and we mention in passing many more that may inspire the inquisitive instincts of fly-fishers. These streams are not necessarily the best that you might choose, if you could wade the 12,500 miles of designated trout waters in more than 3000 streams. But rest assured that we have included a baker's dozen of the premier fly-fishing streams in each state. For every profiled stream, we identify the DeLorme map page number, the county or counties through which the stream flows, nearby cities or villages offering food and lodging, and travel directions.

We have observed, sometimes loosely, a number of criteria in our selection. The habitat should be suitable for the reproduction of at least one of the trout species present, or, if reproduction is marginal, for the overwinter survival and growth of planted trout. The stream should be wadable, at least in part, with variations from deep pool to riffle and run. There must be room for a fly-caster to practice her or his art, and to capture a few trout of larger-than-average size. The stream should be esthetically pleasing, a subjective evaluation that might be characterized by adjectives such as "enchanting," "beautiful," and "quality" water and the like. Of least importance is the need for an extraordinary population of trout, although many of our streams exceed the magic number of 1000 trout per mile.

In general, with all Wisconsin and Minnesota trout streams, you will find your best fishing where the Departments of Natural Resources have purchased blocks of land or leased easements along the streams. The public lands are marked on some maps by overprinted blocks of green, on others by a leaping trout, and by various symbols on Department of Transportation county maps. Public Fishing Grounds are often, but not always, signposted. Easements are often clearly delineated by fencing parallel to the river and 25 feet from the center line. Publicly controlled sections of river are most likely to have been improved by bank stabilization, in-stream structures, and intermittent de-brushing.

Maintaining a trout stream over the years is labor intensive and hugely expensive. The DNRs have neither the money nor the manpower to keep all of the streams tailored for fly-fishing. Some public stretches now will be cramped by brush and fallen snags, or beavers will have interrupted the flow. It's a shame to see some of our beautiful streams degraded by time and neglect—nearly unfishable—and yet the trout will live out their lives unmolested, and maybe that's one way of assuring the continuation of a discrete native stock.

WISCONSIN

Wisconsin has more than 2600 designated trout streams encompassing more than 9500 miles of water. Southeastern Wisconsin has only a few, and there's a big void north and west of Stevens Point, where warm-water streams predominate. Milwaukee County has no natural trout streams, although there are anadromous trout and salmon runs through the city. On the other end of the scale, Marinette County in northeastern Wisconsin lays claim to 196 trout streams. For the convenience of traveling fly-fishers, we have arbitrarily divided the state into five sections.

Beginning in 1980, the state applied a classification system to all its trout streams, and with few exceptions statewide bag and size limits were established. Although the class system was superseded in 1990 with a more sophisticated Category system, the old system still has relevance today for those who really want to interpret the information. We quote at length from *Wisconsin Trout Streams,* 1980, a book that listed, classified, and mapped by county 2674 of the state's streams. It is a fly-angler's bible that we call the "Blue Book."

"Class I. These are high-quality trout waters, having sufficient natural reproduction to sustain populations of wild trout at or near carrying capacity. Consequently, streams in this Category require no stocking of hatchery trout . . . Class I streams comprise 37 percent of Wisconsin's trout stream mileage.

"Class II. Streams in this classification may have some natural reproduction but not enough to utilize available food and space. Therefore, stocking sometimes is required to maintain a desirable sport fishery . . . These streams comprise 44 percent of the total trout stream mileage.

"Class III. These waters are marginal trout habitat . . . Class III streams comprise 19 percent of the total trout stream mileage."

We have profiled no Class III streams. In some instances, relying on the Blue Book together with our experience, we have rated a stream "first class." Such streams should command your attention.

In 1990, the DNR promulgated the new Category system, which was designed to "maximize the potential many Wisconsin streams have for producing trout."

Wisconsin fish managers had identified a number of problems that prevented Wisconsin trout fishing from being as good as it could be. Many streams produced satisfactory numbers, but the trout weren't as large as anglers would like. Stocked fish were caught too soon after being planted, thereby depleting the streams and effectively shortening the season. Fish growth and public access were poor on many small streams. Too many large trout were being caught and killed. In some streams, natural reproduction was poor because the breeding stock was fished out. On the other hand, the report concluded that there was much potential for improved fishing.

Wisconsin streams are distributed widely and are diverse in structure. Water quality is generally excellent, and forage food and habitat are adequate. Angler surveys revealed that the quality of the outdoor experience was more important than the number of trout creeled. And high on the list of factors that determined quality was the chance to catch an occasional trophy.

To allow the new Category system to be evaluated, it was to remain unaltered for five years, that is, through 1994. Fish managers reviewed every stream in their areas and assigned a Category 1 to 5 to each, "based on trout growth rates, trout reproductive success, fishing pressure, location in a watershed, habitat, long-term fish survival, water quality, and other factors. Classifying streams this way statewide would make it possible for fishery biologists to manage streams for specific types of trout fishing."

In its preliminary proposal of December 1987, the DNR wrote: "For instance, in small, headwater streams crowded with native brook trout, size limits that exist may actually be removed because the streams can sustain healthy fisheries even with added fishing pressure . . . On medium-sized streams, which make up the bulk of Wisconsin's trout waters, size limits would be slightly increased and bag limits decreased so anglers could harvest a maximum weight of fish . . . On high-quality wild trout streams, a slot size limit may be used to protect fast-growing spawners while still allowing anglers to take fish smaller or larger than the slot size."

Category 1 streams have no minimum size, with a bag limit of 10 trout, of which only 5 may be either browns or rainbows. Category 2 has a minimum of 7 inches and a bag limit of five. Category 3 has a minimum of 9 inches and a bag limit of three trout. Category 4 has a limit of 12 inches for browns and rainbows, 8 inches for brook trout, with a bag limit of three in total. Category 5, Special Regulations, includes streams where size and bag limits vary by specific water.

The 1987 study proposed that some large and productive streams be subject to catch-and-release fishing only, and managed for trophy trout. They were to be open year-round, but that exciting suggestion did not make it through the lengthy approval process. However, some 50 streams were assigned to Category 5, Special Regulations, in 1990, with bag and size limits tailored for the individual stream.

There is no doubt in our minds, or in those of most of our fellow anglers, that the Category system of 1990 has greatly improved the quality of trout fishing in the state, for which we make obeisance to the professionals of the DNR.

In 1995, the year destined for change, only the early open season in the eight counties of southwestern Wisconsin was eliminated; regulations for the remainder of the state were unaltered. And what of the future? The classifications of a few streams will be changed and possibly some sections will be added to Category 5. Notably, the Wisconsin Department of Natural Resources has recommended that the lower third of the state be opened for trout fishing on April 1. That area would include the eight counties named earlier plus portions of several others. But it's a long and tedious process. Anglers will have to read the regulations and adjust their expeditions accordingly. Whatever the changes, we expect the quality of the trout fishing experience will improve in Wisconsin.

The traditional season for inland stream trout runs from the first Saturday in May through September 30.

MINNESOTA

Minnesota has 3300 miles of trout water distributed among more than 623 streams. Although there are streams throughout the state, the concentrations occur in the secret streams of the southeast and in the Arrowhead region above the North Shore of Lake Superior. In the southeast there are more than 600 miles of trout waters and approximately 100 streams. The North Shore has 179 streams and much of the remainder of the 3300 miles.

There has been less change of regulations and classification of streams in Minnesota than in the neighboring state of Wisconsin. The trout streams are still rated Good, Fair, or Poor, similar to Wisconsin's pre-1990 classifications, but the DNR is unduly modest. Many of the Good sections could properly be rated Blue Ribbon.

Since 1987, when the state DNR issued its Long Range Plan for Fisheries Management, a few miles of quality waters have been placed under Special Regulations during the regular summer season. A number of streams in southeastern Minnesota have been opened experimentally and incrementally for an early season, from January 1 through March 31, with a marked improvement in the quality of the fishing experience for many fly-fishers, including visitors from surrounding states. Shogren and Humphrey are among the many who have enjoyed superb fly-fishing for trout, even as early as the first week of January, in the North Star State. Because only 3 percent of Minnesota trout stream mileage is currently open for an early season, we hope that the experiment will be extended to other streams.

Nor has the DNR been dragging its heels in other ways. Extensive habitat improvement has gone forward, together with the purchase or lease of riparian corridors in and around trout streams. Since 1987,

Dr. Art Kaemmer fishes on Hay Creek in southeastern Minnesota on a late winter day. This was a productive day for Griffith's Gnats and Black Ants!

700 miles of water have been identified or improved as trout habitat. A few streams have been added to the list of designated trout waters.

The traditional season for inland stream trout runs from the Saturday closest to April 15 through September 30.

Fly-fishing for trout is better now in Wisconsin and Minnesota than it was 20 or even 30 years ago. This is due in part to the application of more sophisticated and more limiting regulations.

But regulations are not a panacea. They are only one tool in the hands of the keepers of the streams. Special regulations, categories, or classes are not the answer to acid precipitation, siltation from eroded fields, and thoughtless lumbering and grazing practices. Nor are they the answer to irresponsible applications of pesticides and herbicides, leaking chemical dumps, leaching landfills, and degraded waste disposal systems. Improved habitat is the number-one priority of every fish manager. A clean environment ought to be the goal of all anglers.

Fly-fishers shouldn't expect miracles from the regulations. We must continue to protect and improve the environment for both humans and trout. We must also limit our kill, not kill our limit.

CATCH AND RELEASE

Catch and release of trout by fly-fishers has been practiced for decades. Muskie fishermen have come around recently to the idea that the release of a trophy allows it to be caught more than once. Even walleye fishers are returning selected fish so that they can be eaten later. Back in the dim days of the postwar years, fly-rodders for largemouth bass were known to release a fish or two. Catch and release makes possible the catch of trophy trout several times in a season, thereby sharing the pleasure of the chase among several fishers, or it may permit released trout to grow larger where the habitat will sustain additional numbers of large trout. A big female, if released, can spawn thousands of eggs.

If you wish to join the legions of fishers who are practicing catch and release, here's how to release your trout. (The catching of them is another story.) First, crunch down the barb of your fly. We do not usually carry a net. Play the fish quickly. When it ceases its initial airborne antics, grab the leader, clamp the rod under your arm or between your knees, and pull in the fish hand over hand. Run your hand up under the belly and cradle the trout gently, keeping it still in the water. Turn it belly up and back out the hook. If the hook is inside the mouth instead of in the lip, as is usually the case, pick the hook out with a forceps. If it is deep and difficult to remove, cut the leader short. Right the trout and hold it lightly until it powers its way out of your hand. If it seems to want to tip over on its side, indicating a state of exhaustion, gently move it forward and back to flush water through its gills, thereby pumping lifesaving oxygen into its system. Release the fish in quiet water. You'll get the hang of it soon enough. With luck and skill you'll come back next week to re-create the thrill of the catch and release.

Precise instructions such as these are always subject to qualifiers, or to dispute. So you may prefer to use a net in those mythic waters where the trout are all huge. Some anglers recommend the use of the net in all cases, but our experience has been that a netted trout gets entangled in the nylon mesh, damaging the fish and delaying its release. If you prefer to net your trout, use a shallow-bag catch-and-release net, sold at the better fly shops.

And while we are about it, let us get some acidulous comments off our chests. We have seen fishers derrick a fish out and flop it on the bank to admire. We have seen them dangle their lip-hooked catch at eye level to count the spots. A recent Canadian study demonstrated that mortality of trout increases dramatically with time spent out of water. Even brief exposure to air, 30 to 60 seconds, can cause eventual death. Therefore, release your trout in the water.

Too many Saturday-morning TV shows have filmed smiling anglers sticking their fingers in the gills of fish and then congratulating themselves on being practitioners of C&R. Gills are too fragile to allow for such harsh treatment. Another common visual image that causes us pain (and the fish damage) is that of a bass angler with thumb and forefinger clamped like a vise on the fish's mouth, the body hanging limply at right angles to the clamp.

Catch and release is here to stay, we hope. It's an efficient and enjoyable practice that will help extend our sport into the 21st century. The sizzle of fresh fish in a pan is transitory; the remembrance of a fine fish released to freedom lasts forever.

HABITAT IMPROVEMENT

During the period from 1920 to 1980, the miles of cold-water trout habitat nationwide decreased by as much as 50 percent. Since 1980, we have lost more miles due to an expanding population; mindless development in the watersheds; chemical pollution; fence-to-fence farming; decreased groundwater flow due to irrigation; grazing, which tramples the streambanks; clear-cutting of forests; filling of wetlands; and a thousand other ills the soil, water, and air are heir to.

For example, at the turn of the century there were at least seven native brook trout streams in the Twin Cities. We are now reduced to a last-stage defense of Eagle Creek, which joins the Minnesota River at Savage. As late as 1960, Jim Humphrey used to shoot over there from Bloomington to relax with a brace of brilliant brookies after a hard day in the office.

A second anecdote will serve to illustrate the losses. In the 1950s, Dick Frantes, a plumber by trade, was an inspector for the gas company. One memorable day he was working in the subbasement of a downtown St. Paul commercial building. And there he found, in a concrete channel, a free-flowing stream, one of the early trout streams, that had been paved over in the 1920s, or perhaps earlier.

We won't belabor the point. Every reader must mourn the loss of one of her or his favorite streams. However, there is hope for the future because the environment has become a cause for many Americans. Aroused and articulate citizens are holding the politicians' feet to the fire on behalf of clean air, clean water, and protected trout streams.

Trout fishers have decided that they ought to protect the streams that remain, regardless of what may occur in the wider world. And so we arrive at a discussion of trout stream rehabilitation and improvement. The subject is complicated, the material available for study is extensive, and the opportunity to get one's hands dirty restoring a stream is there for those who care.

We quote from "Wisconsin Trout Stream Habitat Management" on the last page of the *Trout Fishing Regulations and Guide:* "Habitat management focuses on the stream channel and its banks. The idea is to create conditions favorable for trout by adding something to the stream or modifying what's already present.

"Trout need certain environmental conditions, called habitat, to survive and flourish. Cold water, plenty of oxygen, sheltered places to hide and rest, and abundant supplies of insects and forage fish are the most important. For streams supporting wild trout, add gravel

Brush bundles

Brush mats

beds for spawning, water swift enough to sweep silt from developing eggs, and half a dozen other factors just beginning to be understood.

"Leave out one of these conditions and you may still have a trout stream, but it probably won't produce to capacity. Leave out many more and you can forget about the trout. They won't be there."

All is not lost. Scientific habitat improvement can enhance the streams that remain. The techniques are many. This is not an attempt to describe all of them, nor to imply that they can be applied indiscriminately. Our experience is pretty much limited to cutting brush and pulling deadfalls from the streams on winter days—as long as the wind-chill factor is not worse than minus 20 degrees.

The appropriate technology to be applied is best left to the professionals who know what will work, and where. We review a few examples here to give you a taste of the possibilities, and to show how you can recognize them on the stream.

Riprap is usually easy to spot. It's a jumble of broken rock lining the bank, most often on an outside curve of a stream. Riprap stabilizes the bank and provides cover for trout in the interstices among the huge blocks or boulders at the base of the pile. The streambank should be sloped at a 30-degree angle and grassed. (For examples of riprap, see the photographs accompanying Timber Coulee Creek in chapter 3 and Stoney Brook in chapter 10.)

Traditional bank cover structure showing construction stages (side view)

Riprap is most often used in agricultural areas where cattle have eroded the banks. It is often possible to deliver quarry blocks to the pastures with heavy equipment when the ground is hard. In some cases where heavy equipment can't approach the stream, smaller stones can be carried by boat to interior sections of the river. It may take a sharp eye to spot the improvements there after a year or two.

Bank covers may be even more difficult to identify if they've been in for several seasons. These are wooden shelves or platforms set into the bank, then covered with a layer of rock, and topped with small stones and sod. Typically, they will create a cave 2 or 3 feet wide, 8 or more feet long, and perhaps as much as a foot deep. Trout hide from predators back in the shadows, but venture out to feed at the edge of the cover. Such covers may be built in the stream, but many newer ones are assembled on land, then carried to the stream and anchored with reinforcing rods. Variations of the bank covers are called "lunker structures" or "skyhook covers."

Brush bundles and brush mats narrow the stream, collect sand and silt, and provide space for young trout to hide. Half-logs are simple, economical structures used to provide hiding, resting, and security cover for yearling and older trout in reaches of stream having sparse in-stream cover. Hundreds of them have been pounded into the bed of the Willow Race in west central Wisconsin. You are likely to discover them when you tear your waders on the bent reinforcing rods, but waders are cheap compared to the opportunity to catch numbers of brown trout.

Other structures include log or rock sills to create plunge pools, Hewitt ramps, which are artificial waterfalls designed to add oxygen and create pools, and sand traps. Fencing and gravel crossings for cattle are frequently needed to protect a stream. Old wing dams are encountered often. Some wing dams on the upper Kinnickinnic of west central Wisconsin date to the days of the Civilian Conservation Corps, but are still serviceable.

Stream improvements are long lasting but labor intensive. The initial cost is expensive. Professional fish managers must design and supervise the installation, and many hired hands or volunteers are needed to do the bull work.

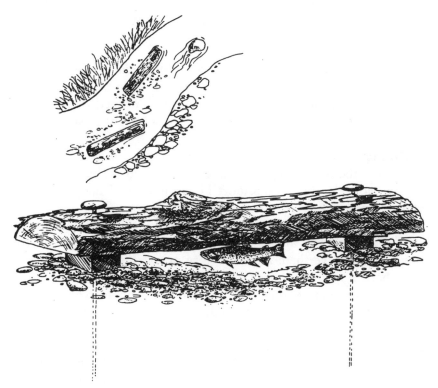

Half-log. Inset shows position of half-logs in stream.

No good result comes cheaply in this world. Stream improvements may be the wisest investment to secure the future of trout fishing on your home stream.

A fine reference for those interested in learning more about habitat improvement is *Trout Stream Therapy* by Robert L. Hunt, a former fisheries research biologist with the Wisconsin DNR (University of Wisconsin Press, 1994).

PLAY IT SAFE

We note elsewhere in this book that our profiled streams are neither intimidating nor, save for a few, dangerous. But there's no point in ruining a good outing for lack of preparation and care.

Only a handful of our rivers are wild and rough—the Wolf, Bois Brule, Peshtigo, and some on the North Shore—but a stout wading staff is always useful to pull or prod yourself out of sucking silt, to negotiate steep and slippery banks, and to probe for drop-offs. We have rescued a fellow angler from a slow and sinking death on a trout lake, when he took one step too far, by throwing our staff to him. He pried himself out.

Felt-bottomed boots and waders are recommended, except on ice. On late-night excursions, carry two flashlights, or at least one that you've checked out. Both Bill and Jim have suffered because their flashlights failed, or because they stayed too long after sunset without a light.

Turning to domestic and wild animals, there is a lot more "bull" than truth about the danger of bulls in pasturelands, but we remember one episode above Bucksnort Dam on Trout Run that set our hearts to pounding.

Bears, badgers, coyotes, wolves, moose, skunks, cougars (aka mountain lions, panthers, and pumas), bobcats, and lynx will leave you alone if you leave them alone. You're not at a petting zoo. Don't stand between a mother bear and her cubs, and don't store your provisions in your tent if you camp out. You probably won't see a wolf, coyote, or cougar that has drifted down from Canada and elected to stay because he likes the provender, but if you are lucky you may hear one howl or growl on a misty night. Moose have been known to run right over a visitor during the rutting season. Badgers are beautiful creatures that inhabit southwestern Wisconsin, but they are surly; when they begin to hiss, keep your distance. You must know the swaggering skunk, which doesn't care who you are or how exalted is your position in the world of men.

Snakes. Don't stick your hands in the crevices of limestone cliffs on the lower Kinnickinnic or in the bases of towers in the coulee country of southeastern Minnesota and southwestern Wisconsin. It's an old dodge to warn neophytes about the rattlers along a particular stream in order to keep them (the neophytes, not the rattlers) out of a favored fishing hole, but we haven't encountered a rattler yet. Not yet.

Our friend Felix Rondeau told us how he fell asleep on his private trout stream in northern Minnesota and awoke a couple of hours later, 300 yards downstream, carried by Minnesota mosquitoes. He surmised that three of them had lifted him. That's a tall story; it would take at least four to transport the big redhead.

Ticks. Yes, we have them. If you push your way through heavy cover, inspect yourself at evening's end. A few cases of Lyme disease have been reported in western Wisconsin. A spray of insect repellent on your boots or waders, on the sleeves of your shirt, and on your trout vest will provide protection.

There is barbed wire lying like snares in farm country, and barbed hooks around anglers. We have twice removed hooks from our pal Dick Frantes, utilizing the monofilament loop technique that has been widely publicized. Loop heavy mono around the bend of the embedded hook. Press down on the eye of the hook. A quick yank on the loop in a straight line with the shank will free the barb with little damage. (See illustration.) It works. Dick continued fishing for hours and with no ill effects. You can, of course, avoid the trauma by pressing down the barbs of your hooks with pliers.

The greatest danger in the Midwest comes from driving your car at

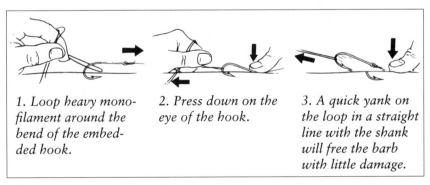

1. *Loop heavy mono-filament around the bend of the embedded hook.*

2. *Press down on the eye of the hook.*

3. *A quick yank on the loop in a straight line with the shank will free the barb with little damage.*

Above: The loop method of hook removal

high speed at night and plowing into one of an overpopulation of deer. We almost wiped out a deer, the front end of our car, and perhaps our lives on Interstate 94 opposite 3M headquarters, not far from downtown St. Paul. We can still hear those hooves scrabbling at the pavement as the deer veered off. We and the deer were lucky. Luck runs out for thousands of Wisconsin and Minnesota drivers every year. In northern Minnesota, your nighttime opponent might be a moose, with disastrous results.

We provide some last words about a staff. Our longtime staff is an aluminum ski pole 4 inches short of armpit length, slung over the shoulder on a shock cord front to back. It has saved us from terrible falls on numerous occasions.

MAPS

Every explorer of our far-flung trout streams will need at least two good maps of his area of interest. No one map will suffice because no single map illuminates all of the detail, and all will contain errors. Streams and roads will be misnamed, the blue lines of streams will run in the wrong places, older maps may not include new roads, and trails may have disappeared.

We have used the DeLorme page numbers under the name of each stream in this book because the finely detailed DeLorme atlases, 16" x 11" in book format for each state, are widely available at sports shops and magazine counters. The DeLorme *Minnesota Atlas and Gazetteer* divides the state into 77 sections; the Wisconsin book contains 81 sections. Both are available by mail from DeLorme Mapping, PO Box 298, Freeport, ME 04032; phone 207-865-4171. Or phone 1-800-227-1656, extension 6404, for the dealer nearest you.

The Milwaukee Map Service, Inc., 959 North Mayfair Road, Milwaukee, WI 53226, phone 1-800-525-3822, sells a series of four excellent maps of Wisconsin, which name most of the minor roads, and block out in green many of the public lands. This is an invaluable aid to fishers who are looking for sections of streams that have received habitat improvement.

Wisconsin trout fishers should be sure to obtain the *Wisconsin Trout Fishing Regulations and Guide* when they buy their licenses and trout stamps. This 8½" x 11" brochure maps all significant designated trout streams in the state and color-codes the trout waters by Category. This one is a must for Wisconsin fishers. Unfortunately, some license sellers may forget to give it to you.

Dedicated fly-fishers who want to explore even beyond the limits of our book may want the "Blue Book," *Wisconsin Trout Streams,* referred to in our "Streams and Rivers" section. It lists and maps by county 2674 trout streams, indicates the trout species present, and classes the stream by quality of habitat and productivity. Although it occasionally falls out of print, it is currently available from Wisconsin State Publications, 222 Midvale Road, Suite 26, Madison, WI 53705.

Minnesota fishers will want "Trout Streams of Southeast Minnesota," a large folded map showing the designated trout streams of the six southeastern counties overprinted in blue. It may be ordered by mail, free, from the Minnesota Department of Natural Resources, Section of Fisheries, Box 12, DNR Building, 500 Lafayette Road, St. Paul, MN 55155. This one contains a wealth of supplementary information—miles of good water, trout species, and shoreline ownership. Don't leave home without it. A companion map, "North Shore Fishing Guide," may be ordered by those who plan to fish the North Shore streams of Lake Superior.

Minnesota also produces for sale a series of Public Recreation Information Maps (PRIM), which show parks, forests, trails, canoe routes, water access sites, designated trout streams, wildlife management areas, and more. They are available from Minnesota's Bookstore, 117 University Avenue, St. Paul, MN 55155.

County maps are available from the Departments of Transportation of both states, and at many map stores and sports shops. These large-scale maps, one-half inch to the mile, are useful but do not give the names of minor roads.

Many counties and communities in both states produce instructive touring maps that we have found useful. State park, wildlife area, and national forest maps will round out your tackle. We obtain our state park and wildlife area maps at entrance kiosks; national forest maps are available for a modest charge at any ranger station within the forest.

Minnesota state park maps are free by mail from the DNR Information Center, 500 Lafayette Road, St. Paul, MN 55155, but with a limit of 10 items. Information on Wisconsin state parks is available from the Bureau of Parks and Recreation at 608-266-2181. Maps for the Chippewa National Forest in Minnesota may be obtained by calling 218-335-8600; for the Superior National Forest by calling 218-

720-5321. For the Chequamegon National Forest in Wisconsin, call 715-762-2461, and for the Nicolet National Forest, 715-362-3415. The current charge for national forest maps is $3.

Because of space limitations we have not been able to provide a map in this book for every stream profiled. We have included maps of the big rivers and of some of the smaller streams that we consider particularly appealing. Where appropriate, we have indicated preferred access points. Our maps are composites, drawing on the various sources described above and illustrating, we trust, those elements that will make for a most successful experience for you.

TRESPASS AND NAVIGABILITY

If you can get into a stream from a bridge or by crossing public land, you are usually safe from challenge, but if you find a fence across the stream, common sense dictates that you request permission from the landowner to proceed beyond the fence. Most landowners are accommodating in our part of the world and permit angling in their stream sections. A few may disagree with the concept of navigability. If a canoe can be maneuvered through a stream during high water, the stream is considered to be a public waterway, but you must stay between the high-water marks. This is still a murky subject; some disputes as to navigability wind up in court.

Stream sections that run through state, national, or county lands are open during the regular trout season, except in a few sanctuaries. Many other streams have signposted easements where the DNR has purchased or leased a corridor on one or both sides of a stream. Wisconsin posts most of its easements with small green-and-white "Public Hunting and Fishing Grounds" signs. Minnesota marks fewer easements. Unfortunately, some signs have fallen or have been deliberately removed. A very few easements have been acquired by public-spirited organizations such as Trout Unlimited.

But what if there are no posted easements on your trout stream? If there's a well-defined path along the stream, you may assume either that the landowner doesn't object or that there's an easement. If there is fencing that parallels the stream about 25 feet from the stream center line, it indicates a public easement. When approaching a bridge, we always scan the open fields for a well-made fence that follows the stream meanders. Look for neat bracing at the corner posts, indicative of careful DNR construction.

Fishing easements permit anglers to walk the stream banks within the fenced corridor, but camping, hiking, trapping, hunting, and other uses are prohibited.

Respect the landowners' rights. Don't break down fences, don't cut or disfigure trees, and take your litter out with you. Above all, close the gates behind you. We know of a few farmers in southeastern Minnesota who now refuse permission to cross their lands because of litter left behind by trout anglers.

2

Hatches, Tactics, and Tackle

THE TROUT FOODS

What do trout eat? Trout eat everything. At times trout are such gluttonous consumers that food will be oozing out of their vents while they are taking more in at the front. At other times they lie quiet, seeming to be interested in nothing edible. One researcher reported that trout may obtain as much as 70 percent of their *annual* dietary needs from the *Hexagenia* mayfly alone, which may account for some streams being notably poor producers except during the Hex hatch.

When actively feeding at the surface, trout are renowned in literature and lore for being selective, which means that often they will target some insignificant species of insect to the exclusion of all other foods. A common occurrence on midwestern streams is the evening rise of small trout to tiny midges. Trout will feed fearlessly at rod tip distance, ignoring both your presence and your larger artificial. If you change to a #20 or #22 midge pupa or dry fly, there is still no guarantee that they will accept your offering. Your fly may be too different in silhouette against the night sky, or just a size off, or may not duplicate the peculiar action of the natural. You might conclude that trout are fickle and fussy as well as gluttonous, and you'd be right on the money.

Trout feed on at least 10 different orders of aquatic insects, plus several orders of insects that are associated with the riparian environment. Fortunately for us, only those genera or species that are important to the trout's diet have been replicated by fly-tiers. Otherwise we'd be carrying thousands, rather than only hundreds, of patterns.

*Jack Haines studying the entomology of the Kinnickinnic River
in Pierce County, Wisconsin*

Trout also feed on chubs, shiners, sculpins, and sundry small fishes, plus crayfish, scuds, leeches, and other swimmers and crawlers. Worms are a favorite. Big trout have been found to have snakes and mice in their stomachs. Trout have been observed by Joe Balestrieri in southwestern Wisconsin, thrusting their heads into a mass of weeds to dislodge snails . Naturally, fly-tiers have exercised their imaginations in the creation of swimming mice, snails, and even articulated worms!

From the menu of aquatic insects, trout take the winged stages of mayflies, caddisflies, and midges—and less often in our area, stoneflies—on the surface. Terrestrials such as beetles, ants, inchworms, leafhoppers, and grasshoppers are taken in the surface film as well. The larvae of mayflies, caddis, stoneflies, and crane flies, together with scuds (freshwater shrimp), leeches, and minnowlike forage fish, are taken subsurface. For smaller trout, the primary sources of protein are the several stages of the mayflies, caddis, midges, and stoneflies, as well as scuds. Large trout require a more substantial diet.

Mayflies present the classic challenge to fly-fishers. When the Hendrickson, *Ephemerella subvaria,* is emerging from southeastern Minnesota and southwestern Wisconsin streams from approximately mid-April to mid-May, trout may restrict their feeding to the nymphal form escaping from the bottom or to the dark, winged dun on the surface. Either an artificial nymph or a dry fly that closely resembles the naturals will be demanded. Similar conditions occur throughout the season when the sulphurs, brown drakes, or Hex are predominant emerging species. Tiny blue-winged olives may be encountered all season long on our streams, but that doesn't guarantee that trout will feed on them continuously.

Caddisflies pose fewer problems of selectivity for fishermen. Caddis hover over our streams from May through the season's close. The pupa rises to the surface, pops out as an adult with wings, and flies to nearby brush. Later it joins a swarm and mates. The female bounces on the surface of the water to release eggs or swims down to deposit her eggs on the stems of waterweeds. Trout take caddis at all stages, but only a handful of artificial patterns are necessary to trick them.

Stonefly nymphs crawl out to some convenient rock, molt, and fly. A day or two later, but rarely observed in our area, the females of some species may buzz on the surface while releasing eggs. Trout feed chiefly on the nymphs migrating through the shallows, so your mayfly nymphs will do double duty for the nymphs of stoneflies.

Scuds (freshwater shrimp) hang out in the weeds and patrol the margins of streams all season long. When swimming they look like arrows, or perhaps javelins. There are scud patterns, but bristly mayfly nymphs are a satisfactory substitute. Leeches are always slinking around and are replicated by the Olive Woolly Bugger. Ants, beetles, inchworms, and other terrestrials fall or are blown to the surface during the warm months and are seized by trout opportunistically. Artificial flies need not precisely match the natural, but size and (sometimes) color are important. One or two standard fly patterns will fairly represent several minnow forms. The Muddler is a sculpin when weighted; dry it is a grasshopper kicking on the surface.

Trout feed down deep, in the mid-depths, and on the surface. The literature of trout fishing has long romanced the rise of trout to specific mayfly hatches. Matching the hatch is a fascinating exercise and worthy of a lifetime of study, but remember that trout take most of their protein from underwater life forms. So study the hatch charts, but fish deep.

MAYFLIES

Because most fly-fishers for trout soon become entranced with the identification, replication, and dating of the times of emergence of significant mayflies, it seems necessary to devote a few paragraphs to these *Ephemeroptera*.

The mayfly begins as an egg; soon it becomes a larva, or nymph, which crawls, burrows, or swims on the bottom of the stream. After a number of instars, which are the periods between the molts of the exoskeleton, the nymph usually swims to the surface. Some species crawl to the shore. It then flies into the brush or trees, if a trout doesn't pick it off as it is swimming up. After as little as an hour or as long as a couple of days of resting, the dun, or subimago, slithers snakelike out of its shuck, unfolds glassine wings, and joins a crowd over the stream for the mating ritual. There are, as always, exceptions to this process. Some duns molt immediately; one species of female dun doesn't molt.

In the final adult stage, the imago, also called the spinner, develops long legs and tails, hyaline wings, and a shiny body that appears to be lacquered. The male grabs a female. They mate. The female deposits her eggs on the surface and drops them like bombs, or crawls down along a stem to deposit her eggs underwater. She then dies, usually with wings outstretched in what is known as the spentwing position.

The above is a truncated explanation of the marvelous process. Professional entomologists would doubtless take exception to our version. But in a careful reading of the scientific literature of mayflies you'll often run into qualifiers such as "generally," "usually," "sometimes," "often." Seldom will you find the word "always," because mayflies, like humans, do not always act predictably or invariably. Nor do entomologists like the use of the word "hatch," which is more accurately applied to something coming out of an egg. They prefer "emergence," and who is to blame them?

Fly-fishers have several opportunities to match the various stages of the mayfly life cycle—nymphs crawling on the bottom or swimming up, emerging duns with forewings rising like sails, females touching down to drop their eggs, and finally spentwings. Some anglers tie flies to represent each stage!

Let's get the numbers out of the way. There are more than 600 species of mayflies north of Mexico. Many of them are not native to our region, and only a few are found in sufficient numbers to trigger the attention of trout or trout fishers.

Approximately 150 species occur in Wisconsin, many of which are rare. (See W.L. Hilsenhoff, *Aquatic Insects of Wisconsin,* 1975.) Our guess is that there are fewer in Minnesota due to the more limited habitat, and many of them are not important to trout or trout fishermen. That makes your job more manageable.

In our charts of significant mayfly emergences we have relied on our own observations and identification, and on the reports of reliable observers. In some stream profiles we have named and dated specific mayfly emergences. Otherwise, the Generalized Emergence Chart will be a guide, but only a guide. In some cases we have missed significant emergences. Even the most definitive text, *The Mayflies of North and Central America,* by Edmunds, Jensen, and Berner, notes the problem that some mayflies may become active when entomologists are home in bed. Similarly, some heavy hatches appear at night when anglers are sitting around the cabin with drink in hand, telling lies to one another.

Hatches also change over time. Anecdotal evidence suggests that the predominant hatches on some of our streams are now composed of smaller species of mayflies, and fewer of them, due to deteriorating water quality or, rarely, improving water quality. Fencing, for example, may eliminate cattle droppings, which enrich the water and produce some larger mayflies. On many streams the major hatches are *Baetis,* called tiny blue-winged olives, or *Tricorythodes,* called tricos, and midges, which are not mayflies.

Emergence dates may also change from year to year. Weeks of cold weather may delay a hatch; warm weather may accelerate the emergence. Other factors known only to God may affect hatch times. In short, emergence charts were not brought down from the mountain by Theodore Gordon, the patron saint of American fly-fishers, or even by Swisher and Richards, nor were they chiseled into tablets of stone or marked with a stylus on wax.

CADDISFLIES

According to Dr. Hilsenhoff there are probably 275 species of caddisflies (*Trichoptera*) in Wisconsin. Without being unduly scientific, one could divide them into two major groups: those with a portable case and those without.

The casemakers may have a rough tube fashioned of plant material, rock particles, or small snail shells, or a case incorporating some silken material.

Those without a portable case are either free-living or living within a fixed retreat—something like a net to catch food.

All start as an egg, which hatches into a larva, which pupates, and then eventually swims or floats to the surface to become an adult, winged caddisfly. Trout will eat the casemakers, but we've had our greatest success with a Green Caddis Larva, which represents the free-livers, with a soft-hackle that looks like a pupa rising, and with the Elk Hair Caddis on the surface. Although we may get an argument from some fly-tiers, color of the adult at the surface is much less important than the size of the artificial.

STONEFLIES

Stonefly nymphs clamber among the rocks and "scatter like rats" (Ann Haven Morgan in her wonderful old book, *Field Book of Ponds and Streams,* 1930) when you pick up a rock.

Stoneflies (*Plecoptera*) are vulnerable as nymphs when they are heading to the shore through the shallows, but we have seldom found trout feeding on the egg-laying adults at the surface. I have seen a large and juicy adult buzzing in the film for more than 200 yards over the lies of hungry trout on the Wolf River, but with never a pass at it.

FLIES AND MIDGES

This very large order of aquatic *Diptera,* two-winged true flies, includes many families that are of no interest to trout fishers, although trout may occasionally feed on black flies, punkies, and no-see-ums. Two families are important—the crane flies and the midges.

Two crane flies afford some interesting opportunities. The larva of the giant crane fly (which we describe in our profile of the Rush River in Wisconsin), when replicated by a yellowish Woolly Worm, may entice very large trout. In our profile of the Kinnickinnic of Wisconsin we describe how John Schorn tied into a batch of trout when fishing a soft-hackle, a representation of the *Antocha* genus, which was swimming to the surface. The *Antocha* is frequently mistaken for a mayfly, but the presentation to trout is a very different case. Observation is all important.

Midges, of the family *Chironomidae,* are omnipresent on our streams all season long and represent a consistent food source for trout. We have taken trout with a Brassie on the bottom or a Griffith's

Gnat on the surface on innumerable occasions when nothing else would satisfy them. We have noted one occasion, on the North Branch of the Whitewater, when the trout were stuffed with midge larvae.

Midges are tiny, #20 and #22, but their presence is too often overlooked by anglers who are casting a #12 Adams. Be advised and be warned.

There are smaller true flies that appear in clouds on our streams. Dick Frantes called them "number 50 dandruff," but if trout are feeding on them, you might as well wind up and go home.

We include two charts, with the caveat that they do not represent perfection.

Other trout foods include the early black stonefly, found as early as March in the southern range; the carpenter ant, in the middle of May; the water boatman in March; the little yellow stonefly or little golden stonefly, toward the end of May; and the giant brown or giant black stoneflies, which appear on many northern rivers. In central Wisconsin, on the Tomorrow River, for example, they will emerge on or about June 1. The black cricket will be chirping during the hot months.

The hatch charts are only a rough guide, sometimes spot-on, sometimes off by as much as two weeks. Hatches may also be interrupted by weather. You may meet a heavy hatch of brown drakes on June 5th, but none in the air on the 6th and 7th. On the 8th they may fly again.

THE ARTIFICIALS

As Izaak Walton wrote, "There are twelve kinds of flies to angle with, which makes up a jury of flies likely to betray and condemn to death all the trout in the river."

But that was England then, and this is the United States now. England has but 50 or 60 species of mayflies; Wisconsin alone has 150. But there is a grain of truth embedded in the wisdom of Walton. More than 2000 fly patterns have been named by their American creators, but many are merely minor variations of historic patterns. The famous Pass Lake of the Midwest, one upon which we rely, is only a slight change from the Trude of western waters. And so, out of our vast experience of fishing the waters of the United States, from the Midwest to the Far West, we have hit upon a Terrific Twenty.

To the newcomer to fly-fishing, the choice of flies is a mystery

GENERALIZED MAYFLY EMERGENCE CHART FOR WISCONSIN AND MINNESOTA

Naturals	Jan	Feb	Mar	Apr	May	June	July	Aug	Sept	Artificials
Baetis species (14 spp.)			xxxx	xxxx	xxxx	xxxx	xxxx	xxxx	xxxx	Tiny Blue-Winged Olive #16 & #18.
Paraleptophlebia (7 spp.)				xxxx	xxxxx				xxxx	Dark Blue Quill, Slatewinged Mahogany Dun, Blue Dun, all #14 & #16.
Ephemerella subvaria				xxxx	xx					Dark Hendrickson, Adams, Red Quill (M), Brown Hen Spinner (F), all #14.
Ephemerella (18 spp. in 5 sub-genera)					xx	xxxxx	xx			Light Hendrickson, Sulphur, Light Cahill, Dark Slatewinged Olive, all #14 & #16.
Stenonema vicarium					xx	xx				March Brown, Gray Fox, Dark Cahill, Ginger Quill, all #12.
Ephemera simulans					xx	xxxxx				Brown Drake, March Brown, Chocolate Dun, all #12.
Stenonema/ Stenacron (10 spp.) Mainly spinner falls						xx	xxxx			Light Cahill, Sulphur, Ginger Quill, all #14.
Hexagenia limbata & H. atrocaudata						xx	xxxx	xx		Hex, Green Drake, White Wulff, all #8, #10, & #12.

Tricorythodes atratus & *T. stygiatus*					xx	xxxx	xxxx	xxxx	Trico, Tiny White-Winged Black, Tiny Gray-Winged Olive, all #18 & #20.
Pseudocloeon (8 spp.)						xx	xx		xxxx	Small Yellow Mayfly, Blue-Winged Olive, Minute Gray-Winged Olive, all #20 & #22.
Isonychia (6 spp.) Mainly spinner falls							xx	xx	xx	White-Gloved Howdy, Slate Drake, Mahogany Dun, all #12.
Ephoron leukon & *E. album*								xxxx		White Wulff, Trailer, White Fly, all #10 & #12.

Note: Each x represents approximately one week.

Potamanthus (Cream Fly) and *Siphlonurus* (Gray Drake), mid- to late-season hatches, are limited to the northern half of the range. As you travel north, the hatches may appear days or even weeks later.

SOUTHEASTERN MINNESOTA EMERGENCES AND OTHER TROUT FOODS

Naturals	Jan	Feb	Mar	Apr	May	June	July	Aug	Sept	Artificials
Midges	xxxx	xxxx	xxxx	xxxx	xxxx	xxxx	xxxx	xxxx	xxxx	Dry: Tiny Blue-Winged Olive, Griffith's Gnat, #18 to #24. Nymph: Brassie and Dark Mottled Grayish Olive #20.
Baetis species			xxxx	xxxx	xxxx	xxxx	xxxx	xxxx	xxxx	Dry: Tiny Blue-Winged Olive #18 & #20. Nymph: Gold-Ribbed Hare's Ear #18 & #20.
Paraleptophlebia adoptiva			xx	xxxx	xxxx					Dry: Dark Blue Quill, Slatewinged Mahogany Dun, Blue Dun, all #14 & #16. Nymph: Dark grayish-brown #16.
Ephemerella subvaria				xxxx	xx					Dry: Dark Hendrickson, Adams, Red Quill (M), Brown Hen Spinner (F), all #14. Nymph: Dark Hare's Ear, Wiggle Nymph, Pheasant Tail, all #16.
Ephemerella spp. plus subgenera Drunella, Attenella, etc.					xx	xxxx				Dry: Light Hendrickson & Light Cahill, #14 & #16. Nymph: Gold-Ribbed Hare's Ear #16.
Pseudocloeon spp.							xxxx	xxxx	xxxx	Dry: Small Yellow Mayfly, Blue-Winged Olive, Minute Gray-Winged Olive, all #20 & #22. Nymph: Yellowish-green or pale olive #20.

Organism								Flies
Tricorythodes spp.				xx	xxxx	xxxx	xxxx	Dry: Trico, Tiny White-Winged Black #20 to #24. Nymph: Any black-bodied #20 to #24.
Caddisflies (various)			xxxx	xxxx	xxxx	xxxx	xxxx	Dry: Tan, Olive or Speckled Caddis, all #14 to #20. Nymph: Green Raggedy Caddis Larva, Peeking Caddis #16.
Crane Fly: *Antocha* spp.			xxxx	xx			xxxx	Dry: Blue-Winged Yellow #12. Nymph: Yellow Sally wet #14.
Grasshoppers				xxxx	xxxx	xxxx	xxxx	Hoppers #12 and #14.
Scuds		xxxx	xxxx	xxxx	xxxx	xxxx	xxxx	Tan, Pink, Olive, Brown, Purple, #12 to #16.
Leeches				xxxx	xxxx	xxxx	xxxx	Black, Olive Woolly Bugger #8 to #12.

Note: Each x represents approximately one week.

Stoneflies are not important in southeastern Minnesota.

Epeorus vitreus is a minor mayfly hatch: April and May emergence. Dry: Gray-Winged Yellow Quill and Light Cahill. Nymph is dark amber #14.

Stenonema/Stenacron spp.: minor mayfly hatches. June 15–July 30. Dry: Sulphur and Light Cahill #12. Nymph: Gold-Hare's Ear #14.

Potamanthus, Cream Fly, is reported mid-July through August.

wrapped in an enigma. It's a daunting puzzle that turns some people off before they really get into the sport.

Some anglers carry as many as 200 different patterns in their fly boxes. Others, out of desperation or despair, have reduced their flies to a mere handful of patterns.

There is a middle ground—20 patterns that we call the "Terrific Twenty" will serve you well throughout the Midwest, and the West, too, for that matter, all season long.

Trout take flies—mayflies, caddisflies, et al.—and terrestrial insects at the surface with a visible rise, the most exciting game in town. But trout feed primarily below the surface on the nymphal forms of various aquatic insects and on crustaceans such as scuds, cress bugs, and crayfish. Large trout fatten on minnows, leeches, and crayfish. Our 20 artificials are reasonable approximations of all these trout foods, except perhaps crayfish. Hundreds of species of aquatic insects take wing from the surface as adults, far too many to replicate, but 12 patterns of dry flies should cover the variety of forms and spectrum of colors displayed by mayflies, caddisflies, midges, and even some common terrestrials.

The Adams is a match for the darker species of mayflies encountered in April and May. The Light Cahill will substitute for the pale mayflies of summer. The Tiny Blue-Winged Olive, sizes #16, #18, and #20, is an exact stand-in for many important species of mayflies and midges throughout the season. The Trico, sizes #20 and #22, is a dead ringer for *Tricorythodes,* which blanket many of our streams early mornings beginning toward the end of June and lasting into September. The White Wulff, size #8, is a generic substitute for any large, night-hatching mayfly, including the fabled *Hexagenia* of July and the *Ephoron* of August. The Brown Bivisible is an all-purpose, bouncy, fast-water fly. The Elk Hair Caddis is an adult caddis; on a #20 hook it is also an emerging midge. The Pass Lake, with its back-slanted calftail hair wing, is both a caddisfly and a mayfly in process of unfolding its wings at the surface. It is a superb attractor, even when allowed to sink. Not least, everybody uses the fanwing or hairwing Royal Coachman at some time during the season. Like nothing else on earth, it is a proven pattern for pounding up trout when they are not feeding on the surface.

The Black Ant is for the slow days of summer when inept ants are falling from overhanging brush. An anomaly: The Ant will often take winter trout when other offerings are refused. Perhaps trout mistake

A Black Beetle perfectly presented under an overhanging bush
fooled this Willow Creek, Wisconsin, brown.

the black body for a rising midge, or for the adult of the tiny early black stonefly. A Black Beetle is also a choice morsel during the warm months.

The Griffith's Gnat, size #20, invented by a founder of Trout Unlimited, is a dry fly that has given us our best catches over several winters on the Whitewater of southeastern Minnesota, including a 13½-inch rainbow trout. It's useful whenever midges are hatching, which is year round on our streams.

The Gold-Ribbed Hare's Ear, Green Caddis Larva, Pheasant Tail, Brassie, and Brown Woolly Worm are sinking patterns that duplicate the underwater stages of many aquatic insects. A Pink Scud should be fished over and through weedbeds on overcast days and at night.

The Muddler is a grasshopper kicking on the surface in July or August, or a minnow when weighted and swimming in the middle depths. For big, stream trout, or for rainbows from the lakes in the fall, the leechlike Olive Woolly Bugger has no peer.

You will want many of the Terrific Twenty in more than one size. Where a size for a dry fly is not specified, buy size #14. Size #16 is about right for the Gold-Ribbed Hare's Ear, Green Caddis Larva, and Pheasant Tail. A #20 Brassie replicates midge larvae. Scuds are sizes #12 and #14. The Brown Woolly Worm, Muddler, and Woolly Bugger should measure about 1½ inches and be tied on a #8 or #10 long-shanked hook.

No doubt you will add one or two killer flies of your own as your experience unfolds.

Because Bill has had so much fun this year with a Hornberg fished dry on the surface or just under the film, I suppose we could add that. Other anglers swear by a Green Beetle. We've had success with a crayfish pattern, if you can find one with claws that don't collapse on the retrieve. Oh, Lord! We have violated our precept already. Well, perhaps you'll wind up with a Thrifty Thirty. We began with Perfect Thirteen some years ago, and here we are with a Terrific Twenty.

As a matter of courtesy and fair trade, it is always a good idea to buy a few flies recommended by a local fly shop in your area of interest. You'll get a warmer reception to your questions.

THE TACTICS

There is no way we can elucidate all of the tactics that we have learned by experience and from reading the magazine articles and books about trout fishing. What follows here are a few of the tactics that we have gleaned by experiment and observation over many years and that we think may be especially helpful to you on Wisconsin and Minnesota streams. We hope that you will add your own and contribute to the literature of our sport.

THE DEADLIEST GAME

Fishers for stream trout have a spectrum of methods by which to lure their quarry out of hiding. Fly-fishermen dearly love the delicate upstream cast with fine leader and dry white-wing to sipping brown trout during the twilight hours. But the deadliest game may be the sinking nymph, cast upstream with a floating line and a 9-foot leader, with a strike indicator strung on the leader. Through the deeper runs and pools, a twist of lead or tiny shot may be needed to place the fly on the trout's nose. On a memorable May day on the Root River I watched Jay Paulson, an expert at the technique, catch and release a 16-inch brown, two 15-inchers, and a half dozen more in the 10- to 14-inch range. His was a textbook demonstration.

The strike of a trout on an upstream nymph is often so subtle that the average fly-fisherman will miss it, hence the need for a strike indicator. The brightly colored indicator signals the take of a trout by going under, by stopping, by darting sideways, or by some other unexpected movement. Experts at the upstream nymphing technique may use a tiny fluorescent cork strung on the leader, a piece of bright floss tied in with a single overhand knot, a pinch-on foam pad, a bushy dry fly tied on a 2-inch dropper, or even a 1-inch two-tone fluorescent streamer tied on a dropper and greased to float. Sometimes the best fish of the day will seize the indicator fly rather than the nymph on the tip. I remember a day on the Willow of Wisconsin when the rascals ignored my nymph on the point, but were like leopards leaping on the fluorescent streamer. A recent improvement is an indicator tied parachute style with upright (mayfly) or back-slanted (caddis) wings fashioned from fluorescent yarn. An indicator fly doubles the fisherman's chances.

Paulson opted for a small fluorescent yarn ball, similar to an egg fly used for steelhead. His results convinced me that a highly visible indicator is the only way to fish a sinking fly upstream.

Of course, the indicator is only part of the story. One must learn how to fish the upstream sinking fly. If you already know where trout are likely to lie, you have a leg up. Paulson fished ever so slowly through the deep pools, adjusting the position of the indicator often, crawling his fly along the bottom. He worked the deeper riffles from lower end to upper. He took one of his best fish from an oblong pocket in the bottom of a long flat that many trout fishers would have passed without a glance. He searched all those spots where the bottom structure was not visible, on the assumption that if he couldn't see the bottom, neither could the trout see him.

A couple or three casts are never enough to cover even a narrow run. Paulson placed his drift at least a dozen times through one run before he connected with the best fish of the day. Be sure to strip the slack out of your line as the fly drifts back to you. Keep your fly on the bottom, even if you must add weight. And watch that indicator for any unusual movement. It's the deadliest game.

IS IT A HATCH OR SPINNER FALL?

It is dusk on the Wolf River of Wisconsin at the Langlade Bridge, on the 4th of June. A cloud of mayflies fills the air, rising and falling over the riffle. They are large and dark with striped abdomens and glassy wings. Gray drakes, I think. The time of emergence conforms with the hatch chart, and the silver and black abdominal rings match the description of the *Siphlonurus quebecensis,* the jawbreaker title that entomologists have given them. I'm in the right place at the right time, I do believe.

I cast fruitlessly with a dry fly until it was too dark to see. I had taken my stance about midway down the riffle, casting a fan across the width, working from close in to far away with a large upwing dry, a reasonable approximation of the natural, I thought. But not so much as a strike tempered my rising frustration.

It was only much later that I realized my stupidity. Important lessons are sometimes learned slowly. Those mayflies were not hatching, not emerging from the surface. They were spinners, adult, glassy-winged mayflies in the process of mating, the females depositing eggs and dying with wings outspread on the water.

Most mayflies emerge at the surface of the stream. The nymphs swim from the bottom, shed their nymphal exoskeletons and unfold their wings at the surface, then fly to some convenient bush to wait for the final change from their dull (dun) form to the glassy-winged, glossy-bright adult form, or spinner. If the emerging mayflies are floating downstream like tiny sailboats while their wings are stiffening for flight, then the fly-fisher is in his glory, casting a dry fly with cocked wings. But if the cloud of mayflies over the stream is a spinner flight, then the trout will feed on the spentwings in the slow water below the riffle.

Not all mayflies emerge at the surface and float leisurely downstream, like a flotilla of sails. The gray drakes of the Wolf in June and the White-Gloved Howdys (*Isonychia*) crawl out of the water to change their dress. Others, such as some species of tricos (*Tricorythodes*), make the change while they are swimming up. Most *Stenonema* and *Stenacron* species, those midseason pale flies (light Cahills and sulphurs), emerge in such an individual and sporadic fashion that they do not trigger the interest of trout. It is only when the *S/S* collect in quantity as spinners that trout turn on. Other species, such as the white fly, *Ephoron,* of August and September, are quick-change artists at the surface, giving a wary trout very little time to examine them.

I was wasting my time on the Wolf that evening. I should have been downstream in the flat water casting a Gray Drake with wings outstretched.

How many times have you thrown the upwing form of the artificial fly to the circles of feeding trout, only to have them ignore the offering? I blush to think of the times I've cast to sipping trout at evening, thinking they were taking #22 midges, when they may have been selecting the spentwings of some spinner fall that had taken place over the riffle upstream.

Spentwings floating in the surface film are difficult to see in good light and almost impossible to spot at dusk, when the majority of mating flights occur. If in doubt, put your nose close to the surface and turn on your flashlight. Hold an aquarium net in the film and examine the drift of material. Rusty or Gray Hen Spinners are usually available in your local fly shop. Be careful to match the size of the natural.

HOW TO BEAT THE HEAT

July and August are tough months for most trout anglers. The streams and rivers are low, clear, and often warm, and the trout are sluggish. Daytime sun and heat are almost unbearable. As a consequence, many fishers give up in despair, hoping that September will bring relief.

Waiting for a change to more clement weather may be the wrong strategy. Not scratching an itch is terribly frustrating. Satisfy your need by going at dawn or dusk, or whenever there's promise of overcast or light rain, even if the temperature threatens to establish a new record. Or seek the feeder streams and snug a hopper up against the banks.

One August day we were on the stream at 7 AM—one of those "lost creeks" that we have mentioned in this book. There are many such streams that are spring-fed and keep their cool even through the worst of a torrid summer. In slightly less than an hour, before the sun had risen high enough to sparkle the water, we had caught and released between us 28 brilliantly hued brook trout. They weren't large but they fought with honest desperation. The air temperature was already into the 80s at that early hour, but we were navel deep in 60-degree water, so we kept cool. The brookies were feeding on rising midges, but they took our #14 hoppers or fat black crickets with abandon. They were too hungry to be selective.

Some of the most experienced fishermen arrive on the stream before dawn. That's earlier than we like to arise, but you may like it. Those early risers hope for a spinner fall of tricos, tiny whitewinged blacks, which begin the death flutter when the air temperature reaches their preferred range. Tricos are omnipresent on midwestern streams into October. *Baetis,* called tiny blue-winged olives, may be early risers, too. Look for them.

Night fishers may run into a hatch of *Hexagenia* or *Ephoron,* the white fly, or *Ephemera simulans,* the brown drake or even a spinner fall of *Isonychia* on the big rivers.

HOW TO CATCH A BIG BROWN TROUT

Let's get the definition of a big brown trout out of the way first. A big stream trout is one longer than 15 inches. Curiously, there are many more big browns reported caught, eyeballed for length, and released by catch-and-release anglers than are counted by Department of Natural Resources crews in electro-shocking surveys. It's all too true that fighting browns appear larger than life. A 16-inch brown from Trout Run Creek on an August evening actually measured a respectable and honest 13 inches. Anglers who keep their fish are assumed to be more exact with their measurements, but sometimes we wonder.

Big browns do not come easily. Putting aside the dubious claims of a special intelligence acquired by certain trout, browns become large by happenstance. When smaller, they wandered into particular niches in a stream that afforded superior cover from predators—man, herons, or otters.

Big browns lurk in the deepest and darkest holes. They hide under tangles of deadfall or underneath root wads. They laze out the daylight hours under bank covers or current deflectors that have been installed by the DNR. While we were watching a DNR crew install lunker structures on the Rush, the first had barely been placed and covered with rock when a 16-inch trout (eyeballed) swam out of nowhere to take possession of that newly created niche.

Large browns feed during the darkest hours. This is not an invariable rule, of course. There are no absolutes in trout fishing. One recent afternoon Bob Linsenman, of the Twin Cities Chapter of Trout Unlimited, observed a brown in the 20-inch class sipping tiny blue-winged olives on the lower Kinnickinnic. But that trophy disdained his artificial. When you find a big brown, he won't bite. Life is hard, brother.

Recently I sat for more than an hour in "The Devil's Seat" (that is, a spot where one may sit, feet in the water, at ease, and cast over a pool) on Trout Run, watching and waiting for one of the several outsize inhabitants to feed at the surface. Finally, one rose to something small. I cast over the lie with a #16 Elk Hair Caddis. A beaver hove into view, swimming downstream. She saw me, banged her paddle, and dove. The brown sank into the weeds, not to rise again anytime soon. The hard treatment—again.

A recent study by the Minnesota DNR is instructive. The study of

A hefty brown caught on a crayfish imitation
on the Wolf River in Wisconsin

511 pools on 21 streams of southeastern Minnesota concluded that pools with three different cover types—undercut banks, deep pools (more than 2 feet in depth), large boulders, root wads, and submerged trees—were most likely to hold big trout. Pools with at least three types of cover were up to 47 times more likely to hold a large brown trout than were pools with only one cover type.

We recall a day of electro-shocking on the Willow River of Wisconsin. Working our way upstream, we were dismayed at the paucity of brown trout in this classic stretch, which consisted of deep pools alternating with some sweet riffles. Finally we came to a deep pool with an undercut on the left, a huge root wad, and a tangle of underwater branches. There we turned belly-up three brown trout, the largest at 21 inches and the smallest about 15. Proof positive that the Minnesota researchers had got it right—four elements, if you count the branch tangle, which we do.

So many years ago, in our salad days, we watched fly-fishers at evening, wading downstream with three big wet flies on a stout leader, taking oversized brown trout from the Namekagon. That's a lost technique in these days of tiny flies and light tackle, but you might think about it.

The best way to catch a big brown is to fish the streams that have produced delegations of lunkers in the past. They aren't spring creeks—there must be depth and volume and forage fish to fatten trout. Be willing to plumb the big pools or deep runs with Black Nose Dace, Woolly Buggers, Muddlers, crayfish, and such. Go from late afternoon into dark, or early morning, well before the sun strikes the water. Don't cast an artificial until you see "the whites of their eyes." Sit and wait in the Devil's Seat. A short prayer will do no harm.

THE TACKLE

Occasionally in this work we must tread where angels fear to tread. So it is with our tackle recommendations. The choice of tackle is personal, depending on experience, sentiment, prejudice, availability, and, not least, the ability to pay. Reasonable fly-fishers will disagree over which fly rod is superior for use on our midwestern trout streams. Anglers, exhausted at the end of a fruitful or fruitless day, will still find time to gather around their pickup trucks to argue the merits of their respective equipment. Even Bill and Jim differ over matters of less than substance.

Therefore, you won't find any dogmatic statements in this section on tackle. Well, perhaps a few.

Before the Second World War, fly-fishers for trout were limited in their choices of tackle. Rods were made of bamboo—most often long, heavy, and slow. Leaders were laboriously hand-tied from short sections of gut, which required preliminary soaking and popped easily, most often, according to myth, on the run of a world-class trout. Silk lines were a misery to keep afloat. Artificial flies were large and gaudy. Creels were both clumsy and capacious, designed to carry home limits of fat trout.

All that changed after the war, thank goodness. Now the varieties of tackle are seemingly endless and often confusing. The trout are smaller on average, but more wily than ever. And many anglers no longer carry creels.

One thing has not changed. The fly rod is still the most important piece of equipment, and merits careful selection. A rod that can be used anywhere in the country is graphite, 8½ feet in length, 5 weight, with a fast action, from any reputable manufacturer or rodmaker. A fast-action rod may require a higher degree of coordination, but the resulting ease of casting is worth the extra practice. A 7½-foot,

3-weight rod has enough firepower for most of our Wisconsin and Minnesota streams. Graphite rods range in price from a low of $50 to a high of $500, and much of the difference may be cosmetic. You can even make your own under the skilled direction of fly shop experts, at considerable savings. But there is something magical about the look and feel of a bamboo rod that probably has more to do with tradition than with practicality. So if you can afford one, go for it.

Most fly-fishers choose two-piece rods because they are cheaper than three-piece travel rods, but some of us have good things to say about the multi-piece rods. They are easier to transport on aircraft, for one. It's our experience that there's no diminution in action due to the extra ferrules.

A single-action fly reel is the first choice of most fly-fishers. There are many good reels, from modest to outrageous in price, that will store a full fly line with a generous length of backing. Here's one instance where Jim and Bill diverge. Humphrey's favorite reel is the #1494 Pflueger/Shakespeare Medalist, which will store all the line and backing you'll need, and will handle the powerful surge of a 2-foot trout easily as it will the tentative tug of a tiddler. Bill Shogren leans toward Scientific Anglers reels, Systems I and II. There are several dozen makes and models of fly reels; one will suit you well.

The fly line must be matched to the rod. That is, a 5-weight rod requires a #5 line. Your first line should be a weight-forward floating line. Ivory, salmon, or one of the fluorescent colors will help you observe and control the drift of the fly. To save money for more important items, partners can buy a 25- or 30-meter double taper and cut it in two, so each can have 45 or 50 feet of single taper and plenty of 15-pound Dacron backing. You are not likely to be casting more than 45 feet of line in this part of the world.

The leader will be at least 9 feet of monofilament, tapered from .019 inch at the butt to .007 inch (4X) at the point. For dainty flies, you can add 18 inches to 3 feet of tippet, .006 (5X) or .005 (6X). Some commercial brands are consistently a millimeter thicker than the diameter given on the spool, so you may want to invest in an inexpensive micrometer or monofilament gauge. Tippets are tied to the leader with the surgeon's knot, aka the double surgeon's knot. For a description of all knots, refer to Mark Sosin and Lefty Kreh's *Practical Fishing Knots,* or to the *L.L. Bean Fly-Fishing Handbook.*

Except for the choice of fly, the above takes care, all too briefly perhaps, of the fly-fishing end of the business.

You may not need them, but surely you will desire other accoutrements of the modern angler.

Hip boots are cooler than chest-high waders during the heat of summer. They are easy to walk in, and will allow you to wade deep enough on 60 to 70 percent of your trips. Hippers with plain old lug soles are cheap enough to discard after a couple or three seasons.

Dedicated trout fishers also own chest-high waders, invariably with felt soles, because the felts grip better on slimy rocks. Felts, however, are never as good as lugs on ice, to which we can attest by a series of pratfalls suffered when fishing the snowbanks and ice shelves of southeastern Minnesota during the special winter season.

Now the selection of wading gear becomes more complicated. Most modern fly-fishers opt for stockingfoot waders, worn with a stout felt-bottomed wading shoe over. A common practice is to wear heavy socks inside the waders, a pair of socks over the waders, and eventually some kind of gravel guard over the top of the boot. Neoprene stockingfoot waders with fitted feet and built-in gravel guards are the current fad among well-dressed aficionados, but tight-fitting neoprenes can be hot under summer skies. Humphrey remains loyal to the boot-foot, ankle-fit, rubber-over-stretch-nylon waders that have been around since the year 1. Body heat is squeezed out of the open top.

All boots and waders leak eventually, so ease of patching may be an important consideration in your selection of a particular style or brand. If you invent an all-purpose glop or tape that works every time on all manner of surfaces, you will have made your fortune.

Last on this fascinating subject: Try on boots and waders before you buy. Different manufacturers use varying combinations of foot size and leg length, a critical consideration with chest-highs. If the waders are too short in the crotch, you won't be comfortable after a couple of hours of wading; if they're too long, the accordion pleats around your knees will abrade the material. Always allow for a pair of heavy socks over your regular socks.

A dark green or camo vest with no reflecting hardware on the front, and not too many pockets, is another necessity for the complete angler. Pockets have a tendency to get filled up, and the vest becomes a millstone. You'll need a ripple foam fly box, Polaroid glasses or clip-ons, a snippers for clipping tippets, a forceps for removing hooks taken deeply by trout, and the recommended staff for tricky wading. An aluminum ski pole makes an outstanding staff. Don't remove the basket. Cut away the outer circle but leave the three or four stubs intact. The stubs prevent the staff from sliding too far into a soft bottom.

You may want a small net and a flat creel with which to capture and carry home an infrequent meal of small, fresh trout. As you develop experience, you will naturally acquire miscellaneous accessories of the modish angler. They might include a thermometer, specimen bottles and an aquarium net for capturing insects in the film, a magnifying glass, and other esoteric items. A packet of pH strips is useful for measuring the acidity/alkalinity of water. Such strips are still used in the boiler rooms of commercial buildings. A grateful fisherman who was a maintenance engineer in a hospital donated a packet to Jim.

And so, here comes the Compleat Angler, fly-casting upstream, all spangled and flashing with the jewels of his art.

We close without comment on the hat he is wearing!

WISCONSIN

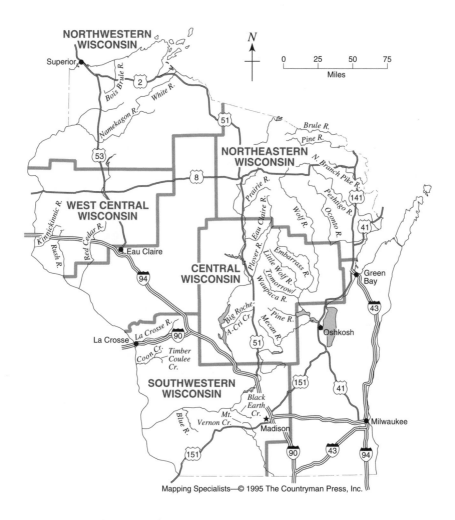

3

Southwestern Wisconsin: Spring Creeks in Hidden Valleys

The winding roads bear such evocative names as Hidden Valley, Hoot Hollow, Dry Dog, Zero Hero (?), Romance Lookout, Far Nuff, Never Sweat, Rattlesnake, and Morning Star. There are Old Mill Roads and countless River Roads—Blue River and Green River among them. In truth, there is a rainbow of colors in the old names.

You'll find Timber Coulee and Spring Coulee and other coulees— "coulee" being a relict French word for ravine. There are ethnic remembrances of the earliest settlers of this hill country: Indian Creek, Irish Ridge, Russian Coulee, Dutch Hill, Swiss Valley, German Flats, British Hollow, and Bryn Gyrwen, a hill named by some long-dead Welsh miner to remind himself of home. There are mountains, too: Tabor, Ida, Zion, Sterling, Vernon, and, of course, Hope.

Among the earliest settlements, Hard Scrabble, Fairplay, Nip-and-Tuck, Shirt-Tail, Shake-rag, Hoff Noggle, Trespass, and Tail-hole have disappeared. Only a handful, such as New Diggings, Lead Mine, Plugtown, Avalanche, and Cataract, remain to remind us of the direct and hard-edged speech of the immigrants. In later, more respectable times, the names were softened and changed to commemorate dead heroes and live governors, or voracious land speculators.

Come late August, winding down from the highlands into the hollows and bottoms, past limestone towers and through bee-loud glades, paralleling fields of corn the color of weathered brass, you'll turn a corner and see at streamside, even now, a woman gathering the huge green leaves of tobacco in tanned and muscular arms. It is picture-book country, with dusty gravel roads and narrow, sinuous black-tops, and long vistas of meandering spring creeks with browsing, drowsing cattle on their emerald banks.

This is the Driftless Area of Wisconsin, which was left untouched by the glaciers, some 15,000 square miles of one-time prairie and oak openings, carved by the rains of time into hills and "mountains," eroded into valleys, hollows, coulees, glens, dingles, and dells, and drained by hundreds of named spring creeks and warm-water rivers. It is a huge, rough right triangle of land, more than 100 miles on each leg, wedged between the Mississippi River and the Illinois border. The bellied hypotenuse is Interstate 90, connecting Beloit, Wisconsin, on the Illinois border with La Crosse on the Mississippi.

Some links of hills are called the Blue Mounds because at the end of day they are just that—blue mounds rippling against a washed sky. There are also names like Castle Rock and Pike's Peak to differentiate one crenellated tower from a distant, limestone spire. There's Wildcat Ridge, named in the 1820s for those sly beasts which roamed the hills when the settlers came up the Mississippi from St. Louis and points east. The homesteaders came in sternwheelers, sidewheelers, and by wagon from Milwaukee, to burn the oaks and plant corn. Welsh and Cornish miners came to dig lead out of vertical shafts and to burrow winter homes into the sides of cliffs.

Wisconsin is known as the Badger State. Folklore has it that it was named for those first soft-rock miners, and that is as good a story as any, although the shy and dangerous badger still mines his hidey-holes in the quiet valleys.

This gigantic triangle, part of which is appropriately named the Hidden Valleys for commercial and tourist purposes, includes portions of 14 counties. A wandering fisher will find trout in all of them, even in Rock County, which is only a couple of hours by car from Chicago.

Twelve counties are of special interest to the footloose fly-fisher. They contain 413 trout streams and more than 1500 miles of brook trout, browns, and rainbows. That's almost enough for several lifetimes of exploration.

For 15 years, 8 of the 12 counties opened for trout fishing on January 1, rather than on the first Saturday in May. It was a cherished experience for us to travel to southwestern Wisconsin to fly-fish for trout, often under blue skies, sometimes in snow or sleet, as early as the second week in January. As of 1995 that wonderful experiment ended.

At first, 10 counties were open for the special winter season. Then that was reduced to eight, because of extraordinary pressure on several first-class streams near La Crosse. During much of this period, fish managers believed that the winter season had no deleterious effect on the stock of trout. More recently, the evidence suggests that trout are vulnerable to fishing pressure when they stack up in the pools during periods of low water. It is true that on some winter trips we found the brown trout congregating in clear pools, but that didn't seem to us to make them any easier to coax out with an artificial fly. Added pressure for closure came from a majority of anglers in the eight counties who attended spring county conservation meetings, and from the State Council of Trout Unlimited.

However, the DNR fisheries researchers have recommended that the lower one-third of the state be opened on April 1 rather than the first Saturday in May. The review process is complex, so we can't guarantee that you will be able to explore the fine streams of the Hidden Valleys that early. We can only cross our fingers, and hope.

Whatever changes in regulations become law in 1996, we respect the careful deliberations of the researchers. It is the goal of the Wisconsin Department of Natural Resources to maintain and enhance the opportunity to enjoy quality trout fishing for legions of fishers.

With so many productive spring creeks from which to choose, it's impossible to guide you on a stream-by-stream tour, so we'll examine 20 streams that are suitable for fly-fishing over educated stream trout. All are classic, spring-fed hardwater streams. Many are exceedingly fertile and produce multiple hatches of aquatic insects. Don't be put off by terms like "creek" or "river." Some creeks are larger than some rivers and some rivers are quite modest.

EIGHT STREAMS OF
THE SOUTHWEST CORNER

We will review first our favorite streams in Grant and Iowa Counties in the southwest corner of Wisconsin. They were among the eight counties that opened early through 1994, so our profiles include a few interesting anecdotes that describe winter fly-fishing. You will find those short stories useful on other streams that may be opened for an early season in the future.

We'd label six of these eight streams as first class. One is marginal, and another is small, with only a few pools. Castle Rock Creek has huge pools that will cause any true-blue fly-fisher to salivate. Seven of them include sections placed under special regulations, Category 5.

CROOKED CREEK
DeLorme 33

Crooked Creek in Grant County, south of the Wisconsin River, is Category 5 from WI 133 to the headwaters, a distance of 5.4 miles. Its browns are wild, that is, naturally reproducing. About 3 miles south of Boscobel on US 61 you will find Town Hall Road. You should be able to see the double-arched bridge way off to the west from US 61. There's a DNR stile at the bridge and a superb pool. We always stop at the bridge to tease the brown trout. Or maybe they're teasing us.

We've usually found trout midging under or in the shadows of the bridge. Maintain a low profile and approach from downstream.

Which reminds me of an incident. I parked the car, climbed the stile, and walked down the east bank, hunched over to keep out of sight of the feeding browns. Aha! I thought. What a way to start a day in early March. Clear skies, temperature in the 50s, no competition from other anglers, and the browns taking midges at the surface.

Fifty yards or so downstream I crossed the riffle and began a stealthy approach along the west bank. When I was close to casting range I dropped to my knees and began to inch forward, painfully.

Just then, two young guys stopped their car on the bridge, got out, leaned over to look, waved to me in friendly fashion, pulled the car off the bridge, hopped the stile, and began to flail the water.

So much for the beginning of a great day. There is such a thing as courtesy to other anglers who have already staked a claim to a promising bit of water, but I guess the kids didn't know any better.

There are a couple of small pools downstream that you must fish on your knees, but generally the stream is narrow and deep, with water plants at the edges. Upstream to the next bridge on US 61 is pasture. It's not posted against trespass, but you'll want to ask permission at the white house.

We can't leave Crooked Creek and Boscobel without leaving you with a bit of history. The old hotel in Boscobel is the birthplace of the Gideons, the folks who supply Bibles to hotel and motel rooms worldwide. It seems that one night, long ago, three traveling salesmen met in the lounge. Discovering, after a conversation that lasted into the wee hours, that they had similar religious convictions, they founded the Gideons. It's a fair guess that they weren't trout fishermen or they'd have been out on the streams.

Boscobel is a quiet town, with comfortable facilities for travelers. The Hotel Boscobel is now home to the Boscobel Heritage Museum and Library and is part of a historic downtown featuring many beautiful stone buildings.

THE BIG GREEN RIVER
DeLorme 32 & 33

From the heights of Mount Ida (junction of US 18 and County Road K), west of Fennimore, one can look down through green pastures, past forested slopes, and into the valley of the Big Green. To the east, only minutes away, lie the broad meadows of Castle Rock Creek and the narrow, twisting glen of the Blue River.

The Big Green, upstream from WI 133 near Woodman, has 11 miles of water, a section of which is Category 5; the remainder is Category 3, planted with brown trout. Snaking through pastureland, sometimes with one edge against a wooded limestone ridge, it is narrow, averaging 12 feet in width. A few expert early-season nymph fishers will take 30 or 40 fish in a morning. They work excruciatingly slowly upstream through the open land, casting a #14 or #15 Hare's Ear Nymph or a Green Caddis Larva.

One March 25 on the upper Green, with the air temperature at 35 degrees and the water at 48 degrees, while I was throwing figure 8s into a powerful breeze (and sometimes 9s and maybe even 10s), the

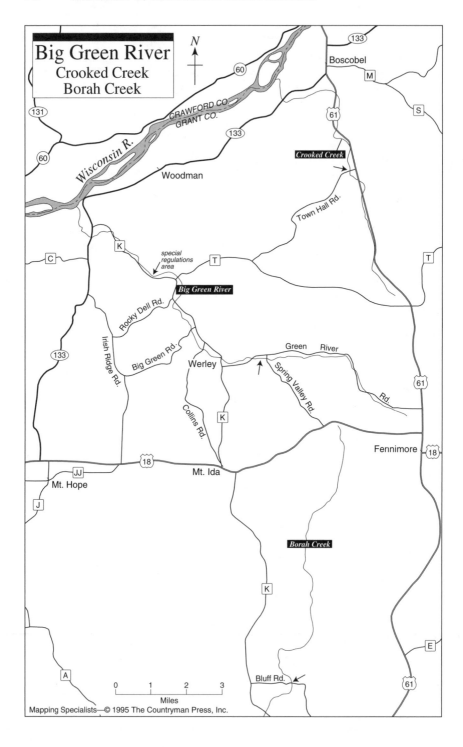

Big Green River
Crooked Creek
Borah Creek

N

133
Boscobel
M
S
131
60
CRAWFORD CO.
GRANT CO.
133
61
60
Crooked Creek
Wisconsin R.
Woodman
Town Hall Rd.
C
K
special
regulations
area
T
T
Big Green River
Rocky Dell Rd.
Green   River
Irish Ridge Rd.
133
Big Green Rd.
Werley
Spring Valley Rd.
Rd.
61
Collins Rd.
K
Fennimore
18
JJ
18
Mt. Ida
Mt. Hope
J
Borah Creek
K
E
A
0   1   2   3
Bluff Rd.
61
Miles
Mapping Specialists—© 1995 The Countryman Press, Inc.

browns began to rise at noon for lunch to a goodly hatch of miserable, struggling *Baetis*. I took just enough trout to satisfy my ego before deciding that life was too short to suffer so for the Art of Fly-Fishing. My emerger had a dark olive/brown body with a ball of gray rabbit dubbing on top. A purist might have preferred to drop a #18 Blue-Winged Olive on the nose.

Take Spring Valley Road into the valley from just opposite the Fenmore Hills Motel and Supper Club (our usual headquarters) on US 18, 2 miles west of Fennimore. Between the two bridges on the Green it's low-profile fly-casting with a 4- or 5-weight rod, .005 (6X) tippet, and tiny flies in the early weeks. A visitor can also find the headwaters of the Green on the Green River Road, 1 mile north of Fennimore, west of US 61, or on County Road K from Mt. Ida to Werley.

Downstream from Werley, the pools deepen and in places the brush closes in. About 3 miles of the Big Green from County Road T to WI 133 is restricted to artificials only and catch and release, Category 5. It's probable that the significant increase there in larger trout is the result of these special regulations. At least one local angler, Roger Kerr, thinks so. He reported the best trout fishing of his life one recent June in that Category 5 section.

Fly-fishing the special-regulations water can produce unexpected results. It's the most beautiful water through pasture, where the DNR has installed lunker structures. Walking downstream, Bill spooked one fish that looked to be about 14 inches. Then, you won't believe what he did. He caught a legitimate 20-inch rainbow, on a Hare's Ear bead head with a little bit of split shot. It must have taken him a half hour to bring her in. It was a real reel screamer. I couldn't believe it either! Evidently our friends from the DNR plant more than browns in the Big Green. A few more browns deigned to look at our offerings after some labor, but none approached that first trophy, which, by the way, was carefully released.

Bill sums up our experience this way: "This Big Green is a wonderful river! There are so many places for big trout to hide. That's what this river must be about—good-sized trout, not necessarily about numbers of trout. I don't know anything quite as nice as this. All pasture, a lot of deep runs, 15 to 25 yards wide in most areas. It's just got to have some amazingly big brown trout in it. You couldn't find an easier stream in the whole wide world to fish. Everything's open: It's really neat."

BORAH CREEK
DeLorme 25

We haven't fished Borah Creek yet because there's so much good water around the Fennimore Hills, but we like the looks of it. Find it south of Mt. Ida and about a mile east of County Road K on Bluff Road. On last report it contains planted browns. Downstream from Bluff Road it's under special regulations, Category 5, for a few miles. You might like to sneak over there one evening after a satisfying dinner at one of the many supper clubs.

CASTLE ROCK CREEK
DeLorme 33

Castle Rock Creek begins as a trickle from a ravine on the east edge of Fennimore in Grant County and winds some 22 miles northeast to its junction with the Blue River. At times past, that ravine was used as an occasional dump, so we've always had some doubt as to the water quality of the upper reaches.

About 6 miles downstream from Fennimore, along County Road Q, find Church Road and turn southeast to the bridge, the beginning of approximately 6½ miles of designated trout water, and the head of about 1½ miles of Category 5, "fish for fun" water, artificials only. The remainder of the mileage is Category 4. There may be some trout upstream of Church Road but the real action will be downstream as far as Witek Road. Access to the designated trout water is excellent because much of the mileage is under DNR easement.

Castle Rock Creek, also labeled Fennimore Fork on the trout regulations map, offers a different configuration from most other southwestern Wisconsin streams. Upstream of the first bridge on County Road Q, east of Church Road, it's a broad pasture stream with huge, slow pools alternating with riprapped corners and a few graveled runs. There's a short section of paving on the northwest side of the first County Road Q bridge, which provides off-road parking. Downstream to the second bridge it's somewhat narrower and heavily riprapped, with a variety of habitat more typical of the other streams in the area. It's possible to park at the second bridge down and, for a small fee, fish through a private campground. As I recall, the last time we fished the campground we paid our fees to the folks at Kohout Farm.

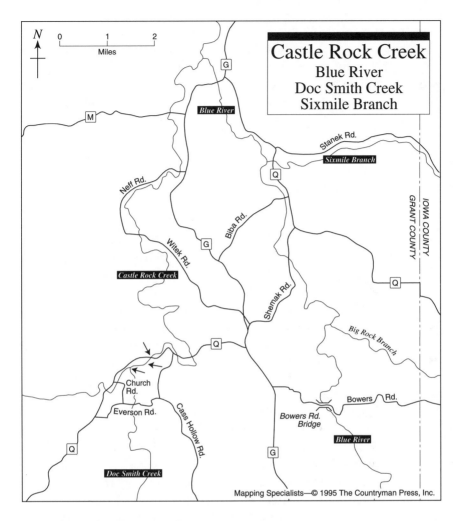

Mapping Specialists—© 1995 The Countryman Press, Inc.

Quick to rise during a rainstorm and slow to fall, the creek is always slightly milky due to runoff from pasture and field and percolation through limestone. Summertime water temperatures are not likely to exceed 70 degrees. Because natural reproduction is poor and the stream is popular with anglers from Illinois and other distant places, all three species of trout are planted.

One expert advises that he's had consistent and quite fabulous success with a Royal Coachman bucktail. A Pass Lake, or any similar white-winged caddis pattern in size #14, will do equally well if the trout are not rising to an identifiable hatch.

The gigantic pools upstream of the County Road Q bridge will have to be approached in an attitude of prayer—on your knees on the bank—not because you implore the intervention of divine beneficence, but because you will be visible against the sky to wary trout that have already tested the metal of a hook. Stay back on a long line and a fine leader. Float your fly close to the jumbled riprap. Late in the year you'll find mats of blooming watercress and the massed tiny pads of lesser duckweed at the margins. Drop your fly there; the trout will lie in shadow and rush to meet your fly, if they like the look of it.

Not so long ago, a DNR survey revealed 200 fish 16 to 18 inches long, and hundreds in the 10- to 14-inch class, all in the catch-and-release section. There were also a few giant browns to 24 inches near the outlet of the big spring, which pumps 3000 gallons a minute into Castle Rock. On one recent occasion, Bob Mitchell, of Bob Mitchell's Fly Shop in Lake Elmo, Minnesota, released a 27-inch rainbow—brood stock from a hatchery, no doubt.

To fatten those superior trout, the creek contains substantial populations of scuds, leeches, and a few species of the smaller stoneflies. That thin hatch of early-April small black stoneflies is probably *Capnia vernalis,* known to the fraternity as the early black, but stoneflies are not common to these spring creeks, and the early black will have gone airborne by May.

You might think that so popular a stream would be under constant pressure. Yet we have been there in the early season in midweek and again during the dog days of August, and have encountered no other fishermen. May and June weekends will see a surfeit of anglers.

On an August evening under a gloomy sky, on the fourth cast against the bank of the first run downstream from County Road Q bridge, a 14-inch brown rose to take a Cap Buettner Stonefly Muddler. The brown was a veritable football in shape, deeply colored and determined to fight. Not one other fisherman was there to witness that titanic struggle.

But we admit we particularly enjoy the early weeks on Castle Rock when the barometer is rising into the green range of "good fishing." The sun is shining. Visibility under washed blue skies is forever. Go fishing! our inner urges yell. Go, go! After all, it's only 250 miles from home. And so our recommendation to you, dear reader: Go and enjoy the great pools of Castle Rock at least once in your life.

DOC SMITH CREEK
DeLorme 33

This 4-mile feeder shows some pretty water above its junction with Castle Rock in the pastures, but the water quality is marginal due to runoff from grazing land and high summer water temperatures. Only the lower 1.8 miles is considered trout water. We've had modest returns from the first ¼ mile above the junction with Castle Rock.

THE BLUE RIVER
DeLorme 33

The Blue River at Bowers Road Bridge east of County Road G twists north to the Wisconsin River through a forested valley. Go east from Castle Rock to County Road G, then south to the first road running east. That's Bowers Road, where there is a DNR parking lot and a stile. You may also be greeted by a friendly dog who always shows up, tail wagging, to share our sandwiches companionably. We've named him Beggar Dog, but he's a good chap.

Between Bowers and Biba Roads, the downstream end of the designated trout water, a fisher may enjoy the solitude of primitive Wisconsin through 6 pretty miles. Upstream toward Montfort there's a stretch of Category 5 water; the remainder is Category 4.

Late one March, Dick Hanousek of the Twin Cities took 13 good browns from the upstream Blue with *Baetis* emergers in a 4-hour period. As he said, "Not bad for openers." Those tiny blue-winged olives will be around in May and June, and on through the season.

On another March day, Bill fly-fished upstream from Bowers Road, where he caught a couple of brownies and a rainbow on nymphs. "It's a beautiful day, in the 40s, I'd say. Overcast most of the time. I ran into a guy who fishes below that bridge. He goes in there quite often. He came out with three browns today; he thought they were rainbows. He was fishing pieces of chub. A 22-incher, a 20-incher, and a 14-incher, and they were shaped like footballs. Obviously, these fish must make a pretty good living in the winter months in these big, deep holes. He said there were many deep holes and good fish, and that he had missed a couple of bigger ones. Can you imagine it? That 22-incher had to be 6, 7 pounds!" This may be one reason why the early season has been eliminated. Only parts of some streams were protected by catch-and-release rules during the special winter season, so bait fishers could plumb the pools outside the limits.

SIXMILE BRANCH
DeLorme 33

Before you leave the Blue River, try the Sixmile Branch, Category 3. Go north on County Road Q to Stanek Road, east on Stanek to Pine Tree Road, then southeast to the Sixmile. All three species of trout are planted; you may find some of them in the pools.

The Big Green, the Castle Rock, and the Blue are a trio of fly-fishing streams as good as you'll find anywhere in the Midwest, but that doesn't mean that your experience will be like shooting fish in a barrel. It's estimated that the Castle Rock trout have been caught an average of four times a season, and those suspicious trout on the Big Green and the Blue have been worked over by experts. And yet they are there, awaiting the drift of your Trico or the kick of a black cricket under the orange-freckled blossoms of jewelweed at streamside. Or maybe you should use a chub tail. We're just kidding!

This part of the world is amazing in many ways. "The supper clubs are alive and well. We got a steak sandwich for $5.95, and the place was absolutely packed; everybody was there. Everybody's friendly; it's so relaxed; it's really neat."

Facilities for the preceding seven streams are at Fennimore, Boscobel, and at the Fenmore Hills Motel and Supper Club 2 miles west of Fennimore on US 18.

OTTER CREEK
DeLorme 26 & 34

Travel east from the Fennimore Hills via US 18 toward Dodgeville to Otter Creek in Iowa County, our eighth stream. Take County Road Q north from the highway, about 2 miles west of Dodgeville. Stop at the bridge on County Road Q and take a look at one sweet run just downstream of the bridge. We've enjoyed tagging those browns with an Adams or a #16 Elk Hair Caddis.

The approximately 8 miles of Otter, from its headwaters down to County Road II, is a wide meadow stream planted with brooks and

A summer day on Otter Creek at the County Road Q bridge

browns. Between County Road Q and the County Road II crossing downstream, a matter of 2 miles, it is Category 5; upstream from County Road Q, it is Category 4.

DNR metal stiles, not always prominently placed, afford access along County Road II. Those tall, narrow ladders, which are also used throughout the Southwest, have been known to tip. Just ask us! Be careful going over.

Otter produces excellent hatches of caddisflies. The Dark Green Raggedy Caddis or Green-Bodied Hare's Ear will do well as underwater searching patterns. Dry caddis patterns will be small in the spring—#14 and #16. In the later months you'll find occasional hatches of larger caddis. At the downstream end near the County Road II bridge, you'll find a narrower stream with bending grass at the margins. This is for hopper time, July and August. We have had some wonderful early fly-fishing days on the Otter with an Elk Hair Caddis under bright blue skies, and later with a hopper or a small dry Muddler fished at the surface.

Facilities at Dodgeville. Mineral Point, about 10 miles to the southwest of Dodgeville, is a historic lead-mining town. You may want to spend some time at Pendarvis, a collection of stone houses. Superior cuisine and tourist facilities there.

FOUR STREAMS OF THE MADISON AREA

TROUT CREEK

DeLorme 34 & 35

Follow County Road T north and west out of Barneveld from US 18 and US 151 to Trout Creek in Iowa County. This stream is approximately 35 miles west of Madison. All 8 miles of Trout Creek are Category 5 and include the three species of trout.

An expert of our acquaintance, Joe Balestrieri, always felt that Trout Creek was better than Grandma's apple pie and Wisconsin cheddar cheese, even though the creek runs narrowly through brush. Joe uses light rods and knotless, fine leaders for delicacy, and a sneaky slow presentation from a kneeling position. Fish downstream with a Gold-Ribbed Hare's Ear on a swimming nymph hook, or with Pheasant Tail nymphs and soft-hackle wet flies tied after the Sylvester Nemes method. Midge dries are necessary, in sizes #22 and smaller. Scud and sowbug imitations, plus ants, hoppers, and beetles, are useful during the hot months. It was here that Joe B. watched a trout nosing into eel grass and shaking its head to dislodge snails, which the brown then proceeded to gobble up. The snails were about the size of a BB.

Recommended dries are small Light Cahills, Blue-Winged Olives #18 and #20, and Sulphur Duns #16 and #18. The many species of caddisflies are represented by the Small Black, Spotted Sedge, and Dark Blue Sedge. The above list reads like a prescription for any of the spring creeks of the hidden valleys.

Trout Creek has long been a blue-ribbon stream, but at this writing we can't rate it quite so highly; the flow appears to have slowed and the water has darkened. The condition may be temporary due to transitory factors. By the time you read this report, Trout Creek may have recovered.

Facilities at Barneveld or at Spring Green on the Wisconsin River, close to Frank Lloyd Wright's Taliesin, the American Players Theater, and Tower Hill State Park.

BLACK EARTH CREEK
DeLorme 35

Black Earth Creek in Dane County, which is one of the four counties that did not open for the early season, is so close to Madison and so famous for its naturally reproducing browns that you'd expect shoulder-to-shoulder fishing, but that's not always true. On one Saturday afternoon and evening in August, we met only one spin-fisherman. He was taking an occasional small trout on a Mepps. Weekends in May and June, though, you'll have to walk away from the bridges and DNR parking lots to find fly-casting room. Weekdays will be quieter, but not much. If you fish over the Hex hatch well into dark, you'll find some breathing room because it's a fact that many fishermen don't care to wait for the sound of a slurp to strike. Bill, together with Bill Haugen and Dave Fass of Minnesota TU, enjoyed some super fishing over the Hex hatch as early as June 13, a week early. This renowned creek is one that fishes best early mornings or late evenings.

Black Earth Creek, 12 miles long, begins as a trickle along US 14 west of Middleton, but gathers water at Festbe Spring east of Cross Plains. A section of it east of the village of Black Earth, from South

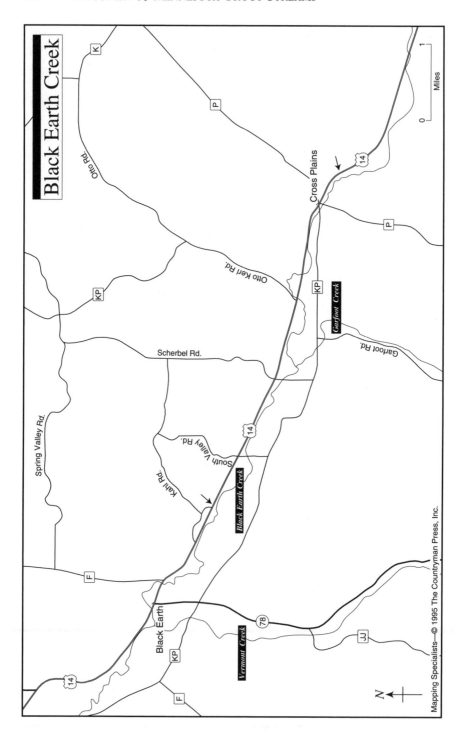

Valley Road to Park Street, is rated Category 5. The creek has been undergoing extensive rehabilitation by the Wisconsin DNR at the request of local chapters of Trout Unlimited. In 1985 TU expressed concern over an apparent increase in weeds, a decrease in weight of fish, increased siltation, and streambank erosion. Electro-shocking confirmed a decrease in weight of trout per acre, but there remained a large and relatively stable population of wild brown trout. Erosion was reasonably well controlled, but siltation was greater than desired.

In the fall of that year, the DNR selected Black Earth Creek as a priority watershed project under the Wisconsin Nonpoint Source Water Pollution Abatement Program. That soon brought to bear a variety of interdisciplinary studies. Since then, great improvements have been made. Easements have been acquired, the banks have been reshaped and riprapped, cattle have been restricted behind 5000 feet of fencing, and many in-stream structures have been installed downstream from Cross Plains. The wild brown trout have responded well.

In addition to the Hex, notable hatches are the early Hendrickson and little black caddis. The tan caddis appears throughout the stream in May and June. Scuds, sowbugs, leeches, and the usual variety of terrestrials are trout fare all season long. There is a DNR parking lot at Cross Plains and access at four or five bridges.

All facilities at Madison and some at Cross Plains and Black Earth.

MOUNT VERNON CREEK
DeLorme 27

Mount Vernon Creek in Dane County, southwest of Madison, is popular with fly-fishers from Madison and is only 150 miles from Chicago. Two miles of it between WI 92 and County Road U are Category 5. Above and below the special regulations section it is Category 3.

This beautiful stream has been tended and manicured by the DNR as a showpiece. Cattle have been fenced out and easements well marked. Joe Balestrieri of Milwaukee, who values that stream above all others in the southwest, stalks the hatches from just above the village of Mt. Vernon to the public parking area downstream. He makes his approach from the bridge on County Road G in town. On

May 28, Joe and his brother Jim found a flight of "sulphurs," but not the typical *Ephemerella*. The brothers caught and released brown trout to 14 inches on a brown nymph and a Sulphur dry fly.

Mt. Vernon Creek is a jewel, known for its hatches of spring creek mayflies, plus a variety of terrestrials—crickets and beetles from May 1 to September 15. Hoppers are abundant from July 25 through September.

This clearwater creek is notable for being exasperatingly difficult; the trout are super-selective. The visitor must proceed with caution, patience, and experience if he intends to finesse any of the three species of reproducing trout. It's a fine stream to visit during a weekday after the May and early-June rush of fishers is past its apogee. In June you'll still find evening hatches of *Ephemerellidae* and *Stenonema/ Stenacron*, although the S/S hatches are never heavy. Toward the end of June and early July the dark-of-the-moon Hex will be on the wing, signaled no doubt by the arrival of bats over the water 5 minutes before. Carry two flashlights, locate a pool, and wait for the long, wiggling lift of the super mayflies of the Midwest. For the night release of big brown trout, barbless hooks are *de rigueur*.

All facilities at Madison, Mount Horeb, and Verona. Specific advice is available at Lunde's Fly Fishing Chalet at Mount Horeb, WI 53572, on WI 92.

ROWAN CREEK
DeLorme 36

Rowan Creek, about 35 miles north of Madison in Columbia County, is intersected by Interstate 90/94 4 miles west of Poynette. The freeway exit to Poynette is County Road CS. Upstream of US 51 at Poynette there is a section of Category 5 water through more than a mile of DNR lands; the remainder of its 8 miles is Category 3. More than ½ mile of it through cattails and bulrushes was purchased by The Nature Conservancy and transferred to the DNR.

Access to the downstream section is by trail from a DNR parking lot on County Road J, which is immediately east of Interstate 90/94. Go north on County Road J from County Road CS about 1 mile to parking. There is a second parking lot on County Road CS about 0.5 mile east of County Road J. Closer to Poynette on County Road CS there's a park from which you should be able to foot it to the creek.

In town you'll find more DNR parking on Main Street on the up-stream side of the bridge; downstream is a picnic ground and ball field. Just east of US 51 on Tomlinson Road find East Road, going south, which will take you into the open DNR lands. At still another DNR parking lot, on Loveland Road east of Poynette, the stream is narrow, dark, and deep, alternating through hay meadows and brush. There you'll find a "Federal Aid In Fish Restoration Project" sign commemorating the work of the Southern Chapter of Trout Unlim-ited, the Columbia County Sportsman's League, the Columbia County Conservation Fund, and the Trout Stamp Fund. You'll also find a spring under a grass mat that will permit you to bounce on it as if it were a trampoline.

Rowan Creek is popular with anglers from a wide radius, so there's no guarantee that you will have the stream to yourself. Best to go on a bad day when other anglers are put off by overcast or rain. We've had it all to ourselves in March in miserable conditions, but we caught trout on the usual small stuff—Brassies, Pheasant Tails, Adamses, and Griffith's Gnats. Our friend Jason Carpenter, from Missouri, on our recommendation stopped on his way north to fish Rowan Creek in September. But he reported that the river was so soggy at the mar-gins that he could hardly get close to it.

Facilities at Poynette.

STREAMS NORTH AND WEST OF THE WISCONSIN RIVER

RICHLAND CREEK
DeLorme 33

Richland Creek in Crawford County is just across the river from Crooked Creek at Boscobel. It parallels US 61 just north of WI 60 and the Wisconsin River. It's a small creek, a bit more than 8 miles in length, and planted with brook and brown trout. If you stay over-night at Boscobel, you could send one of your partners to Richland to fish the evening through the pastureland. Marietta Valley Road is a loop road off US 61 that takes you west of the stream just north of WI 60. From Marietta you can follow Spring Valley Road up-stream.

Facilities at Boscobel.

CAMP CREEK
DeLorme 33 & 41

Curt Dary, an aquatic entomologist and dedicated fly-fisher whose superior wisdom and skill we bow to, states categorically that Camp Creek, east of Viola in northwest Richland County on WI 56, is one of the 20 best streams in Wisconsin—high praise, indeed. Its 5½ miles of natural brook trout and browns are rated Category 5, an indication that the DNR accords the stream special status. Access is at County Roads G and MM bridges or by a short stroll between cornfields from the neat little park on WI 56, 2 miles east of Viola. Another enthusiast swears that his fat #10 Carpenter Ant will inveigle trout consistently.

Our experience on Camp Creek has not been all that wonderful, perhaps because we haven't fished it consistently. And that points up a moral that we will make quite often in these pages: You may find a section of stream that is everything to you that the Good Lord might allow, while Humphrey or Shogren can't "lay up a dime" there. So we don't claim, can't claim, that our streams are the *best* that you will discover in Wisconsin and Minnesota. Our streams are good ones, but you'll find better if you just poke around on your own.

Facilities at Viola.

THE PINE RIVER COMPLEX
DeLorme 33 & 34

The Pine River, Category 3, some 14 miles of water above the village of Buck Creek on WI 80 in northeastern Richland County, includes a complex of seven streams within its watershed. We like the main stem of the Pine around Hub City. It is bigger water than many of the streams of southwestern Wisconsin and absolutely beautiful, winding through fields of hay and corn and around limestone castles. We haven't yet spent enough time on it to prepare a definitive report on all of the feeders, but it's certainly one that demands further attention. A number of feeders and a section of the West Branch of the Pine are Category 5, a sure sign of interest by the DNR, and therefore worthy of exploration. Access is easy at numerous bridges in that tangled country.

Facilities at Richland Center.

*Small flies and fine leaders are required in the still water
of the Pine River.*

TIMBER COULEE CREEK
DeLorme 40

Timber Coulee, Categories 3 and 5, in northern Vernon and southern La Crosse Counties, is just about perfect for fly-fishing, with many
deep runs, easy access, and access points well marked by the DNR. It
lies along County Road P, east of the village of Coon Valley on US
61. Timber Coulee has been tended and improved by the Wisconsin
DNR. Lunker structures, riprap, and a Hewitt ramp have been installed. A mile downstream from Olstad Road Bridge to County Road
P is Category 5, artificials only, with a daily bag limit of one trout of
14 inches or longer. One electro-shocking survey produced a few 20-
inch browns, but a later survey did not. The assumption was that
they had moved downstream into deeper water.

Your best bet, when there is no hatch to match, is to swim a Prince
Nymph or a Dark Green Caddis Larva. Crickets and hoppers are
searching patterns for daytimes after the middle of June. Tricos should
appear early mornings July through September.

There are access points upstream from Olstad Road, and then a
bridge crossing, and suddenly you break out into the open and see—

a surprise, leaning against the sky—the fluid curves of the Snowflake Ski Club ski jump, incongruous in this remote valley, even anachronistic. It's one of the last jumps that take us back to sunny winter boyhood days, with bright flags snapping on shining poles and daring young men (like Bill Shogren) on their flying skis.

RULLANDS COULEE CREEK
DeLorme 40

Rullands Coulee, 4½ miles long, a small feeder to Timber Coulee, mostly in Monroe County, is about 1.5 miles east of Olstad Road on County Road P. It holds naturally reproducing brooks and browns, and is recommended by Dorothy Bergmann Schramm, one of the best fly-fishers and casting instructors.

SPRING COULEE
DeLorme 40

Spring Coulee is another excellent trout stream to explore if you can tear yourself away from Timber Coulee. Access is at the bridge on County Road P east of the village of Coon Valley, where the stream is quite narrow. Or proceed up Spring Coulee Road on the east side of the stream to roadside parking in the meadows.

COON CREEK
DeLorme 40

Coon Creek is an open, lazy creek 8 miles long, formed by the junction of Timber Coulee, Spring Coulee, and Bohemian Valley Creeks. Some maps label Bohemian Valley Creek by its old name, Coon Creek. Coon Creek is planted with brown trout. Although we'd rate it as a third-class stream down from the village of Coon Valley, improvements have been made in the village section. When the Wisconsin Department of Transportation decided to replace the bridge on US 14 and US 61, DNR fish managers Dave Vetrano and Ken Wright seized the opportunity to create a handicapped-accessible fishing area. There is now a park, an 850-foot trail with 10 paved fishing spots,

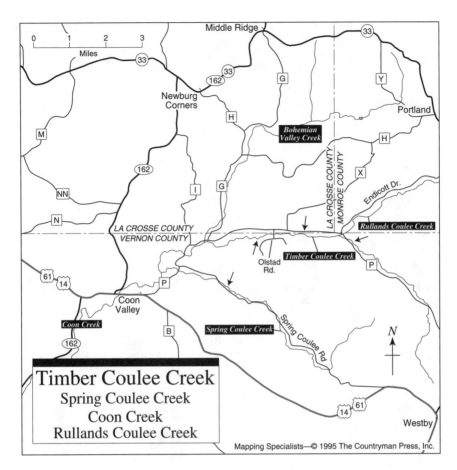

Timber Coulee Creek
Spring Coulee Creek
Coon Creek
Rullands Coulee Creek

Mapping Specialists—© 1995 The Countryman Press, Inc.

and a section of rehabilitated stream, complete with 20 in-stream structures, riprapped banks, and a Hewitt ramp, which is an artificial plunge pool. Many agencies of government and conservation organizations contributed to the effort, including Trout Unlimited.

Bohemian Valley Creek is recommended by fly-fishers of our acquaintance, but we can't vouch for it on our own.

Facilities at Coon Creek on US 14 and US 61, and at Westby.

THE LA CROSSE RIVER
DeLorme 41 & 50

The La Crosse River, Category 2, even though it's a tad north of Interstate 90 in Monroe County, comes highly recommended. It of-

Fly-fishing the edge of the riprap on Timber Coulee Creek

fers more than 10 miles of deep wading from Angelo Pond (northeast of Sparta on WI 21) up into the Fort McCoy Military Reservation. It contains native brookies, planted browns, and rainbows. In June it's possible to fish over evening hatches of the brown drake, *Ephemera simulans*, a central and northern Wisconsin superhatch, and on dark July nights, the giant *Hexagenia* for trophy browns to 20 inches. If you meet fly-fishers arriving early evenings on the river and they're talking about the "shad hatch" or "shadflies," they're referring to the Hex.

Easy access is at the end of a dirt road off WI 21 a bit northwest of Angelo Pond, or at Byron Avenue Bridge farther northeast, and from the west through DNR hunting and fishing lands.

For the approximately 4 miles or more that lie inside Fort McCoy, a special permit from the army is required. It is obtainable at McCoy headquarters on WI 21. The army and Trout Unlimited have completed several stream improvement projects inside the fort acreage.

Facilities at Sparta or at Tomah on Interstate 94.

There, you have 20 spring creeks and rivers from which to choose. They are only a sample of smooth creeks and riffling rivers. You will discover better ones, we know. As you can't tell a book from its cover, you can't survey a stream by a glance from a single bridge. Crowded by brush and slow at the first bridge, at the next it may open into a garden of delight.

We enjoy all of the pastoral streams of southwestern Wisconsin. We can see an August afternoon, with the sun casting long shadows over the upper valley of the Green, and a lone angler, a latter-day Robin Hood in Sherwood green, throwing a cocky dry on an open loop and delicate drop to dimpling trout. In the distant background, a chalk-white farmhouse, a crimson barn, a steel-gray tower of silo, all framed by the purpling hills of Earth. In the foreground, black and white patchwork Holsteins laze in the shadow of a rusty bridge. We recall, instantly, an evening on Castle Rock under a lowering sky, so near it seemed that one could touch the bellied clouds. A Stonefly Muddler, yellow under with a blue wing, dropped within an inch of the duckweed: a short, slack drift, then a wiggle. Then that explosive bulge in the slick surface that shouts, Trout on! The netting of the brown, the lift of net, water drops like diamonds streaming. And the last act, the gentle release of a fine fish to freedom.

Your bright trout is there, in Castle Rock, the Big Green, Mt. Vernon, or in one of the more than 400 spring creeks deep within the Hidden Valleys.

4

Central Wisconsin:
The Ice Age Streams

This collection of streams lies on the northeastern border of the Driftless Area, a huge and unique area covering parts of several states that was bypassed by the glaciers that once covered all of Canada, the northeastern United States, and the central states south to what is now St. Louis. To identify and commemorate this phenomenon, the state of Wisconsin has defined and is acquiring rights of way for the Ice Age Trail, which roughly follows the glacial edge. Inside the Driftless Area of central Wisconsin, the streams carry a burden of sand and gravel that is outwash from the edge of the glacier. Within the former limits of the Wisconsin Drift of the Labrador Ice Sheet, the streams flow over a bed of gravel strewn with boulders that were rolled south by the terminal thrust of the glaciers. Some of our profiled streams meander over outwash sand and gravel, with silt at the margins where the trout lie in shadow; some streams reveal stretches of sand alternating with pitches around boulders. A few of them, such as the Little Wolf, rush downhill sporting and sparkling among the rocks and over ledges to the mighty Wolf River.

Going north from Westfield in northwestern Marquette County, the traveling fly-fisher will find a succession of productive streams: Lawrence, Caves, Tagatz, Chaffee, and Wedde Creeks, the Mecan River, Lunch Creek, the White River, Willow Creek, the Pine River, the Tomorrow/Waupaca, the several branches of the Little Wolf River, and the Lower Plover, plus many others of lesser reputation.

We are unable to describe all of them but we want you to know that many have been improved by the DNR with help from volunteer organizations through stretches owned by or under lease to the Wisconsin DNR. The Milwaukee Map Service map of southeastern Wisconsin indicates the DNR lands in overprinted blocks of green. A word to the wise, then: If you arrive at one of the streams not profiled, begin your exploration in the green lands, where the stream is usually small but improved, and generally productive of brook trout; then work downstream into the heavier water, which is the domain of larger brown trout.

LAWRENCE CREEK
DeLorme 43

Lawrence Creek in Marquette County, a popular stream, has been studied and improved under the direction of Robert L. Hunt, formerly of the Wisconsin Department of Natural Resources, for more than 30 years. Many of the in-stream structures first tested on Lawrence have since been used elsewhere. You'll never have it all to yourself during the trout season, but every devout fly-fisher should see it once, upstream of Lawrence Lake on Eagle Avenue about 3 miles west of Westfield, as an example of what can be done to improve habitat. There are about 4 miles of Category 2 water for naturally reproducing brook trout through those tailored waters above Lawrence Lake in Marquette County, including a bit in Adams County. There are two main access points: one on Eagle and a second on 1st Avenue.

This sweet creek is a place for light rods, fine leaders, small flies, and a stealthy approach from downstream. Avoid the weekends, if you can.

In recent years, 6 or 7 miles below the lake have been added to the list of designated trout waters, Category 3.

Facilities for travelers at Westfield on US 51.

MECAN RIVER

DeLorme 44 & 53

Tread carefully the sandy track of the Mecan in lower Waushara County and upper Marquette—you may hook up with something that you can't handle on a fly rod or anything else. In May 1994, anglers or canoeists reported seeing a hippopotamus in the Mecan River. Crazy! said DNR personnel, but they had to investigate, eventually, to find a dead hippo being winched out of the river at the business end of a pickup.

It seems that the camel let the hippo out of his corral at a game farm and the hippo hightailed it for the water to frolic. Every time the owner of the game farm tried to lasso the hippo, the happy beast swam downriver. Finally the owner shot it and winched it out.

The Mecan is a sand stream some 17 miles long, from Mecan Springs downstream to WI 22, one of those that has received outwash

Jim Humphrey nymphs upstream on the Mecan River at the JJ access. Is there a hippo lurking under the bank cover?

PHOTO BY JOYCE HUMPHREY

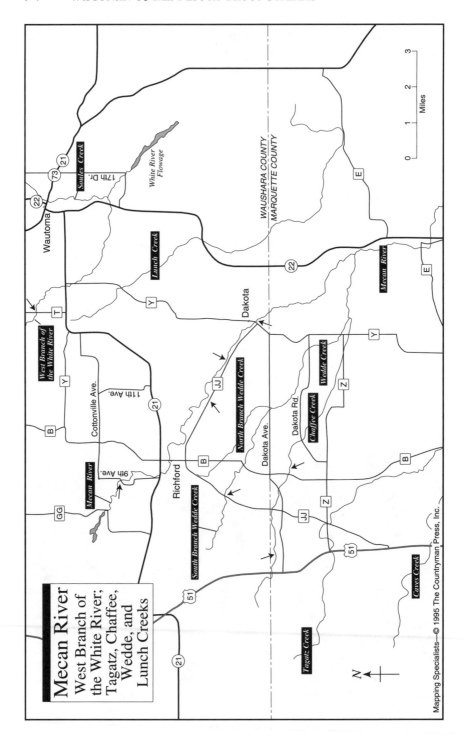

Mecan River
West Branch of
the White River;
Tagatz, Chaffee,
Wedde, and
Lunch Creeks

Mapping Specialists—© 1995 The Countryman Press, Inc.

from the glacier. It has been improved with wing dams and other structures at a number of locations. There is easy access on DNR lands along County Road JJ upstream from the village of Dakota, at the bridge on 11th Road, and up from Richford at 9th Avenue in the state fishery area. Or you can check the outlet of the springs at County Road GG.

Approximately 12 miles at the upper end are rated Category 3; the lower 5 miles are Category 5. All three species of trout are reported to be naturally reproducing, although we wouldn't stake our lives on the likelihood of catching a native rainbow.

Facilities for travelers at Wautoma.

WEST BRANCH OF THE WHITE RIVER
DeLorme 53

The West Branch of the White River, west of Wautoma in Waushara County, is favored by fly-fishers for many miles around. Although not much more than 5 miles long above its junction with the White River proper, and not wide, it has been rated first class by the DNR. Our favorite access is at County Road T, 3 miles west of Wautoma, where there is a DNR parking area. A second recommended entry is on the main White River, at the bridge on 17th Drive and Cottonville Lane, 3 miles south of Wautoma. You can fish upstream to the junction of the two streams through some very enticing water. There is DNR parking just above the bridge off 17th Drive. Downstream is the head of the flowage, which will be difficult wading for more than a short distance, but we recall one August evening when a very large trout gulped a very large something at the surface only a few yards below the bridge. That one refused our several oversized mayfly artificials; nevertheless, it was a heart-pounding experience and we have that brown marked for a return engagement. The nighttime Hex appears on the river, usually toward the end of June and early July.

Both the West Branch and the main White are Category 5, Special Regulations, although the regulations differ between the two streams. The West Branch contains the three species of wild trout; the main has natural browns and rainbows.

Complete facilities for travelers at Wautoma.

WILLOW CREEK
DeLorme 53

Willow Creek in Waushara County is one of those anomalies that we have mentioned elsewhere. Although it is called a creek, it is larger than many rivers. About 10 miles of water, from the origin just east of WI 22, 2 miles south of Wild Rose, to the bridge on Blackhawk Road south and east of Mount Morris, are granted a first-class rating. The next 10 miles down to the Auroraville mill pond are somewhat less productive, but all of Willow Creek contains native brooks and natural browns. Brook trout will dominate the upper half, where it is rated Category 2; the lower half, Category 3, will cough up some decent browns. There is a state fishery area in each section, but we prefer the open stream at the bridge where County Roads S and Z intersect 2 miles north of WI 21, particularly during grasshopper time. There is also easy access upstream to DNR parking on the east side of the creek along 24th Road where the water runs slow and smooth. The mud banks signal the possibility of a Hex hatch.

However, you may choose to begin upstream in the green DNR lands marked on the Milwaukee Map Service map, at 21st Drive or Badger Court. Another entry is at the bridge on Beaver Avenue.

Facilities at Wild Rose, Wautoma, and Redgranite.

THE PINE RIVER
DeLorme 53

Wild Rose has long been a staging point for fly-fishers. One can fish Willow Creek and the Pine River and its several feeders, including Humphrey Creek (no relation).

The Pine River begins as the Upper Pine west of Wild Rose in Waushara County, drifts through town, where it becomes the Pine River, loops north through DNR lands, where it picks up volume from three cold feeders, then meanders southeast through Saxeville to Poy Sippi. Its approximately 20 miles contain wild native brook and naturally reproducing brown trout. The best fly-fishing will be found from the north loop on County Road K in DNR lands and on down to Saxeville. You can also reach the DNR lands from Apache Road. It was in this section that a 27-inch brown was creeled recently.

We've fished the Pine as far down as County Highway H and 28th

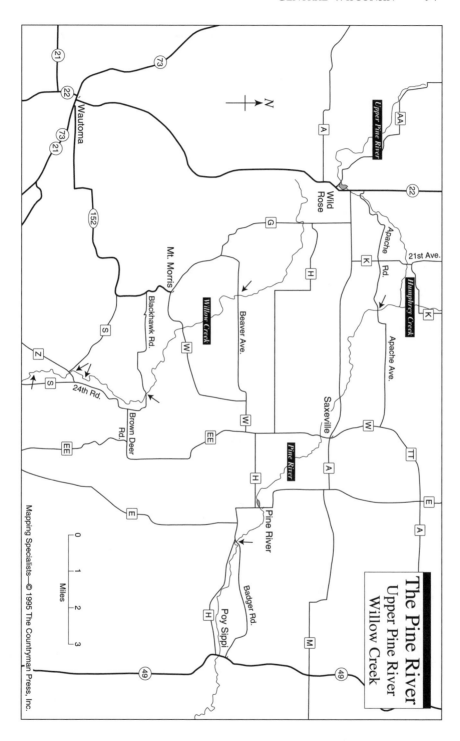

The Pine River
Upper Pine River
Willow Creek

Mapping Specialists—© 1995 The Countryman Press, Inc.

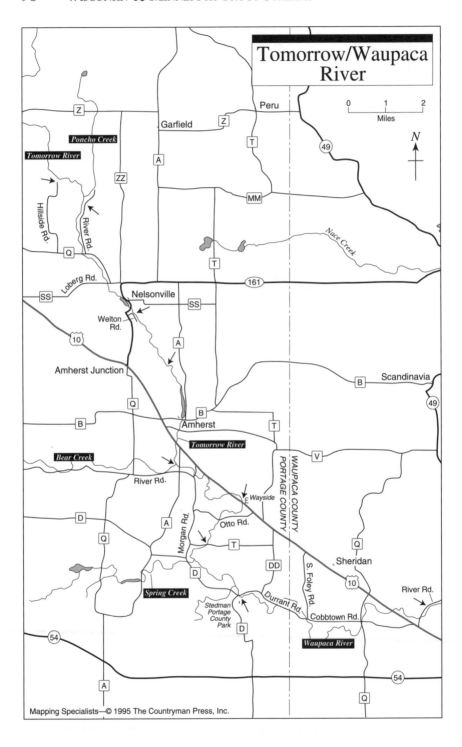

Tomorrow/Waupaca River

Court, but with indifferent success at that end. The bed there is thick sand with little in-stream cover. If there's any action, it will occur on an early-season evening, or possibly in the late season with terrestrials.

From Wild Rose down the stream is rated Category 3, with a daily bag limit of three trout of 9 inches or longer.

The three reference maps we've used to define the Pine disagree as to the names of the feeder creeks. We judge the DeLorme map to be the most accurate.

Facilities at Wild Rose.

THE STREAMS OF WAUPACA
AND STEVENS POINT

Going north toward the city of Waupaca and the termination of the Tomorrow/Waupaca River, you may cross Radley and Emmons Creeks and the Crystal River. All three are small but notable trout streams. We have not yet fished Radley, and the last time we were on Emmons it was so brushy that we couldn't find water with a worm rod, but recently the DNR elicited the help of the Central Wisconsin and Fox Valley Chapters of Trout Unlimited to remove fallen elm trees and debrush the banks. Unique to Emmons is an annual fall spawning run of large brown trout from the Waupaca Chain O' Lakes. Trout to 7 pounds have been taken in September.

You should, though, see the Crystal River, a Sunday canoeists' paradise and a delight for spectators who congregate at the narrows at Smith Road at Parfreyville to watch the canoes turn belly-up and dump their contents.

If that amusement doesn't appeal, you must not miss visiting the village of Rural, with its graceful 19th-century homes, most on the National Register of Historic Places, the Crystal River flowing brightly through, a tea shoppe, a bed & breakfast, and a village store where Sunday visitors purchase old-fashioned ice cream cones.

THE TOMORROW/WAUPACA RIVER
DeLorme 53 & 65

For purposes of convenience we will begin at the top of the Tomorrow River and follow it south to Waupaca. Its name changes to the Waupaca

River at the west Waupaca County line. Alternatively, a visiting angler could begin on River Road, which joins US 10 about 4 miles north of Waupaca, and proceed upstream from bridge to bridge.

The river rises north and east of Stevens Point in Portage County and flows for 37 miles to WI 54 north of Waupaca. In the upper reaches it contains wild brook and natural brown trout, as well as planted browns. Lower down it contains planted brown and rainbow trout.

The river is divided into three Categories. From the headwaters to County Road SS in Nelsonville it is Category 3; from County Road SS to the railroad bridge upstream from Amherst Pond it is Category 5; the remainder is Category 4.

At County Highway OO it is much too small to fish. The first recommended entry is on River Road about 10 miles east of Stevens Point, on the east side of the river upstream of County Road Q. About 1 mile north is the Richard A. Hemp State Fishery Area. We have had fabulous success there fly-fishing to native brook trout, with an occasional brown trout to whet the appetite. Only a few yards north of the fishery area, you'll find a short road that stops at an abandoned bridge. Upstream is narrow and deep; you'll probably want to fish from the banks, which have been brushed back in recent years. Downstream is wader-deep. Wade the center of the river and cast to the edges of the brush for a breakfast of brook trout.

You can also obtain access to the upper Tomorrow from the west on a DNR dead-end road going east to public fishing grounds from Hillside Road north of County Road Q.

Next downstream access on the east bank is Clementson Road, with easy wading down through shallower water over gravel bottom. About the second week of June we found a good hatch of sulphurs at the bridge. Next down is the County Road Q bridge—posted upstream and posted on the west side downstream, but wadable from the east bank. There are some deadfalls and sweepers that can be negotiated by an experienced fly-fisher through this picturesque stretch.

It is likely that in 1996, from Clementson Road up to County Road I, the Tomorrow will become Category 5.

Next down is Loberg Road Bridge, where the river is posted on both south banks. We have taken brook and brown trout upstream through some beautiful wading water over a gravel bottom.

Rising Star Mill bridge in Nelsonville is the next stop. And that's worth a digression. Ten years ago, Vern Hacker, a fish manager with

Two anglers emerging at the end of a day on the upper Tomorrow River

the Wisconsin DNR, told us that the Tomorrow could become the best trout stream in the state if the dam at Nelsonville were removed. Five years ago the state purchased the mill and removed the dam. The old millpond, which was a slack, black heat sump, is now a stretch of meadow stream. The Tomorrow is not yet as good as Vern Hacker hoped it would be, but it is improved and improving. Now, if we could only get rid of the Amherst flowage, another shallow pond and heat sump in the village of Amherst! But that project is resisted by local residents, who like to look out over still waters of an evening.

Next, go south of Nelsonville on County Road SS. About 100 yards south you'll find Welton Road, a dead end running east toward the river. Follow that to the first south bend of the road, where there is a DNR access with parking for two cars. Do not attempt to drive down the path; one of our fellow anglers, who shall remain nameless, mired his four-wheel-drive and had to be chained out. A few yards' stroll to the river takes you to a snowmobile bridge. Watch the water from the bridge for feeding trout. We fish upstream to Nelsonville because a mile of river has been narrowed and improved with boom covers.

Proceeding south along US 10, we like the County Road A bridge below Amherst, the River Road bridge a tad west of US 10, and the wayside on the highway where Buchholtz Road comes in from the east. There is also roadside parking on the west side of US 10 just north of the wayside bridge.

The river is wide and open through these several access points and perfect for fly-fishing, with a chance at larger brown trout. A long riffle at the wayside may produce brown trout even during the day; some slow water and pools at the upper end of the wayside should be reserved for an evening. The giant brown and giant black stoneflies, together with a variety of *Stenonema/Stenacron* mayflies, inhabit the riffles. The various species of *S/S* will emerge from May through August; the large stoneflies will have taken wing by June 1, but a large, dark nymph or brown Woolly Worm is always a good choice for plumbing the riffles and pools.

About 0.25 mile south of the wayside go west on Otto Road to the bridge to find cobble bottom and pretty water. The stream here is narrow and fairly open. Then, left on Morgan Road south is the next crossing. It appears there is a DNR easement upstream. When you find a fence paralleling the water about 25 feet from the center line of the stream, you can assume that it is a fenced easement. There is a rough canoe landing on the downstream side. Continue on Morgan to County Road D. You'll cross Spring Creek first, then arrive at the junction of County Road D and County Road DD. Just south of the intersection you'll find Stedman Portage County Park, a very pretty place to pause for lunch. The stream is rocky and narrow here. Our preference is to work upstream with a dry fly among the boulders.

Now, go back to DD and proceed south on Durrant Road to the first bridge. It was here on one fine evening that we met three fishermen, a father and two sons, who volunteered that the upstream path on the right side led to some good holes for larger brown trout. We noted, though, that they were going downstream to fish. However, we returned the next day and took several colorful brown trout upstream of the bridge in tiptoe water, which means that you wear chest-high waders over a sand bottom and search for holding water at the margins, in the riffles, or within the deadfall.

Next down, Durrant ends at the intersection of Cobbtown Road and Foley Road. The river here is about 50 feet wide. On Foley Road east of the intersection you can walk to the river at the Ice Age Trail.

Next down is Cobbtown Road to Frost Valley Road. This is more canoe stream than fly-fishing stream, so we'll go on to the east side of US 10, to the River Road about 4 miles north of Waupaca, as our last stop on the Tomorrow/Waupaca River. There is one bridge crossing on River Road between US 10 and Larson Road to the east. The river at the bridge is slow and deep, and roadside parking is doubtful, but go east about three-quarters of a mile toward Larson Road and you'll find roadside parking for three or four cars at river's edge. This is big, tough, challenging water—the kind of habitat preferred by large brown trout and determined fly-fishers. We like this stretch upstream of an evening, working slowly with large Hare's Ears or dry flies.

All facilities for travelers at Waupaca at the lower end or Stevens Point at the upper.

PETERSON CREEK
DeLorme 53

We include Peterson Creek in Waupaca County, about 5 miles east of Amherst on Gurholt Road, less than a mile north of County Road V, because it is typical of dozens of small brook trout streams in central Wisconsin. Just north of the junction with Gilman Road a gravel farmhouse road leads to a bridge and a Wisconsin Public Hunting and Fishing Ground. This is probably the only fly-fishable spot on the stream. Downstream ends soon in a fly-fisher's nightmare; upstream is negotiable for a ways for anglers who favor the short rod, short leaders, and small flies for small wild trout. Peterson is Category 2 for wild brooks and browns.

Facilities at Amherst.

SOUTH BRANCH OF THE LITTLE WOLF RIVER
DeLorme 53

Peterson Creek feeds into Sand Creek and thence into the South Branch of the Little Wolf River near the junction of WI 49 and County Road V just south of the village of Scandinavia in Waupaca County. The approximately 13 miles of the South Branch, Category 3, from Iola on the north, through Scandinavia, over WI 49 to the termination of the designated trout water at the West Waupaca Road, contain wild brown trout, and according to local advice you may run into some bass.

Acceptable access points aren't frequent in sections of the stream best suited for fly-fishing, so we suggest the second bridge south on

Elm Valley Road, below the junction with Blueberry Road, which comes in from the north. The bridge is approximately 6 miles north of Waupaca. Go downstream on the righthand side through abandoned pasture. We'd fish it here, moving cautiously, with a slack cast. It's the kind of place we thoroughly enjoy early mornings, early or late evening, or under overcast skies or in a light rain. If thunder booms in the sky, exchange your graphite rod for bamboo to ward off the lightning, but don't get your hopes up. Our experience is that thunder puts down the trout.

The third bridge south promises action upstream and down. Both directions are fairly open. Upstream you'll see the buttresses of an abandoned bridge. The narrows around old bridges are always productive. A few large trees lean over the downstream section—place your terrestrials in under the trees.

Facilities at Waupaca and Iola.

FLUME CREEK
DeLorme 65

Flume Creek in Portage and Waupaca Counties, a tributary of the Little Wolf River, is a first-class stream, by which we mean it contains natural brooks and browns all the way through its 18 miles of Category 3 water. It rises above Rosholt north of WI 66, but the section we find most productive for native brook and brown trout is between Lund Road (east of WI 49 and a quarter mile south of County Road C) and Ness Road about a mile east of Lund and also south of County Road C. If we were forced to choose between the two entries, we would take the Ness Road access where the stream is open, knee-deep over sand and silt, with overhanging grass at the edges where trout hide.

On the other hand, a fly-angler who likes deep and difficult wading up a rocky, western-style stream with holes over his or her head will wade up from Lund into amazing water where we nailed the brookies on a Pass Lake.

A most interesting development has occurred at the crossroads village of Northland, upstream from Lund Road on WI 49. The old low-head dam has been removed and the pond drained. Now there is parking for a dozen cars, a picnic table, an old iron footbridge, and at least three-quarters of a mile of unobstructed fly-fishing above the WI 49 bridge. We will return to that charming reach, but not on a hot, bright day. Downstream, the river closes through brush over gravel and sand toward Lund and Ness crossings.

Facilities at Iola.

THE LITTLE WOLF RIVER
DeLorme 65

The Little Wolf River is a heart's delight for a fly-fisher who looks for that typical western-style freestone stream. For most of its length of some 24 miles, from southeastern Marathon County through the northeast corner of Portage County to Big Falls in Waupaca County, it rattles around rocks and riffles over gravel. By no means is it the most productive stream in central Wisconsin, but certainly it is one of the most beautiful. At the upper end it contains wild brown trout; at the lower, natural brooks and planted browns. It is Category 3; browns and rainbows must be 12 inches or longer; brook trout, 8 inches.

We begin our fly-fishing on Wigwam Road about 0.25 mile east of WI 49, in extreme northeastern Portage County, where Wigwam makes a sharp right-hand bend. A sign there takes you to parking for three or four cars; then follow the foot trail less than an eighth of a mile to the river. It may be only 20 feet wide and it will test your wading and fly-casting skills, but you must revel in the sight and sound of a tinkling freestone stream.

There is an indication of another Wisconsin Public Hunting and Fishing Ground at the east end of Wigwam Road, but we don't recommend it now. There is no beaten path to the river, and where there's no path, experience tells us not to proceed. You might like to try it, though, and thereby find your honey hole.

Go west to WI 49, south to County Road C, then east, then north on Ness Road—we've been here before in our profile of Flume Creek—to the Little Wolf River Fishery Area at a corner where Ness Road strikes north again. Perhaps three cars can squeeze into the lot. A short walk takes you to the river where it runs sweet and golden over gravel. There is one deep pool on the right, with a promising root wad, then downstream is a long, variegated run. The river here is not much wider than it was upstream, but it was another visual delight on our day, with the sun slanting through the trees, the water shimmering, and, downstream through a tunnel of trees, the promise of trout taking our dry flies.

Back in the car again, go north on Ness to the Little Wolf River Road. Traveling east, find the next access at Wrolstad Road, a south spur off meandering Little Wolf River Road. And this is worth another digression. Several years ago there was a short canoe carry from the east spur at the end of Wrolstad Road. On our last visit, a trailer house with a cropped lawn had obliterated the canoe trail. Consternation! That is a magnificent stretch of water, wide and wadable among the boulders. Fortunately, now you can take the west spur to DNR parking at the turnaround and, on the south side of the road, a sign announcing Public Access. The access is so new that there is no well-defined trail. Make your own trail for less than 100 yards to some fine fly-fishing water. Good luck to you, or good skill, as the case may be. Our hearts fell when we saw the canoe trail had disappeared, but we feel better now. We assume that a 10-year easement had run out, but our friends from the DNR have arranged for another.

Our last stop takes us to another DNR parking lot, at the junction of County Roads C and J. An easy trail follows the Little Wolf on the north bank to the slab rocks and rapids above. We've fished over this complex bottom on numerous occasions, as have many of our friends. We've picked up respectable brown trout, but on a recent June day Jason Carpenter, a friend and fly-fishing guide from Missouri, reported the catch and release of a dozen brook trout taken during daylight.

Forget about it downstream of the bridge. It is narrow, very deep, and ends in a gorge and rapids that are best reserved for kayakers and expert canoeists.

The Little Wolf River, sometimes called the North Branch of the Little Wolf—but by any name a rose is a rose—is not an easy stream to fish. It is a miniature Wolf River, with some easy wading over gravel, but with more difficult stretches that will tax the ingenuity of any fly-fisher. It is a stream to which we return in the hope that eventually all of its secrets will be revealed. And isn't that the essence of trout fishing?

Facilities for travelers at Iola and Stevens Point.

THE LOWER PLOVER RIVER
DeLorme 65 & 77

We might call the Lower Plover one of our "sleepers." It is not celebrated in the literature of trout streams of the Midwest, nor do any of our friends whisper of its magic in our ears. You will find a profile

Two young anglers on the lower Plover near Bevent

of the Upper Plover in chapter 5 (Northeastern Wisconsin). The division between the Upper and Lower Plover is arbitrary. The Upper, celebrated by Bill Shogren, can be reached from Antigo on the north or from Wausau on the west; the Lower, of a size and configuration Humphrey prefers, is only a half hour's drive from Stevens Point.

This is a long river of some 26 miles, and in the lower reaches, a wide one. It rises in Langlade County and flows through the upper two-thirds of Marathon County to the village of Bevent on WI 153, the lower end of the designated trout water.

We'll travel the route upstream from the bridge on Bevent Drive, 1.5 miles west of County Road Y and south of WI 153. This is outside of the designated trout water, and you will wonder why. Here the river is more than 100 feet wide, and there are deadheads, islands, sandbars, and rocks. And on our last visit, caddis were swarming and what appeared to be trout were rising for as far upstream as we could see. (They may have been chubs.) At the bridge, three young men were picking huge crayfish in the shallows. We have had some spectacular fishing in the heavier, warmer waters of Wisconsin with a crayfish imitation. Your imitation should not exceed 1½ inches in length: For some strange reason the larger versions will not attract large brown trout. Perhaps the defensive mechanisms of 4-inch crayfish are too formidable.

Upstream in the village of Bevent there is parking on the northwest side of the bridge. The river is rocky and wadable, with a good riffle downstream making for a fine fly-fishing reach. It will be more difficult wading up.

Next up is the Kristoff Road bridge, with gravel, cobble, and boulders downstream, rocks and deadfall up. On our last visit, during the second week of June, a spinner flight of sulphurs hung over the bridge. The males rose high overhead, then spread their wings and dove straight down into the mass. Birds came out of the tops of trees to pick off the mayflies. The brown trout, no doubt, were waiting impatiently for the spinners to fall at dark. But we had to continue our survey, alas!

At the Plover River Road the trout were feeding greedily upstream, possibly on a spinner fall. "Wow!" is the exclamation that slipped out. "Look at them!" And not another fisherman in sight.

This is spectacular fly-fishing water. It's 60 feet wide, smooth water with overhanging brush at the banks upstream, and perfect wading around boulders down.

Scratch the Esker Road bridge; there is wire across the stream.

At Bridge Road you'll find pretty water over bedrock. Downstream is your best bet, through channels, around islands, and into the pockets.

The Town Line Road Bridge area is open, rocky, nice, but deep and tough to wade.

At Konkel Road there's a Wisconsin Public Hunting and Fishing Ground. The easiest action will be downstream, where you will need waders, and you may have to loop out onto the west bank from time to time.

We recommend that you skip the several bridges in Hatley on WI 29, although we found brookies feeding right through town.

Next up is Pine Road Bridge east of County Road Y. On the southeast side of the bridge a residence shows a fine, sheared lawn to a riprapped edge. Utterly charming, but we don't like to fish through somebody's front yard. Upstream is another story. At least 50 trout were feeding around islands and among rocks through clear, cold water. The bottom rocks are smooth, requiring felt soles. Use light tackle, because these were mostly brook trout, but there was one large trout feeding on the west bank in a side pocket—a brown, we discovered.

And now we come to County Road N, about 15 miles east of

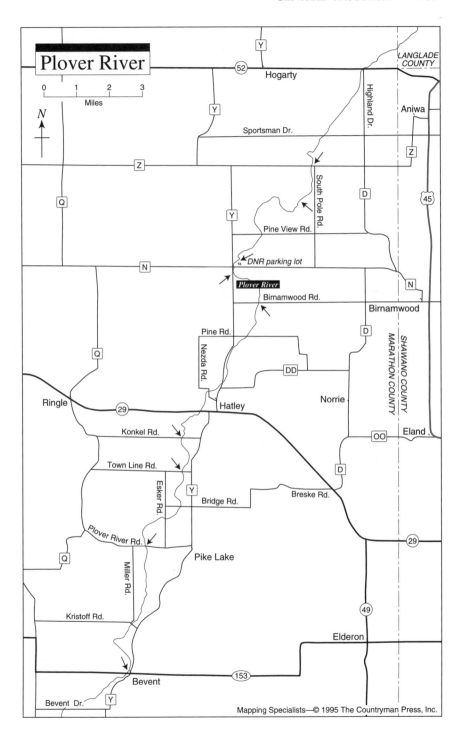

Wausau. For some of you this may be paradise. Both wild brook trout and large native browns are the product of these immaculate waters. It is a location that Humphrey lost many years ago, and now has found again. You could conclude that this is the end of the Lower Plover and the beginning of the Upper Plover. No matter. It is absolutely magnificent.

There is a Wisconsin DNR Public Hunting and Fishing Area with parking northeast of the bridge.

Those of you who cherish native brook trout, with a few browns thrown in for good measure, can proceed upstream into the quality water of the Upper Plover. Those who are after brown trout can work upstream from Bevent or downstream from County Road N. The brooks and browns are naturally reproducing; there may also be some planted rainbows.

Three Categories apply here: The upper few miles are Category 2; a short section is posted for Category 5; and the remainder is Category 4.

You won't find a more varied river anywhere. You pays your money and you takes your choice.

Facilities at Stevens Point, Wausau, and Antigo.

THE DITCHES OF WISCONSIN RAPIDS
DeLorme 52

If you will examine your *Wisconsin Trout Fishing Regulations and Guide* for Portage and Wood Counties you will note a curious pattern of streams—a pattern not repeated elsewhere. South of Stevens Point and east of Wisconsin Rapids you'll find a series of parallel ditches running east to west, all Category 2–designated trout streams.

This peculiar arrangement piqued our curiosity, so we had to investigate. Long ago this outwash flatland may have been a prairie laced with sinuous streams and spotted with marsh. Possibly, the flat was covered with dwarf oak and pine. The early maps we have studied do not tell us precisely.

In the early days of the 20th century, when every flatland was being drained for cropland, the streams were straightened, and small diversion dams were added for irrigation. Aldo Leopold, author of the revered *Sand County Almanac,* called the period from 1910 to 1920 "the decade of the drainage dream." Since then the land has been intensively farmed through a succession of crops, with some range given over to cattle. Currently hay, corn, and potatoes are the preferred produce, although a very large area has been acquired by the state for prairie chicken habitat and booming grounds.

The majority of these ditches hold naturally reproducing brook trout; a lesser number contain planted brown trout. The lower ends of several of them were never ditched, or they have reverted to a more natural state, winding and brush-lined. The best advice to trout fishers comes from a resident who fishes the ditches early and often. He says you should fish the ditches just below the diversion dams, but be there early in the morning or the trout will have been fished out by earlier risers.

We have examined Five Mile, Seven Mile, and Ten Mile Creeks, the lower ends of several of the ditches, for short distances above their junctions with the Wisconsin River. There is fair habitat for both trout- and fly-fishers, and even a Category 5 section on the last stretch of Ten Mile Creek, but in general we'd not grant any of them a high priority. Buena Vista Creek, downstream of Ditches 1 and 2, is planted to brown trout annually—600 of legal size per year is typical—but we suspect that they are snapped up by anglers from Wisconsin Rapids during the early weeks of the season.

In short, there are too many better streams in the area for you to waste your time on the ditches, but we knew that you'd be curious, as we were. Our duty demands that we sometimes tell you which streams to avoid.

Facilities at Wisconsin Rapids and Stevens Point.

BIG ROCHE-A-CRI CREEK
DeLorme 52

The Big Roche-A-Cri, a tributary of the Wisconsin River, rises near US 51 in western Waushara County and flows approximately 16 miles through northern Adams County. The nearest city of any size is Wisconsin Rapids to the north. The village of Friendship, near Little Roche-A-Cri, Fordham Creek, and Roche-A-Cri State Park, is south of the lower end of the creek on WI 13. This is all flat country, so you won't find much in the way of tumbling rapids and rippling riffles.

Fly-fishers, like everyone else, develop prejudices in favor of some streams and against others, often as a result of subtle effects rather than because of the numbers of trout taken. Our favorites include the Kinnickinnic, the Wolf, and the Namekagon of Wisconsin, and Trout

Run and the South Branch of the Whitewater in southeastern Minnesota, each for different reasons that are more emotional than physical.

The ambience is all, for some of us. Some like the wild and rough Wolf; other fishers become ecstatic when searching the pockets of a brook trout stream like the Tiffany or the Upper Plover.

Big Roche-A-Cri, Categories 2 and 3, is a perfectly respectable stream, but we don't like it. The upper 6 miles above County Road W contain wild brook trout, and browns are planted down to Roche-A-Cri Lake. Why don't we like it? "Sullen" would be the adjective to apply if it were human. It's slow, narrow, deep, and murky, and drains some of the most unprepossessing flatlands ever seen. It's also unduly posted against trespass by folks whose small holdings are littered with the rusted hulks of cars and other assorted junk. If we were to compile a list of streams to avoid like the plague, this one would be on it. There is a state fishery area west of US 51 in northwest Waushara County and a mile north of County Road O that might intrigue some of you.

Little Roche-A-Cri to the south has wild brook trout; Fordham Creek's 6 miles are reputed to hold wild brooks, browns, and rainbows. Wild rainbows are a rarity in interior streams, so Fordham is worth a look.

Facilities at Friendship, Wautoma, and Wisconsin Rapids.

THE LITTLE PLOVER
DeLorme 52 & 53

The Little Plover, which joins the Wisconsin River at Whiting, a suburb of Stevens Point, is a tiny Category 2 stream about 3 miles in length, containing naturally reproducing brook trout. It's sweet and petite from Kennedy Avenue downstream to a bit west of US 51. It runs through a park that you'll find downstream of Eisenhower Avenue, and it's the site of intensive rehabilitation by a class of high school students. If you look closely in the park stretch you'll find brush bundles to narrow the stream and speed the flow, and riprap of round stones covered with dirt and seed. It is an example of the work that can be accomplished by ordinary folks with educated guidance from the Wisconsin DNR fish managers.

If you have an opportunity to work on a stream under the direction of a DNR fish manager, seize it. It may be even more exhilarating than catching and releasing a trout.

5

Northeastern Wisconsin:
The Wilderness

Northeastern Wisconsin covers a vast area and contains a glorious variety of topography, flora, and stream profiles. It includes the gracious and well-named Prairie River on the west, the huge, wild, rocky, and dangerous Wolf above Langlade, and to the east the enormous tailwaters of the Peshtigo below Johnson Falls Reservoir near Crivitz. In the far northeast near the Michigan border you may search for brook trout in the inner reaches of the Pike, Pine, Popple, and Pemebonwon, rivers that twist through remote and tangled wilderness. The eastern Brule, which separates Wisconsin from the Upper Peninsula, is a big river and a photogenic masterpiece.

There is a stream for every taste or persuasion, from open meadow to secret silver rivulet at the end of a lonely trail through jackpine stands and blackberry brambles. You can't experience the spectrum of streams in this area in a day; even a week won't suffice. And we can't tell you all that we know in the pages allotted. Some streams and rivers we've fished intensively; others have received only cursory attention. We must leave it to you to discover some treasures of your own.

Jim Humphrey recalls his first look at the North Branch of the Pike: "It remains one of the clearest memories of my fishing life. I was standing at the top of Eighteen Foot Falls with my 8-foot, 9-weight bamboo bass rod in hand and some kind of attractor dangling from a stout leader. Upstream for as far as I could see, perhaps 300 yards, the glide was spackled with the rings of rising, feeding trout—and me a novice, or novitiate more properly, without the least idea how I could coax them to strike. I was smart enough to know when I was licked, so I went down to the foot of the falls and winkled out a brace of trout with a small streamer. That was 40 years ago, when I was enamored of bass and not yet hooked on fly-fishing for trout.

"I hope that I know a bit more about trout fishing now, and I know that the falls pounds down from the heights. I suspect that the trout will still confound even an expert."

We'll come back to the far northeast later on in this survey.

SEVEN STREAMS OF THE ANTIGO AREA

Bill Shogren recommends that you establish your initial base at Antigo in Langlade County while we wade you through the first collection of streams at the southern end of the northeast section of Wisconsin. Bill, who likes the companionship of a few fly-fishing friends, says that you could send members of your party out in several directions for a variety of experiences, then share tall tales at the end of a day.

During the dog days of August, this area of Wisconsin offers wonderful trout fishing. Daytimes, you can fish the fabulous Prairie River, the East and West Branches of the Eau Claire, and the Upper Plover. At night in early August the best game out of town is the white fly hatch on the Wolf or the Prairie. The Big Hay Meadow, a tributary of the Prairie, offers superb wade fishing all day long and into the evening. "Get your fishing buddies and head for Antigo, Wisconsin," Shogren advises. "There are ample accommodations at reasonable prices, and the variety of streams offers fishing for every type of trout fisher—the old, the young, experienced and inexperienced, all can catch trout."

THE PRAIRIE RIVER
DeLorme 76 & 77

"Gleason, The Trout Fishing Capital of the World." The sign is weathered, a relic of Babbitt boosterism perhaps, but on a June evening when the air is alive with the flutter of mayfly wings, when a great brown trout bangs at a #10 White Wulff and pops the leader on his second leap, we can believe, almost, that Gleason may be in the running for that exalted title.

The sign dates back 40 or 50 years, when the Prairie was a renowned stream. Then the deterioration began, perhaps from the warming of water due to the gradual silting in of Prairie Dell Pond, perhaps as a result of poor farming practices and other development along the river. Perhaps it was only that the big trout were pounded to death by experts casting three wet flies by night.

The Prairie River rises in wild, cutover, sand-and-bog country in northeastern Langlade County and lazes in a southwesterly direction through Lincoln County for more than 40 miles to join the Wisconsin River at Merrill. The Prairie is a big river, averaging 64 feet in width with a flow of 15 to 40 cubic feet per second, according to a Department of Natural Resources survey. It is comparable in width to the Bois Brule, Namekagon, Wolf, Peshtigo, and Tomorrow/Waupaca. The first 12 miles in Langlade County contain wild brook and brown trout, but access above the village of Parrish requires that you put one foot ahead of the other. The DeLorme map does show some unimproved roads or fire trails leading to the headwaters east from County Road Q north of Parrish, but we can't guarantee their utility. The river from Parrish down to US 51 at Merrill was described by "Dry Fly" Dick Frantes, Jim Humphrey's fishing partner for many years: "I was very favorably impressed by the absence of litter, the niceness of all the fishers we met, the high percentage of fly-fishers, the ease of fishing and accessibility, and all the convenient parking areas. Lots of hip-boot water; wide-open river." Access is indeed easy at many bridges and across public lands and easements. It is all Category 4.

Above the village of Dudley on WI 17, where the river has been improved with riprap and bank covers by the DNR with the help of Trout Unlimited, brook trout predominate. From Dudley down, brown trout come to hand more often.

You could begin your exploration at the County Road C bridge upstream from Merrill and about 25 miles west of Antigo if you wish

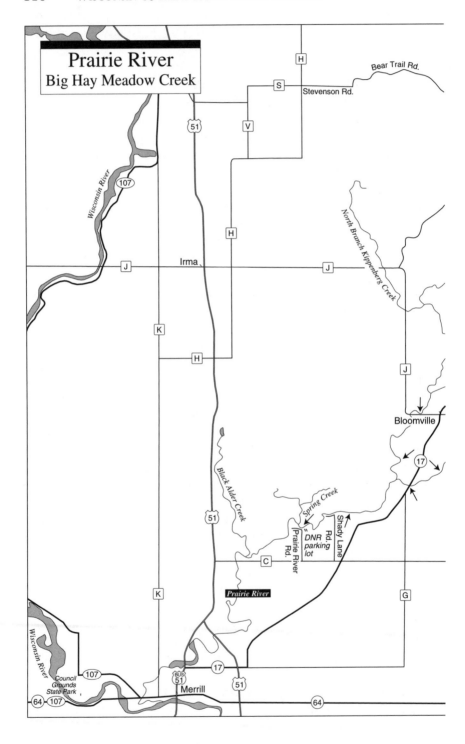

Prairie River
Big Hay Meadow Creek

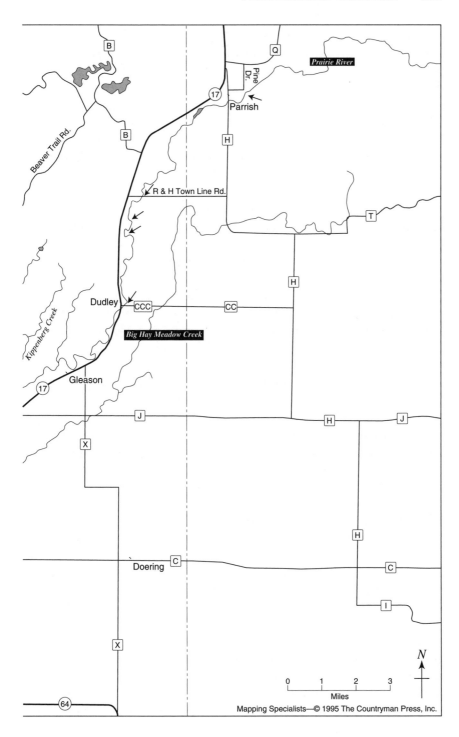

Mapping Specialists—© 1995 The Countryman Press, Inc.

to follow Bill's advice to center at Antigo. It's big, slow water at the County Road C bridge, about 4 miles northeast of Merrill, and on opening day the roadside parking will be jammed for sure. On off days you may find a couple of parked cars. We know that there must be some very large browns in that section, but esthetically we prefer to begin at the Prairie River Road DNR lot, 2.5 miles east on County Road C, then north to the river. There you will find Yankee Rapids upstream and several superb long pools down. In the first long pool and beyond, if you are lucky and skillful, you may tie into an oversized brown.

We enjoy most those early August evenings when the white fly (also known in the eastern US as the trailer because the male dun sometimes trails its shuck like a skywriter's banner) patrols close over the river. Often the browns will leap clear in their attempt to snatch it.

The white fly is a spectral late-evening hatch that appears on many large northern Wisconsin rivers where there is silt for burrowing. It patrols a length of 10 feet, back and forth, inches above the water. It is one of our largest mayflies, not far behind the brown drake and Hex. A diligent fly-fisher may want to hang around for the spinner fall after dark.

This *Ephoron leukon/album* is unique. The male has two tails, the female three. The female does not molt from dun to spinner.

One August 11 the white fly appeared between 6:30 and 9 PM. I released a couple of modest browns and lost one huge brown on a #12 Blond Wulff. I didn't say this was easy fishing; large trout never come easily. On the big pools of the lower Prairie, if mayflies and caddis don't do their stuff, swim an artificial crayfish on the bottom.

Other hatches include the Blue-Winged Olive, *Baetis* genus, season-long; pale evening duns, not identified but probably one of the *Ephemerella;* the March brown, *Stenonema vicarium;* the brown drake, *Ephemera simulans,* June 1–18; the light Cahill, *Stenonema/Stenacron,* June 8–12; tricos, from July 8 to August 4, when the morning temperature reaches 68 degrees; the White-Gloved Howdy, *Isonychia,* from late July through the middle of August; and the blue dun, *Paraleptophlebia,* from the end of August through September.

Other notable trout foods are the giant brown, giant black, and golden stone stoneflies, as well as chubs, sculpins, and crayfish. Caddis appear all season long, but the most remarkable of that group is the black dancer, *Mystacides alafimbriata,* with antennae so long they appear to be tails. We spotted the amazing black dancers at Dudley on June 11, tied on a Black Caddis, and immediately caught and released five small brook trout.

The second entry east off County Road C is at the end of Shady Lane Road. It's broad and flat here. Downstream is the head of Yankee Rapids. On a recent excursion, Shogren found the interstices among the boulders in Yankee Rapids filled with sand, which had drifted down as a result of the removal of the Prairie Dells Dam. And that's a story worth some comment.

In a number of places in this book, you'll find good reasons why dam removal is generally desirable on our midwestern streams. We won't repeat that information here, but we'll summarize the results of the removal of this particular dam. First off, the river temperature below the dam has fallen by an average of 7 degrees—remarkable. Tons of sand and silt have moved downstream—not good. But the DNR has constructed a sand trap downstream. A sand trap is a rectangular trench dug lengthwise down the river. It may be 40 feet long and 4 feet deep, and must be dredged periodically. Thousands of tons of sand and silt have been removed from the Prairie Dells sand trap. In 1992 alone the trap was dredged four times; 1500 tons of sand was removed at a cost of $2400 each time. The cost was borne by local chapters of Trout Unlimited.

There are differences of opinion as to the result. One frequent angler told Bill that Yankee Rapids "has been fishing well this year." Bob Talasek, who runs The Wolf River Fly Shop in Langlade, said that the dam removal had hurt the lower Prairie, but that the upper river was fishing great.

Bill experienced strenuous wading around the boulders in Yankee Rapids, but found not much in the way of trout. A pod of trout were feeding on some small stuff, #22 midges, he thought, in a slick above a boulder, but he couldn't get them to take. Water temperature was 68 degrees. A few large yellow mayflies also appeared, but the trout ignored them. These could have been *Stenonema/Stenacron,* which always appear sporadically. It's our guess that the river below the sand trap will gradually flush out and that the fishing will improve. Max Johnson, area fish manager for the DNR at Antigo, loves the Prairie. That is high praise, indeed, because Mr. Johnson has devoted more than 20 years to the study and improvement of his streams.

A few years ago, Pat Hager, a skilled fly-fisher and student of aquatic insects, took me down below Prairie Dells Dam, before its removal, for the evening fishing. We didn't break any records, but I was impressed by the spectacular scenery in the gorge—the overhanging cliffs, the deep pools, the quiet, and the feeling that I was distant from all the cares of civilization. If only the trout had cooperated! But, we reiterate, trout fishing is not only the catching and releasing of trout. Trout fishing is often a matter of place, and of timelessness. The dells will be found off a loop road near the junction of WI 17 and County Road G.

At Yanda Road, also called County Road J, upstream there is a big eddy in the pool, and a riffle below the bridge. Upstream of here, on an overcast Sunday morning in mid-August, Bill fished a 200-yard stretch full of trout splashing for tricos. "Geez, it's a blast," he said into his tape recorder. "It's about 8:30 AM; trout are everywhere, and this one might be a good one; it's a brookie, about 12 inches. See if I can get him to splash for you. Can you hear him?"

I heard the reel zip, but it was a brown. Bill reported that the trout preferred a poly-wing rather than a feather-wing Trico, which makes one ask, Why? It's one of the unsolved mysteries of our game, thank goodness. If we could solve all the puzzles and conundrums of the sport, we'd soon tire of it.

There are some other upstream entry points that we recommend. Try upstream from Gleason Bridge, which Bill called "enchanting," and where he did connect with several brookies on a scud and a Royal Coachman streamer. Also good is the footbridge area in DNR land on the east side of WI 17 opposite Echo Lake Road, as well as the stretch upstream from R&H Road, which is highly recommended by Royce Dam, a skilled fly-fisher and fly-tier from Wauwatosa.

Jim also enjoyed memorable brook trout fishing at Heineman Road Bridge, north of the junction of the Prairie and Big Hay Meadow Creeks.

BIG HAY MEADOW CREEK
DeLorme 76 & 77

Bill Shogren goes rhapsodic over his hours spent on Category 3 Hay Meadow in August. "It's really nice—gravel bottom, deep holes. My first fish was a 10-inch brown on a Black Beetle. You could keep going and going all day."

Our suggestion is that you pack a light lunch and wade Big Hay Meadow up from WI 17. Take your sweet time. There is no canopy to contend with and you can wade for 3 or 4 miles under open skies. Or you could drop a pal here for an all-day experience.

BIG PINE CREEK
DeLorme 76 & 88

Big Pine Creek crosses County Road D north of Harrison 6 or 7 miles northwest of Parrish. It's a small, tight stream, recommended by an angler whom we met on the Prairie. We found some eager brookies willing to snatch at a foam beetle fly in the pasture. Above the pasture is heavy canopy and difficult casting. It could become a learning stream for a novice who's overwhelmed by the big-water Prairie.

Anglers on the Prairie, Big Hay Meadow, and Big Pine Creek could also establish their base at Merrill, which has complete facilities. Lodging and dining are also available at the intersection of US 51 and WI 64.

WEST BRANCH OF THE EAU CLAIRE
DeLorme 77

You'll find this stream on WI 64 a few miles west of Antigo. Its 24 miles of marginal water contain planted brook and brown trout. We can't give you a definitive report, except to remark that it is a long, pretty stream with many upstream access points. This may be one that you will want to explore; or better still, assign it to one of your partners!

EAST BRANCH OF THE EAU CLAIRE
DeLorme 77

At the risk of being accused of hyperbole, we could characterize this river as awesome. This beautiful river has been improved by the DNR and TU. It has been narrowed, crib shelters or lunker structures were added, and boulders placed midstream. Eleven miles of water above WI 64 contain native brook trout and planted browns. Much of it flows through agricultural land, but all the riparian margins are tree lined. You should be able to take brookies galore on attractor flies. Usually the trout are small. Larger brookies will respond to nymphs and more sophisticated imitations. Bring your waders because this one is cold and deep.

This is another stream that DNR Area Fish Manager Max Johnson is proud of, and rightly so. It's a showpiece and an example of what can be done to improve a stream through dedication and the cooperation of public officials and volunteer groups.

THE UPPER PLOVER
DeLorme 65 & 77

About 10 miles south of Antigo on WI 52 in Marathon County you'll find the Upper Plover in heavily wooded and bog country. Much of the top 10 miles is owned by the DNR, but the best fishing is probably upstream of County Road Z, where the river has been meticulously improved. The brown trout are beautifully colored and they jump like crazy. Both brook and brown trout are wild. Water temperature was 38 degrees on the occasion of our last trip. Wear waders here, too. You will find a profile of the Lower Plover and a map of both sections in chapter 4 (Central Wisconsin).

Facilities at Antigo.

THE WOLF RIVER
DeLorme 77 & 78

In 1755, when Lieutenant Charles Michel de Langlade, in the service of France, summoned his Indian warriors to march against Braddock at Fort Duquesne (now Pittsburgh) in the first battle of the French and Indian War, the country of the Wolf was the very heart of darkness on the maps of British America.

There's an intriguing bit of history, partly speculative. Langlade led the Indian ambush against Braddock. Colonel George Washington, of the Virginia Militia, organized and saved the British retreat. Could Langlade have taken a shot at Washington? In that battle Daniel Morgan, the "Wagoneer" and hero of Cowpens, drove wagons, and Benjamin Franklin scrounged supplies and wagons for Braddock's advance.

In 1763, Langlade was present at Pontiac's attack on Michilimackinac, where Langlade saved the life of the trader Alexander Henry in one of the more remarkable episodes in American history.

The village of Langlade and Langlade County are named for that redoubtable lieutenant, half French, half Ottawa, who fought against the British, later fought with the British as a partisan leader against the upstart Americans, and finally became a respected American citizen and the first white settler of Green Bay, Wisconsin. Fantastic! Langlade's history reads like an improbable novel.

In 1863 President Abraham Lincoln ordered the army to build a military road from Fort Howard on Green Bay, Wisconsin, to Copper Harbor on Lake Superior. It was still a dark and wild country then, when the engineers camped on the Wolf at what is now the Military Wayside on WI 55 north of the village of Lily. The roadmaking was rough, through tamarack thickets and swamps, fording a hundred streams and uncounted beaver brooks, through tangles of birch, maple, and hemlock, and under the brooding vaults of white pines 5 feet in diameter and towering to 150 feet.

Black bears snuffled through the scattered glades for bushberries, eagle and osprey caught spiral drafts in sweet blue skies, and river otters hunted speckled trout in crystal pools. Panthers and gray wolves howled threats on cool and misty nights.

It is wild and lonely even now along the banks of the whitewater Wolf in Langlade County at evening's end when the canoeists and rafters have gone from the river and mayflies ring the water with their rises. The panthers have gone west, but wolves still ululate to distant mates. The river whispers menacingly around gigantic boulders, and blackness moves under the twisted, phantasmagoric cedars. From downstream you hear that rhythmic swish-swish of fluorescent line writing ephemeral words against the sky; you are reassured by the presence of your partner. Suddenly, there's that startling splash close to your drifting Brown Drake. You lift rod and strip line. Fish on! It's a Wolf River brown, shaking luminescence as he leaps. It is a wonderful night to be alive, matching the hatch on the fabled Wolf of Wisconsin.

A peripatetic fly-fisher may count his blessings that the Congress of the United States, the state of Wisconsin, and local political subdivisions, acting in rare concert, have preserved this historic and scenic river for the enjoyment of 20th-century anglers.

More than 60 miles of the upper Wolf, from the village of Pearson at the north end of Langlade County downstream to the southern border of Menominee County, have been characterized by the Department of Natural Resources among those trout waters that "show good survival and carryover of adult trout, often producing some fish of better than average size [but] stocking sometimes is required to maintain a desirable sport fishery." Because water temperatures are not ideal for the reproduction of trout, some 30,000 brown trout are planted each year in the public waters with help from the Wolf River

Wolf River
Hunting River

Chapter of TU and the Wolf River Conservation Club. The trout are scatter-planted from rafts over 26 miles in order to utilize the tremendous range of habitat.

Early in the season, a fisherman is bound to pick up an occasional brook trout in the public waters, but as the water warms, most of the "specs" will retreat to the cooler feeder creeks. Stunted smallmouth bass are found in gentler currents around the boulders. Wild rainbows no longer inhabit fast water, but Herb Buettner, of the Wild Wolf Inn, is leading an attempt to reintroduce reproducing rainbows.

In Langlade County, 34½ miles of the Wolf are under the protection of the DNR, which pursues an aggressive program of acquisition and control. No further development of the shoreline is permitted. Property owners are not free to expand or materially alter their facilities. During the past 25 years, 75 percent of the shoreline has been purchased by the state, at a cost in excess of $5 million.

Approximately 27 miles of the lower Wolf through the Menominee Indian Reservation (coterminous with Menominee County) have been designated by Congress as a National Wild and Scenic River. Although that section is closed to outsiders by order of the Menominee Tribal Council, it is a valuable ecological resource. Its many miles of spring-fed streams are nurseries for trout that stray into public waters, and the DNR obtains some wild rainbow eggs from the Council.

The Wolf is a pristine freestone river, more typical of a large western stream, averaging 150 feet in width and 3 or 4 feet in depth. Through 20 named rapids and rips, from Lily to the Menominee line, the river drops 430 feet. In the flats and runs between the rapids, around the islands, and in the channels between huge boulders there are miles of superb wading water and an immense number of lies for watchful and hungry trout. But entry points to the Wolf River are few. Walking in to the river and wading in solitude are part of the wilderness experience.

Beginning in the north, there is easy entry in DNR lands at Pearson on County Road T, then downstream at the County Road A bridge. The Military Wayside on WI 55 offers a superb variety of bottom types for wading fly-fishers. The river near WI 52 at Lily is a bit more placid. Next down is the Wolf River Road, which makes a loop from WI 55 to a Soo Line Railroad crossing and a dead-end road to DNR parking on the river. This is one of our favorite locations, even though it is deep and difficult wading upstream, and not easy downstream either, through the rapids, but we've spent some wonderful hours here.

Going south, find the spur road that runs south from west-running Hollister Road off WI 55. Hollister at WI 55 is a single building on the northeast corner of WI 55 and Hollister Road. Due west, approximately 1.25 miles, is Burnt Point, giving a spectacular view of flat water spotted with boulders upstream and rapids down. Be sure to see Burnt Point, but we prefer to fish at the end of the spur road, where there is a canoe access. Look for the south-running blacktop a couple of hundred yards before you get to Burnt Point.

Six miles of the Wolf, from the Soo Line trestle below the Hollister spur to Dierck's Pond, are restricted to fly-fishing, currently Category 5. This superb wading stretch may also be reached from the parking lot on WI 55 about 2 miles north of Langlade.

The flats above and below the Langlade bridge can be an evening delight, and have been for us on many occasions. There are two other entry points downstream in Langlade, along Rocky Rips Street and farther downstream at County Road M, the last of our recommended stops.

There is also access by a combination of gravel road and fire lane on the west side of the river. The road, which begins at Four Corners on WI 64 about 6 miles west of Langlade, touches the river at the Oxbow, a renowned fishing hole, but you may need a four-wheel-drive to make the last couple of miles on the fire lane section. Consult your maps for other trails to the river. A *Troutland* map, which shows much of the Wolf in detail, is available at local commercial establishments.

From Pearson up, the main stem of the Wolf through the two Post Lakes is a warm-water fishery, but at Pearson the spring-fed Hunting River adds more than 15 miles of trout habitat. Two branches of the Lily River add 13 miles. Ninemile Creek enters the Wolf at Hollister. Several short feeders contain wild brook trout. Excluding the streamlets, there are nearly 75 miles of trout water open to the public.

The Wolf is aptly named. In the spring, surging through the rapids and runs, it is the White Wolf, hungry and cold, licking its chops, hoping for an errant fisherman to challenge the wild rips and slick boulders. In the low water of summer under a bright sky it seems more like a tabby cat, sleepy and purring, but, for all that, it is ready to slash with a claw if trifled with. Dress in belted waders and use a staff. If you intend to fish the hatches into dark, reconnoiter the bottom first by day.

On bright midsummer days, following a couple or three days of 80-degree ambient temperature, water temperature may reach the

Joyce Humphrey on the Wolf at Wolf Road access south of Lily

mid-70s. Cap Buettner, now deceased, a master fly-fisherman and active TUer, once said that a hot-weather fisherman had better learn to drift a Muddler or streamer deep under the fast currents. A local expert fishes the pockets around boulders in fast water in July and August. Nights, though, are always cool in this north country. The river will also remain cool under cloudy skies—of which, one may be sure, there are many. A summertime fisherman might probe with a thermometer downstream from feeders in the shaded runs.

Another way to avoid warm water and sluggish trout is to take a long siesta at noon, then fish afternoons in the shadows of the cedars on the west bank.

Spring is a different story. One day in early May, fine trout were feeding on Diptera at high noon in less than a foot of water right up against the bank in view of Buettner's Motel at Langlade, where we had been enjoying our midday R and R. Inducing those trout to accept a #18 Blue-Winged Olive, which matched the hatch, became a frustrating interruption.

Cap Buettner always said that the river is rich in aquatic life. Typical of Wisconsin rivers, it has minor hatches of *Baetis*, tiny blue-winged olives, throughout the season, tricos from late June, and a minor hatch of *Isonychia*, White-Gloved Howdy, or mahogany dun, which appears between June 15 and July 15.

One late May evening on the flats at Langlade, I encountered simultaneously two different species of caddis, #16 and #12, one #22 microcaddis, two species of *Ephemerella* (Hendrickson and a pale evening dun), a single advance scout of the *Ephemera simulans* (brown drake), and two crane flies, one of which was identical in color to the pale evening dun. After frantically changing flies over those picky trout, I finally took four trout—two brilliant, prime browns and two recent plants, all on a #14 Hendrickson. Later, attempting to raise a large trout that hung out midstream and willing to experiment, I hooked and released two more on a #12 Ginger Bivisible. The next evening around 7 PM, a satisfactory hatch of *Baetis* appeared and the trout sipped on the Blue-Winged Olives.

The river contains two species of the great black stonefly, *Pteronarcys;* the great brown stonefly, *Acroneuria,* which hatches around the first of June; the stonefly, *Phasganophora,* known as the night creeper; and the large golden stone. Because various species of stoneflies hatch throughout the season, stonefly nymphs are always an excellent choice for bottom-bumping the runs by day and creeping the shallows toward evening. The Green Stonefly Muddler, Cap's creation, should be cast among the sweepers. We can't tell you how many times his Muddler has saved the day on other rivers. Weighted Muddlers and Matukas are good imitations of the three species of sculpins that hide among the pebbles. Chubs here grow to huge size. Even Izaak Walton would be pleased to feed a small wet fly to them in slack water. Big brown trout must relish them as well. Hoppers and ants are traditional summer fare.

Of major importance are five mayfly hatches, plus a sixth that Cap numbered on his personal list. Emergence dates may vary according to temperatures and hours of daylight, perhaps even lunar attraction, and other factors known only to God. All are evening hatches.

Siphlonurus quebecensis, known locally as the gray drake, #10 and #12, emerges May 28 to June 9, duration about three weeks. We think of this one as a dark chocolate quill, but perhaps it doesn't need another colloquial name. Cap Buettner designed an emerger for this hatch that we have used successfully on other rivers as a searching pattern.

Ephemera simulans, #10, the famous brown drake found on many Wisconsin rivers, also known as the March brown and chocolate dun, hatches from June 5 to June 15. One recent June 2 the duns appeared at dusk and the spinners mated at 2 PM the following day.

Stenonema vicarium is Buettner's sixth selection. Use a Gray Fox #10 or #12. Elsewhere it goes by as many as 10 names: dark Cahill, ginger quill, March brown, sand drake, and many more. June 5 to June 10 is the usual period.

Potamanthus, or cream fly, hatches from June 7 to July 1, though the species is in doubt. A Light Cahill #12 is almost a dead ringer for the cream fly. The nymph is sometimes called the golden bull.

Hexagenia atrocaudata, the green drake #8, emerges from July 15 to August 25. Known elsewhere as the big slate drake or great leadwinged drake; in most places, just Hex. This *Hexagenia,* which is a tube maker, is about a third smaller than the *H. limbata* found on many silty Wisconsin rivers, and it appears here a couple of weeks later.

Ephoron leukon, White Wulff #8 and #10, appears from August 1 to August 20. (See our description of the white fly hatch in the Prairie River profile.) Bob Talasek, of the Wolf River Fly Shop, described one hatch as "a blizzard on an evening in August." Cap Buettner called it a "superhatch."

On the evening of August 15 Bill Shogren found the white fly hatch in the fly-fishing section down from Hollister Landing. "Jim, the hatch is on; it's about 8:15. The flies are coming up all over the place, they're towing their shucks. I've got a fish on right now." There sounds Bill's reel, and Bill panting with excitement. "Oh, what a nice fish! Got another one on, Jim. That first one was 16 inches. My God! Amazing to see the white flies coming upriver. A guy I met told me that last night he caught a 12, a 13, a 14, and two at 15 inches. Even allowing for him maybe being a plus-twoer, that's spectacular fishing. You've got to be set up to do your business. These hatches don't last long. It seems to me this lasted about 45 minutes."

Coming out after dark was another experience that Bill won't soon forget. "The joys of trout fishing late at night. The challenge is to find the path, then to stay on it. Jim," he called with a quaver in his voice, "I trust there are no weird creatures along this river. It's getting pretty spooky!"

If the surface of the Wolf is temporarily lifeless during your time on the river, fish blind through the riffles and runs with a Hare's Ear on the point and a Cap's Stonefly Muddler tied short on the butt to serve as both indicator and attractor. At evening, switch to a large nymph on the point.

The Wolf between Lily and the iron bridge at County Road M is a popular summer weekend exercise for canoeists and kayakers. Those even-more-intrusive rubber rafts put in at the Hollister spur road and take out at Langlade or at County Road M.

It's a fact of life that fishermen must share the beneficence of nature with other enthusiasts. Fortunately there are a number of ways for fly-fishermen to enjoy a share of unalloyed pleasure in wilderness surroundings. Visit during the week rather than on weekends. Search the trout lies upstream from Hollister, thereby avoiding all the rafts and many of the canoes and kayaks. Get on the river at early morning or at dusk. However, as a matter of personal observation, even a large and fastidious trout resumed feeding within 10 minutes after a raft went over his lie.

By local ordinance, raft trips may not begin before 8 AM and must end by 7 PM. Experienced Wolf River fishermen wade the lower river in the morning while the rafts are still upstream, then transfer their activities upriver in the afternoon. Other fishermen find runs and braids away from the main channel and pursue their sport in relative serenity. Or if you wish, join the throng, rent a raft, and fish at will between Hollister and County Road M. It's an experience that you may live to regret. If the water is high and hard you risk a dunking; if the water is low, you'll surely hang up on some of the gigantic rocks.

Hollister to Langlade is a drift of 4 or 5 hours. Hollister to the County Road M bridge is an all-day float. Midweek under lowering skies or in a light rain can be untrammeled days on the Wolf.

Rafters and fishers have established a *modus vivendi*. Rafters prefer sunlight and heat of day; fly-fishers opt for overcast and cool of evening. When the rafters are fingering their frosty cocktail glasses in a supper club, the fly-fishers are hiking in to their secret places.

Local authorities and townsfolk are proud stewards of the river. Littering is subject to fine; bottles and cans are not allowed aboard watercraft. Twice each summer, Boy Scouts traverse the river in rafts furnished by the Wild Wolf Inn to pick up flotsam and jetsam.

Dedicated trout fishermen everywhere have learned to accommodate themselves to circumstances. It is always too wet or too dry, or the river is too clear or too murky, or too hot or too cold, or thunder has put the trout down. There are too many fishermen or too few trout. It is a litany of pain that goes back to the days of Dame Juliana Berners and before. But a serious angler will always find trout in the Wolf River of Wisconsin. And even if not, the beauty and magic of this mighty river are compensation enough for the vagaries of weather and humankind.

We shall never see the river exactly as Langlade may have known it, nor as the beat-out army engineers saw it in 1863, but over time the few remaining cabins will disappear, the pines will reach for the sky, and our children will get a sense of a primal magnificence that once was. Aspen and willow will shade the margins and cool the water, eagles and ospreys will make their nests in skeleton cottonwoods; and otter kits will rest their forepaws on a fallen cedar to peer with childlike curiosity at strange, two-legged interlopers.

When the shadows come out of hiding and the twisted cedars bending assume the shapes of phantom French irregulars and Chippewa warriors, turn, turn resolutely into the gathering dusk and cast your big Brown Drake upon the molten pewter water. Listen for the reassuring hiss and swish of your partner's cast. Splash! Trout on!

The Wolf may be at risk. In 1986 Exxon Minerals Company proposed to construct and operate an underground zinc and copper mine and mill at Crandon, Wisconsin. Some intercepted groundwater would be treated, then discharged into Swamp Creek, a tributary of the Wolf. Local environmentalists and trout fishermen opposed the plan, but state agencies appeared to be ready to approve. In 1987 Exxon put the construction on hold due to low world prices for the minerals. In 1994 the proposal was resurrected. Conservation and trout groups may hold their collective breaths and cross their fingers.

Facilities at Antigo, Buettner's Motel at Langlade, Herb Buettner's Wild Wolf Inn on the river (White Lake address), at Langlade and White Lake, plus American Plan and European Plan resorts in the area. There are two campgrounds in the Nicolet National Forest, 10 miles east of Langlade. In addition to Talasek's fly shop, Mike's Mobil Service in Langlade provides both information and an excellent selection of flies.

THE HUNTING RIVER
DeLorme 77

Our old friend Eino Tutt of Wausau was a master at rolling big brown trout from northern rivers on a Hornberg. He was also a specialist at swimming a live minnow on the upper Namekagon above Cable, but that's another story. One of his favorite rivers was the 16-mile Hunting, a major tributary of the Wolf that joins it in DNR lands at Pearson.

A salute is due here to Frank Hornberg, Portage County game

warden from 1920 to 1950, and creator of the fly that has captured the interest of thousands of big brown trout.

The river, which averages 44 feet in width and is cooled by mammoth springs near Summit Lake and others along County Road T, contains wild brook trout and planted browns. It has been extensively improved by the DNR west of Pearson. Our favorite location for early morning, late afternoon, and evening fly-fishing is the slow, broad water at the County Road T bridge, but you may prefer to begin your exploration at Pearson and at the roadside park west on County Road T, where the stream has been narrowed and deepened. Fish it at dusk with a Hornberg.

As of this writing, a long section of the Hunting River, from the mouth upstream to Fitzgerald Dam Road, is Category 5, artificials only, brown and rainbow trout 20 inches, brook trout 14, and a bag limit of two trout in total! That must tell you something about the quality of the river.

Facilities at Antigo, Langlade, and Crandon.

THE FIRST SOUTH BRANCH OF THE OCONTO
DeLorme 78

Traveling east from Langlade on WI 64 you will cross several good-looking streams, including the Second South Branch, a first-class stream for naturally reproducing brown and brook trout. About 9 miles east of Langlade in Oconto County you'll find the First South Branch of the Oconto. Approximately 12 miles of it, from above WI 64 to the Menominee County line, where it enters the Reservation and fishing is not allowed, are split between Categories 2 and 4. The river has been improved with riprap and bank structures at the WI 64 bridge. Try it here. Brook trout are wild; browns are planted.

Facilities at Langlade and at Mountain on WI 64 and 32.

NORTH BRANCH OF THE OCONTO RIVER
DeLorme 78 & 79

The North Branch of the Oconto consists of 24 miles of first-class water, Category 2, above WI 32 at Mountain in Oconto County. It contains wild browns and brook trout. Rainbows may be planted

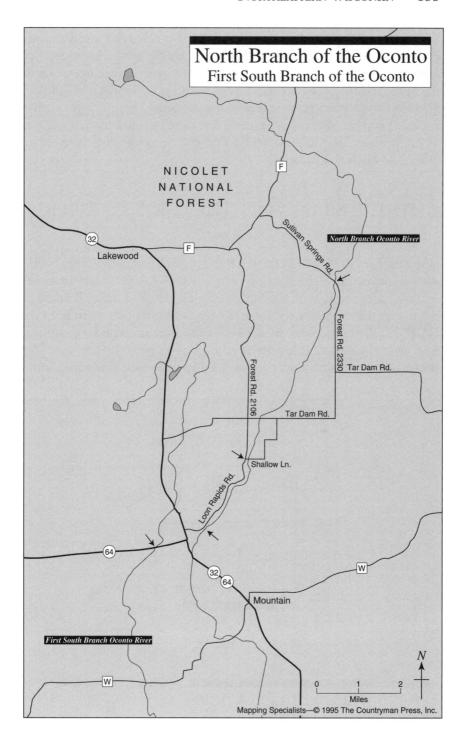

North Branch of the Oconto
First South Branch of the Oconto

NICOLET
NATIONAL
FOREST

F

32
Lakewood

F

Sullivan Springs Rd

North Branch Oconto River

Forest Rd. 2330

Tar Dam Rd.

Forest Rd. 2106

Tar Dam Rd.

Shallow Ln.

Loon Rapids Rd.

64

32 64

W

Mountain

First South Branch Oconto River

W

N

0   1   2
Miles

Mapping Specialists—© 1995 The Countryman Press, Inc.

some years, depending on the availability from hatcheries. Roadside parking is at the bridge on WI 32, and additional entries are up-stream along Loon Rapids Road. We also like it farther upstream at the Sullivan Springs Road bridge. Between Loon Rapids and Sullivan Springs the Oconto is wide and generally smooth and deep, with a broken bottom. Waders are required for the evening fly-fishing.

Facilities at Mountain, north at Wabeno, or south at Suring, all on WI 32 in Oconto County.

SOUTH BRANCH OF THE OCONTO RIVER
DeLorme 79

Seven miles of the South Branch of the Oconto River, a few miles north-west of Suring on WI 32, from County Road AA downstream to WI 32, are Category 5, artificials only and a bag limit of three. Because of the quality of the water the river has received attention from both the DNR and dedicated fly-fishers. Much of the stream is under easement, and several substantial blocks of acreage are owned by the state. We prefer to fish it from County Road AA down the west side along South

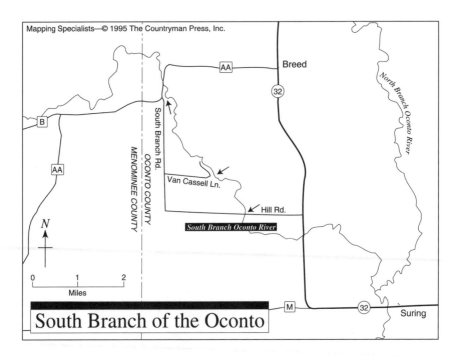

Branch Road, finishing at a DNR parking lot and trail to a particularly charming stretch at the Hill Road bridge. The bridge is about 1.5 miles west of WI 32 if you are coming from the south.

Facilities at Suring and Mountain.

THE LOWER PESHTIGO RIVER
DeLorme 79

The Lower Peshtigo, west of Crivitz in Marinette County, with access from either County Road A or County Road W, has an unusual history. In 1955, Lyle Kingston, an engineer with the Wisconsin Public Service Corporation, and Virgil Muench, a conservationist and fly-fisher from Green Bay, convinced the Corporation to grant an easement to the then Wisconsin Conservation Department (now DNR) on about 5 miles of the lower Peshtigo between Johnson Falls and the foot of Spring Rapids. The purpose was to establish an open season restricted to fly-fishing. This was the first Special Regulations stretch of river in the state. It still is special, rated Category 5.

The Peshtigo down here is huge and often dangerous due to fluctuating water levels from the operation of the dams upriver. We've been on the river at the head of Spring Rapids when the water rose a foot in a matter of minutes.

Because of the changing water levels, natural reproduction of trout is nil, but the experience of fly-fishing for stocked browns and rainbows can be exhilarating. This is a wild river through what appears to be primitive country, although it was logged and burned in the late 19th century. A respondent to a creel survey described his day this way: "This is a beautiful area with the grandeur of a western stream and a bonus of seeing various wildlife while working the river." And so it is for us.

Access from the east side is at Bizjak Lane off County Road A and at Medicine Brook via County Road A to Newton Lake Road, then to High Falls Road. We prefer, though, the west side entries from County Road W out of Crivitz to Kirby Lake Road, thence by 0.8 mile of single-lane sand road to the head of Spring Rapids, or upstream to Seymour Rapids from Kostreva Road. You will want the brochure and map "Your Guide to Public Service Recreation Land," available in the area or from the Wisconsin Public Service Corporation, 700 N. Adams, Green Bay, WI 54301.

Because aquatic insect life is also disturbed by fluctuating water levels, we can't pinpoint any hatches. Better to fish the big river with Hornbergs, Muddlers, Woolly Buggers, and similar artificial baitfish. If trout are feeding on the surface, use a Brown Bivisible in fast water and a Spider on the slicks.

Facilities at Crivitz and in many of the resorts in the area around the impoundments. History buffs may want to visit the museum and graveyard at Peshtigo, Wisconsin, commemorating the catastrophic Peshtigo forest fire of October 8, 1871, which claimed 800 lives and ravaged more than 2400 square miles of cutover country. This fire occurred on the same day as the Great Chicago Fire; both were driven by cyclonic winds.

NORTH BRANCH OF BEAVER CREEK
DeLorme 79

The 6 miles of the top of the North Branch of Beaver Creek are worth a visit to the domicile of native browns and brooks. Go south from Crivitz on US 141 to the village of Beaver, then west on 14th Road, then north on 19th Road to the bridge. Fish upstream here between 19th Road and 25th Road. With the cooperation of the Green Bay Chapter of Trout Unlimited, the state has installed a platform for handicapped fishers in a wide, slow spot. Just to check the quality of the habitat, Bill was the first to pitch in a Hornberg and immediately took a lovely 12-inch brown, which he returned unharmed. We like to see accessible fishing paths and casting platforms installed around the state, because some day we'll all be old.

Facilities at Crivitz.

THE UPPER PESHTIGO RIVER
DeLorme 79, 90, & 91

The Upper Peshtigo is an enigma. Its long complex of branches and creeks comprises one of the major tributaries to Green Bay. It should be one of the biggest and best trout rivers, and it may be to those who know exactly where the trout congregate in colder water in summer. The problem is that the water is too cold in winter to support substantial natural reproduction of trout, presumably due to an excess

A handicapped access area near the town of Beaver
on the North Branch of Beaver Creek

of beaver dams on the many tributaries. But rivers are complex organisms. Warm summer water temperatures may stress the trout; the Peshtigo has many sections that are shallow and slow. Anchor ice in winter may scour aquatic life; various types of pollutants can raise havoc. There may be other factors too subtle to be measured.

We have labeled this long complex of branches and feeders above the several impoundments the Upper Peshtigo, in order to distinguish it from the Lower Peshtigo below Johnson Falls.

The main Peshtigo River begins officially close to Argonne, in Forest County north of US 8, on WI 55 and WI 32, at the junction of the Middle and South Branches. The North Branch adds volume a few miles to the east, a mile or so north of County Road G. While the Middle and South Branches are fairly easy to access around Argonne, the North Branch rises in the bowels of the Nicolet National Forest, with very limited access. Bill says you may need a helicopter to get back in there.

The main river flows, often turbulently, for 40 or more miles in Forest County, then for 25 miles in Marinette County to the Cauldron Falls Reservoir, the first of the Wisconsin Public Service Corpo-

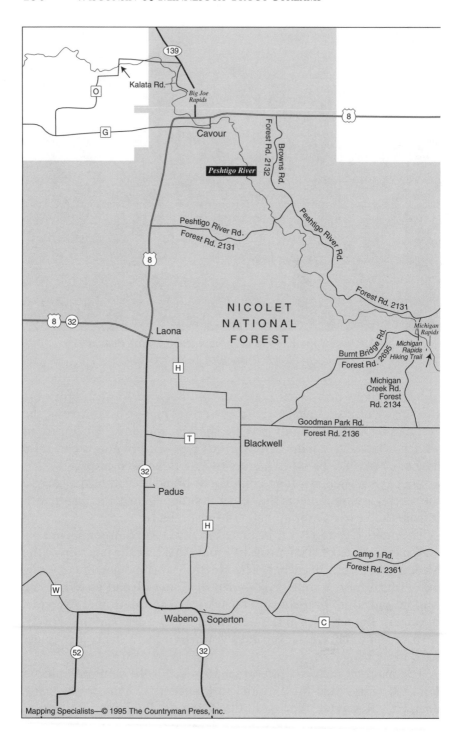

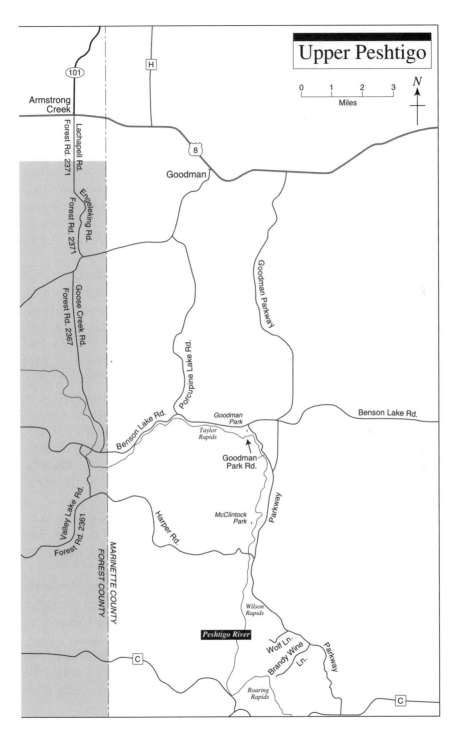

Upper Peshtigo

0   1   2   3

Miles

N

ration impoundments. The tributaries are too numerous to tally, but many will provide first-class fishing for wild brook trout.

There's no way that we can give you a step-by-step tour of this magnificent river. Access points are many, although widely spaced through some of the most remote country imaginable, but we can direct you to five or six places that you won't want to miss.

First, we've had good fishing for brook trout along County Road O on the main Peshtigo northwest of Cavour. Or you might begin your long exploration at the campground at Big Joe Rapids on Kalata Road, a couple of miles north of Cavour on WI 139. (WI 139 leads north from US 8.) It was there on June 5 that we found a marvelous hatch of brown drakes hanging like berries from streamside brush. Upstream from WI 139, the river is Category 2; the remainder to Cauldron Falls Reservoir is Category 3.

Next, go downstream from Cavour to Michigan Rapids via Browns Road (Forest Road 2132) from US 8 east of Cavour, then south on the Peshtigo River Road (Forest Road 2131), then south to the Michigan Rapids hiking trail on Michigan Creek Road (Forest Road 2134). The hiking trail begins at the junction of Forest Roads 2134 and 2695 and loops for 2 miles along Michigan Rapids. The trail can also be reached from the west by Burnt Bridge Road (Forest Road 2695).

A fellow enthusiast, who fished the river for 33 years, mainly in July and August, reported fabulous success in the rapids. We won't repeat the numbers and sizes of trout he caught because they boggle the mind. He also used some unorthodox tactics in that heavy water, but big-fish fly-fishers should be able to find the pockets. When he mentioned Coleman coolers filled with 16- and 20-inch browns extracted from the rapids and in the flat below, we have no reason to doubt, remembering similar catches on other rivers in northern Wisconsin. We doubt that anyone could duplicate his results now, but his advice is still valid. Fish the rapids and the tails but avoid the long, warm flats between.

Next down past many miles of river is Goodman Park, in Marinette County below Taylor Rapids, via Goodman Parkway. The Parkway is listed as one of Wisconsin's Rustic Roads. You'll have to navigate by map to get from Michigan Rapids to Goodman Parkway. Visually, this immaculate park, with its island and Japanese bridge, is a trout fisher's paradise. On opening weekend it becomes a gathering of fly-fishing aficionados, but later in the season you may have it all to yourself.

Next downstream is McClintock Park, not quite so prepossessing but offering a mix of excellent habitat through and above the park. McClintock Falls is a series of rapids with bridges for exceptional views. Marinette County boasts 12 falls, all with easy access and most located in county parks. Anglers will find trout in the oxygenated water below the falls, and quite often in the glides above.

The Peshtigo is a popular summer canoe trail—fly-fishers will sob— but be cheered that most trips begin at County Road C below McClintock Park.

The Peshtigo should be one of the best, and may be again if the beaver dams are removed from the feeders, but for now you will have to search for trout in the oxygen-rich water through and below the many rapids and falls; fish early season or late, or cozen the river at nightfall and after.

Facilities for travelers at motels along US 8, and at the many motels and resorts around the impoundments.

THE NORTH BRANCH OF THE PIKE RIVER
DeLorme 91 & 99

As we promised in the introduction to this section, let us begin with the North Branch of the Pike River as representative of the streams and rivers of the far northeast. The several falls are in Marinette County, about 7 miles west of Pembine and a few miles south of US 8. Look for Lily Lake Road and the signs to Twelvefoot Falls County Park. The 25 miles of the North Branch is first-class water for wild brook and brown trout. You'll always find trout in the turbulence below the falls, but that's no real test of a fly-fisher. Try the glides above the falls for that spackle of trout rising to midges or other small fare.

The North Branch of the Pike still runs free and clear from Railroad Pond just north of US 8 in Marinette County to the Menominee River. Above Amberg on US 141 it is Category 4; below Amberg it is Category 5. Approximately 29 miles of first-class water contain wild brook and brown trout. Our preferred section is still that which runs above and through Twelvefoot Falls County Park where one will find Twelve Foot and Eight Foot Falls. Eighteen Foot Falls is located about a mile north of the park. Access points upstream of the park are few, with some reachable only by long foot trails. Entries are closer to-

Twelve Foot Falls on the North Branch of the Pike River
in the county campground

gether downstream, particularly along the Pike River Road. That is
the way you ought to go for brown trout.
Facilities at Pembine and Amberg.

OTHER RIVERS OF THE NORTHEAST

We might treat the other branches of the Pike River, the Pemebonwon,
the Popple, and Pine Rivers, as a group because the fly-fishing conditions are so similar on each. The country through which they wind
their way to the Menominee River is huge, dark, and tangled, access
bridges are separated by miles of swamps and thickets of aspen and
tamarack, and the rivers are not rich in aquatic life.

Access is generally easy in the upper reaches of the rivers in the
Nicolet National Forest, probable at state and county road bridges,
but probably not possible where a "Lane" ends at the river. Oddly,
much of the land at the ends of these short lanes is posted against
trespass. It is an unusual and disheartening experience to discover, in
friendly Wisconsin, a narrow track through the deep woods that

leads—you're sure of it—to a stretch of roaring rapids and leaping trout, only to find a primitive cabin and a warning to keep out. We suggest that you always cross-check between the DeLorme and Milwaukee Map Service maps before you go hiking off toward that distant waterfall or rapids.

These streams tend to warm during the summer months and the trout become lethargic. During the dog days use a stream thermometer and test for the upwelling of in-stream springs.

THE PEMEBONWON RIVER
DeLorme 91 & 99

The South Branch of the Peme rises in Marinette County and cuts south of Pembine to join the huge Menominee River, the border between Wisconsin and the Upper Peninsula of Michigan. It embraces some 19 miles of first-class water and 8 of the second class, all of it producing wild brookies and planted browns.

Some years ago the Peme was the subject of a 5-year research/management study designed to determine if removal of beaver dams would prevent habitat deterioration and declines in wild trout populations. Four hundred eighty-five dams were removed on the 10½ miles of the North Branch and on 24 miles of tributaries. The results on the North Branch were disappointing, but the numbers of brook trout increased in the tributaries, which goes to prove that habitat improvement is both expensive and sometimes inconclusive.

The North Branch of the Peme includes about 23 miles of somewhat lower-quality water containing wild brook trout. Our suggestion is that you fish around Smalley Falls and in the 2 miles below Long Slide Falls. Take Spike Horn Road east from US 141 about 5 miles north of Pembine for parking near Long Slide Falls. Hike upstream by maintained path to the smaller Smalley Falls.

Facilities at Pembine, Niagara, and Iron Mountain.

THE PINE RIVER
DeLorme 91

The long and complex Pine River reaches the Menominee River at Iron Mountain, Michigan, on US 2 and US 141. Although several of

The Pemebonwon River in Marinette County is home to wild brookies.

its feeders are first class, the 31 miles above LaSalle Falls in Florence County are of marginal quality for trout. However, our friend from Missouri, Jason Carpenter, did extract a 20-inch brown from Snaketail Rapids on the upper Pine one recent early June near Tipler and close to the junction of WI 139 and WI 70. Although we would advise you to avoid the Pine River, we are often confounded by our friends.
Facilities at Iron Mountain.

THE BRULE RIVER
DeLorme 90, 91, & 99

This is the eastern Brule, not to be confused with the Bois Brule of northwestern Wisconsin. This great river begins at Brule Lake in Michigan and meanders for more than 50 miles to the Menominee River. The Brule is big and beautiful, and shows a variety of water types. Browns and brook trout are naturally reproducing. Access is not easy on the Wisconsin side because so much of it runs through the Nicolet National Forest, where the roads are few and far between. You can, however, fish with a Wisconsin license from the Michigan side. We had a blast near Nelma on WI 55 in August, where the river is wide with a slow, even flow. Along the banks under the alders, big browns can be taken during the doldrums of summer. During the day, slide your terrestrials under the sweepers; at night, feed the big browns a Muddler. More detailed information is found in *Michigan Trout Streams,* by Bob Linsenman and Steve Nevala, also from Countryman Press, Inc., 1994.

The country of the northeast is deep and dark and wild. Some long sections of rivers have not seen the fall of an artificial fly since the beginning of time. The native brook trout are there in the fastness of the mysterious woods; the imported brown trout have gone native in many streams. You will find them if you slide on moccasins to the end of the trail, respect the habitat, and connect with the universe.

6

West Central Wisconsin:
A Green and Gentle Land

The streams and rivers of west central Wisconsin offer a pleasing variety, from the placid, intimate brook trout streams north of Eau Claire on the east, to that fine trio of brown trout streams within striking distance of the Twin Cities on the west. McCann, Duncan, Tiffany, and others are productive small streams. The Kinnickinnic, which joins the border St. Croix above Prescott, is one of the best brown trout streams in the state. It is Janus-faced: Above River Falls it is narrow, cold, and wader-deep, with thick blue-black silt at the margins, and is frequently pinched by brush; below the city it is wide and open to easy fly-fishing in hip boots through a riffle and pool sequence for more than 8 miles. The Rush River is big-fish water, partly open, partly flanked by heavy undergrowth and limestone cliffs, with huge pools and long, frustrating flats. The most productive sections of the 40-mile-long Willow River lie in or close to the Willow

River State Park at Hudson, offering solitude and serenity for early-morning and evening fly-fishers.

A SCHOOL OF BROOK TROUT STREAMS

"It's a bluebird day!" shouts Bill. Indeed, it is a rare clear day this late summer. Blame all of the rainy days this year on El Niño, that intermittent oceanic and atmospheric change off the coast of Peru. It is an example of the chaos effect—a change way down there means bank-full streams and saturated topsoil here, in northwestern Chippewa, northeastern Dunn, and southern Barron Counties.

But water, not too much, mind you, and never in torrents, please, gives our native brook trout wiggle room in these gems of streams. Water also encourages the mosquitoes to multiply, unfortunately.

McCANN CREEK
DeLorme 73

"Fantastic!" yells Bill as he releases another water-bouncing brookie from the crystal waters of Category 2 McCann Creek upstream of Old Mill Lane Bridge, a few miles northeast of Bloomer off WI 40. There! We've pinpointed your first stop.

From here on, refer to your maps and don't lose your cool. Some bureaucrat, we suppose, at Madison, the state capital, is rationalizing the road signs in this part of Wisconsin. Or perhaps bureaucrats in the county seat are responsible. At any rate the old, picturesque names, such as Corkscrew Road, which was aptly named, are being replaced with 1210th Avenue or 270th Street, or some such. Friends, we're losing our history under the guise of progress. We'd guess that a computer somewhere can locate 1210th Avenue on a grid easier than it can find Sheridan Road (270th Street). Probably Sheridan was named for the Civil War hero when a deer trail to a homestead was compacted into a wagon track that led to a coach road shortly after the War Between the States. Goodbye, General Phil Sheridan. We hardly remember you anyhow.

We'll use the old, descriptive names in the course of our itinerary out of respect for an area rich in history, with occasional brackets for the new street numbers where we have them.

Enough of the asides: Let us return to McCann. It's grasshopper time on the brook trout streams. A #12 Joe's Hopper is about right. Put on your waders—you'll need them on these narrow and deep little streams. Take your time, wade slowly up the middle, splatting your hopper fan-like from margin to margin on a .006 (5X) tippet. Don't send a bow wave ahead of you and be sure to absorb the beauty of this rolling country, with its prosperous farms, green forested ridges, and sumac bushes now touched with russet. Stalk those rising trout upstream from Old Mill to Morning Crest Lane and there sit and eat a sandwich. It's a bluebird day and all's right with the world.

Bill waxes enthusiastic over these friendly streams. This is where you should bring your daughter to introduce her to the joys of fly-fishing, he says. Or a son. The streams are modest, not dangerous or intimidating. The problems presented to the neophyte are pretty forth-right, not complex. The casts are short and the rods light and easy to handle. The hoppers float high and dry, and the take is topwater and aggressive. If not a daughter or son, introduce a friend to this art.

Bill allows that he saw hundreds of trout between Old Mill and Morning Crest, many of which he caught and released. They're not large, but gorgeous, and they come out shaking water as if they are scattering diamonds. What more could one ask?

You can fish downstream to WI 124, some 7 river miles, but below WI 64 the stream flattens and the trout habitat is less inviting. Below the WI 64 bridge we scared up at least 1000 mallards and a gaggle of geese, a sight to behold, but only one trout came to net. We weren't too impressed with the stream in that stretch, but you might tread lightly there and uncover a variety of deeper pools and larger trout.

Complete facilities for travelers at Bloomer.

DUNCAN CREEK
DeLorme 72

Now drive west about 5 miles to Duncan Creek (Category 1 upstream of WI 64; Category 5 downstream to the Lake Como dam) to the bridge on County Road SS north of Bloomer near Horseshoe Road. There's a good run above the County Road SS bridge, then a neck, then a magnificent pool that will warm the cockles of any fly-fisher's heart. Downstream is easy going through a mix of riffles and small pools.

Bill, who is not given to overstatement, says that this is even better than McCann. "It sure is a beautiful stream; I just fell in love with Duncan Creek."

There are just as many trout here as in McCann, but it seems to us that they run a bit heftier. We took them on a grasshopper and an Adams. Every time we dropped the fly into a likely spot, Bingo! The Coachman streamer also worked well as an attractor.

It's deep, clear water; temperature 56 degrees; cooperative fish. Sometimes they slash at the fly, sometimes up and out of the water and down on the fly, next time a sip. Some go crazy when they leap. Beautiful!

There are three bridge crossings above County Road SS before you get into Department of Natural Resources land in the headwaters. Bill fished down from County Road SS almost to Lake Como at Bloomer through country open to fly-fishing. There are many more miles of designated trout water below Bloomer, all the way to Tilden, but we don't recommend streams below impoundments, as they are subject to damaging water temperatures.

Facilities at Bloomer.

SAND CREEK AND THE RED CEDAR RIVER
DeLorme 72

Next, go west from Duncan about 10 miles to the village of Sand Creek in Dunn County, about 2 miles north of WI 64 on County Road M. Centered at this charming little community, which looks like something out of a Norman Rockwell *Saturday Evening Post* cover or a Currier and Ives print, you'll find a few miles of Category 5 Special Regulations water, including about 5 miles of the Red Cedar River and about a mile of lower Sand Creek. The Red Cedar and Sand Creek contain brown trout, some of which are trophy size. The Special Regs limit you to a maximum of three browns over 12 inches, but only one over 18 inches. That "one over 18" should be enough to inspire any fly-fisher.

Just east of town you'll find a small parking lot on lower Sand. Since there is no beaten path on either bank you will want to wade your way up slowly through a succession of riffles and pools. We found the brooks and browns cooperative, willing to attack a Coachman streamer, an Adams, or a Hornberg, all without prejudice. This stream is not as big as Duncan but it is a quality fishery. We know of an 18-inch brown that was caught and released in one of the pools in the 5 miles of upper Sand Creek beyond the Category 5 segment.

The Red Cedar is primarily a smallmouth stream, but a few larger browns hang out at the mouths of the feeders. There are a few places in the Special Regulations stretch that are wadable. Fortunately, they are where the feeders join the river. Fly-fishing from a canoe will cover more territory.

Facilities at Bloomer, and at Chetek to the north.

UPPER PINE CREEK
DeLorme 72

Next proceed northwest out of Sand Creek on County Road U, winding through the green hills of earth to Dallas in Barron County, where the three branches of the Upper Pine Creek converge. The main stem (Category 2) downstream from WI 25 is pasture fishing in ice-cold water for about ¼ mile; below that alders and willows crowd the banks. The brook trout are cooperative and an occasional brown is willing to rise. The Upper Pine Creek between Dallas and the Red Cedar River is not designated trout water, probably due to the warming effect of the Dallas millpond.

Generally, on all Wisconsin and Minnesota trout streams you will find your best fishing where the DNRs have purchased blocks of land along the streams. The blocks are shown in green on the Milwaukee Map Service maps. Those stretches are most likely to have been improved by bank stabilization, in-stream structures, and intermittent de-brushing. But some stretches will be cramped by brush, and fallen snags and beavers will have interrupted the flow.

Facilities for guests of the Upper Pine, at Chetek to the east and Barron to the north.

MORE STREAMS WEST OF PINE CREEK

Blairmoor Branch, a feeder of Otter Creek, is beautiful where it slides through culverts under WI 64, and downstream there is a section of old meadow. But beyond that, within sight spreads a huge, greasy beaver pond. If you want to try for trout under the scum, you are welcome to them.

When you study the comprehensive map that accompanies your Wisconsin trout license, you'll spot three more streams that are intersected by WI 64. Going west from Sand Creek, they are the Otter, Big Beaver, and Bolen. All three are now nearly impossible to fly-fish due to an accumulation of brush and beaver dams over many years. Even bait fishermen will have trouble fighting the scrub. We should admit, however, that in the spring before the brush is fully leafed out a diligent angler may find pockets to fish.

That same diligent angler will note that Bolen Creek joins the South Fork of the Hay River about a mile south of WI 64. Access to the Hay at 1205th Avenue and at two more bridges downstream is easy, but the fork water is slow-moving—not good trout habitat, although there might be a few big trout in the deep holes.

At the upper end of Bolen Creek, if you should wander that far, you'll find an old, faded, DNR sign, half obscured by brush, announcing a fish restoration project. An angler's record for the years 1972 through 1987 lists Bolen as a first-class stream, open and easy for fly-fishing, but it's a tangle of thicket now.

In the spring and early summer months on these brook trout streams, the trout will respond to Tiny Blue-Winged Olives, Adamses, ants and beetle patterns, and a variety of small colorful flies. Trout that feed on those ubiquitous midges all season long will take a Griffith's Gnat most days.

There are many other streams in this general area that you may want to explore on your bluebird days in west central Wisconsin.

THE WILLOW RIVER
DeLorme 58 & 70

The Willow River wanders for 40 miles through the green hills of western Wisconsin in St. Croix County to join the St. Croix River at Hudson. Its prime trout waters lie about 4 road miles north of I-94 near Hudson and only 25 miles from the Twin Cities of St. Paul and Minneapolis, a metropolitan area of more than 2 million residents. Although the lower Willow is one of the most popular trout streams in the state, it is seldom crowded. A fly-fisher who is willing to walk in from one of three bridges, or along Trout Brook Trail from the beach parking lot in Willow River State Park, will usually find a section on which to while away a couple of hours without conflict.

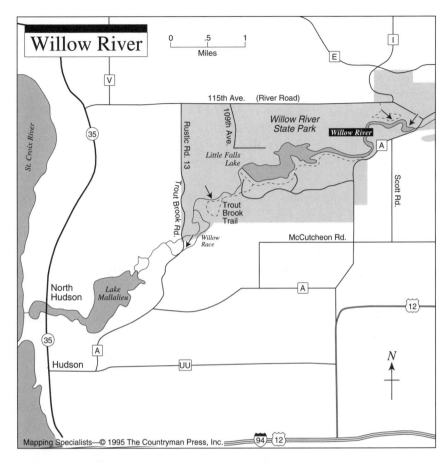

Opening weekend and the last day of the season will always find anglers stumbling over each other, but when those wily brown trout and less-than-wily rainbows do not come easily to net, many casual fishermen return to one of more than 10,000 lakes for amusement.

Approximately 25 miles of the Willow have been identified by the Wisconsin DNR as waters of the first or second class. More than 5 miles of the best waters are included within the boundaries of the park, from the bridge at the junction of County Roads A and I at Burkhardt downstream to the twin bridges on Trout Brook Road on the outskirts of Hudson. A daily activity fee is charged for entrance to the park and for parking in two lots at the east end of the park, one at the Burkhardt Bridge, the Willowby lot, and a second about 0.5 mile west on 115th Avenue, the River Road lot. At the present time it is still possible to fish without a fee upstream of the twin bridges at the western boundary of the park on Trout Brook Road. To find the bridges, take County Road A east from the north end of downtown Hudson to Trout Brook Road. This is also labeled Rustic Road on some maps.

The Willow is known by three designations. The Willow River is the long upper section from the headwaters to the bifurcation in the Willow River State Park. There it divides into the Willow Race and the Willow Branch; where the Race and the Branch rejoin, below Trout Brook Road and east of Lake Mallalieu at Hudson, it again becomes the Willow River.

Less than a mile downstream from Little Falls Dam, by Trout Brook Trail from the bathing beach parking lot in Willow River State Park, the Willow separates into the Race and the Willow Branch. But in your hurry, don't neglect the river below Little Falls Dam. We've had some spectacular fishing there, with the brown trout like leopards leaping.

The mile-long Race, which is the better of the two named sections, has undergone intensive research and habitat improvement during the past 15 years. With the herculean hands-on cooperation of the Kiap-TU-Wish Chapter of Wisconsin TU, the Wisconsin DNR has added riprap, bank structures, brush bundles, and hundreds of half-logs. The Race, which averages 39 feet in width and 12 inches in depth, is now perfect for fly-casting. Although the fishing for brown trout is good, it is not too easy; many have already tasted steel. The Race is Category 5, artificial lures only, daily limit one trout. Brown trout must be 20 inches or longer; rainbows, 12 inches.

The Willow Branch, a bit more than a mile in length, is Category 3, with a daily bag limit of three trout on lures or bait, minimum length 9 inches. The Willow Branch has always posed a problem to both DNR personnel and anglers. Although it's deep and wide, with what appears to be quality habitat, it has never been as productive as the Race. However, an angler who insists on solitude may prefer to wade the Willow Branch all the way to the lower junction with the Race and downstream almost to Lake Mallalieu. On one electro-shocking survey, we didn't find many trout in the section of the Willow Branch that closely parallels the Race, but we did bring to the surface a few very large brown trout from the root wads and under the sweepers. Bob Reynolds, a master fisherman who has solved the problems of the Willow Branch as well as anyone else we know, will put his large fly smack on the bottom of the pools, even if this requires a short section of lead core. We have been chagrined to watch Bob release hefty browns from a pool that we had just laboriously fished by more conventional methods.

None of the several sections of the Willow supports much in the way of natural reproduction, so both browns and rainbows are planted, but some will survive a number of winters. Years ago a 27-inch brown was taken on a spinner from the Race; more recently a 24½-inch brown was taken on a fly. Twice. The second fisherman creeled the fish and was nearly drummed out of the Twin Cities Chapter of TU.

The section of the river from the Burkhardt Bridge at the junction of County Roads A and I down to Little Falls Lake in the park is new trout water. In 1991 the state legislature appropriated funds to remove the Willow Falls Dam at the head of Little Falls Lake. The dam was disintegrating and the pond was a silted heat sump. The following year the dam was breached, the pond drained, and subsequently more than a mile of new stream was partially riprapped at a cost in excess of $100,000.

The river here has already developed character. It has carved its way down through 4 or 5 feet of silt and sand. Points and pockets and islands are forming. There are some picture-perfect riffles at the Burkhardt Bridge, where fly-fishers congregate to exchange anecdotes and prevarications, and riffles and pools at the end of mowed trails from the 115th Avenue parking lot.

Net-spinning caddis, midges, minnows, and small, crawling mayflies have colonized it. Even the white fly has appeared near the Burkhardt Bridge in August; it probably drifts down from the slow water above. Trout will probably never reproduce in this stretch, so the DNR thoughtfully plants brown and rainbow trout for our edification and amusement. We have seen spin-fishers coming out with their limits of three rainbows to 15 inches. Larger browns have been caught and released. The fishing may become more difficult as the season wears on and as anglers extract their limits of three from the planted stock, but we will always enjoy fly-fishing the pools and riffles down from the second lot, regardless of the catch or time of year. This is big and beautiful open water, so enticing that we have not yet walked all the way to the dells where the dam was removed. You may wish to explore it. The foot of the old dam can be reached by going upstream along the Pioneer Trail from the park office or by Willow Falls Trail from the campground.

Conservationist Al Farmes nymphing on a fall day on the Willow Race

Marty Engel, DNR fish manager at Baldwin, notes that "there is no guarantee that a cold-water fishery will flourish above and below the dam site . . . The Willow has had a general warming in it overall. Loss of spring flow is a likely answer . . . from many sources, including human development in the area." Nonetheless, that new 1½-mile stretch of fly-fishing water receives the accolades of all trout fishers.

Anglers may also walk the banks or wade the lower river downstream from the twin bridges on Trout Brook Road into wider and deeper water. Counting the two branches, there may be as much as another mile of excellent water and a few 6-pound browns that cruise between the lake and the lower river. Many of our friends always take the downstream reaches to hunt for larger brown trout, while we prefer to go up into the park along the Race, and even beyond the bifurcation to "Slaughterhouse," the island, and "Humphrey's Pool," where he learned how to fly-fish still water.

Other than the white fly that has appeared on the Willow at Burkhardt Bridge, the dominant hatches along the Willow are caddisflies, midges, several species of *Baetis,* which may appear almost anytime, the fluorescent *Stenonema/Stenacron,* seen most often above the bifurcation in July and August, and the Trico, a reliable morning hatch from approximately June 20 through September 26. Other fly-fishers have reported the sulphur mayfly hatch in June, but we haven't been able to confirm that from our own experience. An entomological survey of recent years notes the presence of four species of *Ephemerella,* as well as *Centroptilum,* a minuscule mayfly.

The Spider on a .004 (7X) tippet settles more lightly than a September milkweed seed, and there's an ache in my mind when I fish this gentle complex of currents below the island in the park along Trout Brook Trail. I blink my eyes camera-like to record the images—the fall of sunlight through shimmering leaves of cottonwood, the liquid silver filigree of water flowing, and the brassy flash of a brown trout under my ephemeral fly.

Facilities at Hudson and on I-94, at River Falls to the south, and at Stillwater, Minnesota, a historic river town on the St. Croix. Superb overnight and dining at the Lowell Inn, a world-famous inn in Stillwater. There is a campground with more than 70 spaces in the Willow River State Park.

THE KINNICKINNIC
DeLorme 58

Trout were sipping midges or minuscule mayfly emergers on the glide above the river ford, but the browns were indifferent to every artificial, no matter how artfully presented. Dusk crept from the willow thicket toward river's edge and a wraith of mist formed over the stream.

At 9:09 PM precisely, bats began to circle the run below the ford. The river had become a sheet of pale, watered silk. A scimitar of moon slashed the tops of pines. Some nocturnal beast padded through the woods, invisible. A great blue heron beat upstream on the hunt for rising trout, its wings like damp sheets flap-flapping.

Under the quarter light—moonlight and starlight and afterglow—exactly at 9:14 PM, the first Hex wig-wagged from the darkling stream. The emerging duns that followed were pale green, long green woolly worms with outrageous wings. They writhed in the film for 20 or 30 feet. When they rose, clumsily fluttering, they skipped again and again like an overloaded plane trying for liftoff. It was the beginning of that spectral hatch of the great night mayfly *Hexagenia limbata,* on the upper Kinnickinnic River of Wisconsin.

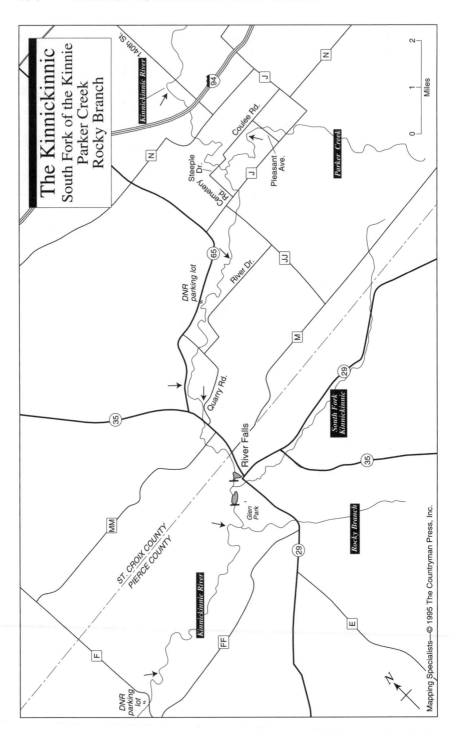

The Kinnickinnic
South Fork of the Kinnie
Parker Creek
Rocky Branch

Mapping Specialists—© 1995 The Countryman Press, Inc.

The first brown to take a #12 Blond Wulff was a slim 12 inches. The next half dozen, all in the 8- to 10-inch range, responded eagerly to a wiggling downstream float. Air temperature was a calm 75 degrees, water 60 degrees, typical of this superb spring creek.

By 9:35 PM the hatch was over in my 100 yards of river. Twenty minutes of fly-fishing for quality trout, and the river went dead. The Kinnickinnic is only 45 minutes east of the Twin Cities and its trout are finessed by experts, but I had encountered not one other fisherman.

I folded up and followed the edge of the potato field through powder-dry dust. The farmers needed rain. Fishing is like farming, it occurred to me, not for the first time. It is either too hot or too cold, too wet or too dry—or something. Maybe fishing promotes even more frustration. Sometimes on the Kinnie, the name given to it by its familiars, the air is so still and close that mosquitoes eat you alive and trout belly down in the weeds; or it's so windy that you can't control the cast. Or the water's so low and clear that you spook the trout, even beyond the reach of "far and fine." Or something. Ah well! Who ever said that life or fishing would be all pony rides on a May morning? A raucous night bird made me look back over my shoulder. Was it a salute or a touch of the raspberry?

Twenty miles of the Kinnickinnic River are superb trout water, from the spring holes above I-94 in St. Croix County to County Highway F near the St. Croix River in Pierce County.

It is the premier trout stream of west central Wisconsin. Or rather, it is like two streams. For approximately 10 miles above the city of River Falls, the Kinnie is narrow, cold, deep, and clear, flowing over sand and gravel down the middle, with silt at the margins. It is a typical spring creek. Chest-high waders are necessary up there. Access is very easy: At least 17 access points, including a DNR parking lot on WI 65, and more than 75 percent of the streambank is either owned by or under easement to the Wisconsin DNR. To keep visitors from having to chase all over the map, be advised that the spring holes are upstream of the bridge on 140th Street, which is about a mile north of I-94. Although the river appears on the maps above that point, it's gone underground during the past 30 years due to dewatering.

Very few forage fish are indigenous to the upper section; consequently the trout do not grow to trophy size above River Falls. A 15-inch brown trout is rare. The upper river, including the mile or so through town, is Category 2: daily bag limit of five, minimum 7 inches for both brooks and browns. DNR fish managers have asked us kindly to return all brook trout.

In past years electro-shocking surveys have revealed astounding numbers of trout in the upper river—one year as many as 9000 per mile at one survey station (the numbers are down in recent years)— but that doesn't mean that they will be easy to take. In the spring, before the waterweeds are up, the trout can see an angler coming from a mile away. Once the weeds are up, the trout will lie in the channels among the weeds. Pinpoint accuracy is necessary. Fly-fishers should wade upstream so as not to send a thread of silt ahead of them to put down the trout.

Below the last dam in Glen Park in River Falls, through the valley that some folks call "the gorge," the lower Kinnie is more like a freestone stream—rubble-strewn, with dark pools at the bends, long, challenging flats, and a succession of riffles where small trout are plentiful and feed aggressively on midges all season long. Anglers can get by with hip boots in that lower 10 miles.

Large numbers of brown trout also inhabit the lower river, 2000 to 3000 per mile on a recent survey, through Category 5 water, Special Regulations, five trout under 12 inches or four under 12 inches and one over 16 inches. The entire river is of such quality that planting of trout was discontinued in 1974, and that last plant was only a token to satisfy put-and-take anglers.

Slightly warmer water below the dams has permitted development of several species of minnows, as well as leeches and some crayfish, through the gorge; consequently, the trout grow faster. An occasional trophy trout in excess of 16 inches will surprise a diligent angler if he will hike into the remote reaches and fish in the shadows of the cliffs.

Downstream through tangled country, entry points are few and far between. Fishermen walk in from a pair of locations in the city— by easy trail from Glen Park to the foot of the dam (park at the tennis courts) or down the public trail from River Ridge Road. A third option is to work up from County Road F, some 8 river miles down the valley. If anglers are persuasive, they may make the acquaintance of some farmer who'll let them walk in on one of the long, steep trails between the city and County Road F. Several of the trails are dangerous, and coming out after dark is hazardous.

Many anglers thoroughly enjoy fishing right through town with access at the County Road MM bridge, at Heritage Park, and at a

PHOTO BY JOE MICHL

Federation of Fly Fishers member Ellen Clark readies herself
for the sulphur hatch on the Kinnickinnic.

couple of bridges in town. We've never been enthusiastic about fishing within sound or sight of backyards and roadway traffic, but you
might like to sample the Kinnie there.

Except for the giant *Hexagenia* mayfly, which hatches on or about
June 21 on the upper Kinnie, the more significant mayflies run to
small sizes, generally #16 and #18. We should warn you that the
Hex have not been so plentiful or predictable in recent years, due
perhaps to falling water temperatures or to a reduction in siltation,
or some other factor or combination of factors beyond our ken.
Tiny blue-winged olives of the *Baetis* genus are omnipresent. A few
March browns, *Stenonema vicarium,* appear sporadically on the
lower river between mid-May and mid-June. A persistent angler may
run into slate drakes or White-Gloved Howdys (*Isonychia*) on the
lower KK in July and again in August, but because the nymphs crawl
to the shore to emerge, the fly-fishing is at nightfall to spentwings
and not to the duns. Caddisflies appear in quantity on both sections, but most of these downwings are also small. A #16 Elk Hair
Caddis is recommended. A #20 Griffith's Gnat or Adams will replicate the prolific midges. Trico spinner falls occur most mornings
toward the end of June, when the air temperature touches 68 degrees, and continue through season's end. Scuds are present in enor-

mous numbers on both sections. Small yellow stoneflies are present both up and down. Giant brown stoneflies emerge around June 1 on the lower river.

On or about May 15 on the lower river, an angler may encounter the sporadic emergence of a #14 or #16 "blue-winged olive," which he might take for a mayfly. But this one is a crane fly, probably of the *Antocha* genus. It becomes an adult underwater and flies to the surface, where it rises like a helicopter, straight up, with its forelegs held upright like a spike. Although in the air the insect may appear to be a #16 or larger, due to its long legs and wings, underwater it's actually closer to a #18. These babies don't waste any time at the surface, so a soft-hackle is the ticket to success. The crane fly is common to many of our streams, but often missed by anglers who try to imitate it with a dry fly.

On May 25 at around 7:30 PM, John Schorn of the Twin Cities Chapter of TU found clouds of caddis in the air and some trout slashing at but not taking his caddis. He captured a fly, discovered it was a crane, switched to a grayish #18 soft-hackle with yellow floss and began to take trout.

An entomological survey of the upper river records the presence of *Danella simplex,* five species of *Baetis, Pseudocloeon,* and four species of *Stenonema.*

Two miles of water from County Road F to the St. Croix through the state park are very pretty. Some large trout are taken on Rapalas and bait, as are smallmouths and walleyes, but the hunt is usually not worth the effort due to the lack of sufficient cover for trout. It's a lovely place for a summer picnic, though.

This is Shogren and Humphrey's home stream. J.R.H. numbers the Kinnie among his baker's dozen of the best trout streams anywhere.

Twenty miles of superb trout water await the fly-fisher who is willing to tread lightly the deep and narrow track of the upper river, matching the hatch with a tiny fly at the end of a spiderweb tippet, or one who is willing to walk into the lonely reaches of the lower river.

Those marvelous miles are the precious jewels of the fly-fisher's memory. We'll give 2 hours of our lives, anytime, to fish our separate 100 yards of the Kinnickinnic on a sultry summer evening, with rising expectations when the bats begin to play.

A Kinnickinnic River Land Trust has been formed to protect the watershed of the Kinnie. The goals of the Trust are to involve the community in conservation, protect the natural resources and scenic areas, improve water quality, and enhance the wild trout population. Nonprofit land trusts, countrywide, have developed unique methods to protect watersheds and other natural wonders from unbridled development. The Kinnickinnic River Land Trust can be reached at N8203 1130th Street, River Falls, WI 54022 (phone: 715-425-5738; fax: 715-425-1746).

THREE TRIBUTARIES OF THE KINNICKINNIC

PARKER CREEK
DeLorme 58

The native brook trout of Category 2 Parker Creek in St. Croix County have received the attention of the DNR and Trout Unlimited in recent years. This fine little tributary to the upper Kinnie can be reached from Pleasant Avenue, a short road between County Road J and Steeple Drive (Coulee Road on the DeLorme map!).

SOUTH FORK OF THE KINNIE
DeLorme 58

The South Fork of the Kinnie, Category 2, joins the lower river at Glen Park. The South Fork has limited access through farm fields and degraded water quality, but there is hope for the future as the University of Wisconsin, the city, and Trout Unlimited cooperate in its resuscitation.

ROCKY BRANCH
DeLorme 58

Rocky Branch, or Rocky Run, as it's known locally, closely parallels the lower Kinnie at the fallen No Trespassing sign about ¾ mile downstream from Glen Park; then it curves away through some beaver ponds to join the river at Richard's Riffle. The run pitches down sharply from its origin near County Road FF. There are several stairstep pools upstream that contain small naturally reproducing brook trout.

Comprehensive lodging and dining facilities for the Kinnickinnic and its tributaries at River Falls, at I-94 on the east bank of the St. Croix, and at Hudson.

THE RUSH RIVER
DeLorme 59

Around the middle of May one recent year a 13-pound brown trout was taken from the Rush River by Walt Anderson, a member of the Eau Galle–Rush River Sportsman's Club. That was a champion fish, but not unexpected. The Rush River, wholly within Pierce County, has produced outsize browns for many years. Usually they are caught on live bait, frequently "water worms," the larval stage of the giant crane fly. The crane fly adult looks like a huge mosquito; the larva looks like a small banana. Those dug from sodden debris or from leaf packs are approximately 1½ inches long and dirty yellow in color. A yellow Woolly Worm with hackles trimmed is a reasonable facsimile. The late Jim Loga of St. Paul, a master at enticing large trout on flies, took his last 22-inch brown on his Wobble Ace, a minnowlike fly with a silver belly.

In the summer of 1985, when a DNR survey crew was counting trout on the Rush above the village of El Paso, a 24½-inch, 8-pound brown and an 18-inch companion were shocked from a small, shaded depression at bankside under bright sun at midday. We did not expect to find large trout in the shallows, but the rubble of the long flat contained incredible numbers of crayfish. Obviously, the lazy browns come out at night to scarf up the crawdads and then retreat to digest their fare during the day. Wisconsin does not permit the use of live crayfish as bait, so fly-tiers can test their crayfish creations on the Rush, but keep them small; about 2 inches is maximum length.

That long flat upstream from El Paso at the junction of County Roads N and G has since been trenched and bank covers installed to improve the holding areas for greater numbers of trout. We were shooting pictures on the day of installation of the first bank cover. The top boards had barely been covered when a 16-inch brown swam up to take possession of the hidey-hole.

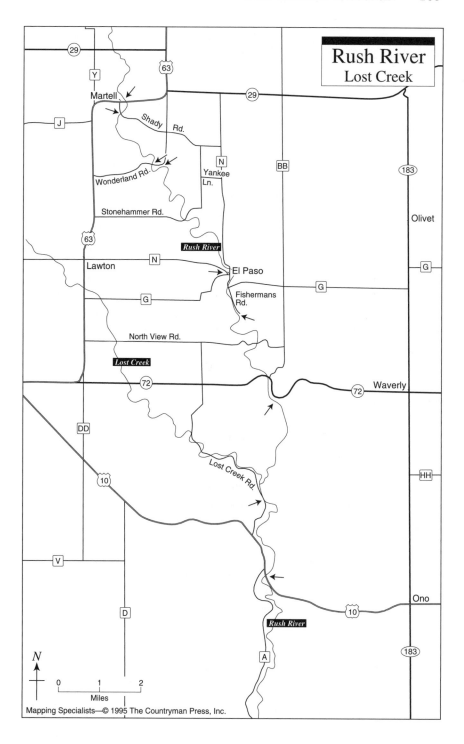

Brown trout inhabit the river from a mile above the fishermen's parking lot on WI 29, 11 miles east of River Falls, downstream to 3 miles south of US 10, a river distance of 23 miles. It is all Category 4; brown and rainbow trout must be 12 inches; brook trout, 8 inches.

The best stretch of trout water is from 0.75 mile north of Martell on US 63 to the iron bridge a mile upstream of US 10. Fly-fishers wade up from the top bridge in Martell or enter the river at one of eight other river crossings downstream.

We have several favorite spots that are worthy of your attention. We'll begin at the north end. Go up far enough from the upper bridge in Martell and you'll discover a long pool; keep to the right side and fish the left bank. A staff will be useful because the bottom is gummy. The pool will not disgorge its trout under clear skies.

There is consistently good fishing between the upper and lower bridges in Martell, although the trout are generally small. It's a favorite quarter mile for novice or elderly anglers; some of us eschew it for them. Next down is the Wonderland Road Bridge where you can fish up through pasture or down through riffle water.

The river from Stonehammer Road Bridge (next down from Wonderland) to the walk-in stretch below the dead-end road (Fishermans Road on DeLorme) at El Paso is picture perfect, and in several places will test the tenacity of wading anglers. But that's not to imply that those 5 miles are the best of the river. Jim Humphrey's personal choice is the tough ¾ mile upstream from Stonehammer where he finishes in a pasture. Other fly-fishers will disagree vehemently with our choices. It all depends. A DNR fish manager advised that the fish are not distributed uniformly; they are "clumped," meaning that a fisherman may have to search for visible or rising trout from his lookouts on the bridges. In 1993, 2400 trout per mile were counted at the Martell station.

The Rush River has all of the attributes of a broad, classic fly-fishing trout stream—deep pools, runs over rubble, limestone cliffs, shady glens, a complex of hatches, and plenty of rainbow darters, sculpins, leeches, and crayfish to grow huge trout. It has all of the attributes, that is, but one—sufficient natural reproduction. The Rush receives its water primarily from surface runoff down steep slopes rather than from groundwater seepage. It's too cold in winter to allow for the complete development of the eggs. So trout numbers must be augmented by annual plantings, a continuing project of the Sportsman's Club, whose members are friendly to strangers but fiercely

DuWayne Fries, fly-caster extraordinaire, on the Rush River

protective of their river. No club works more diligently.

Rainbows are also planted annually. Brook trout, which reproduce naturally in Cave and Lost Creeks, drift into the main river early season and late when the water temperature hovers around their ideal 58 degrees.

The Rush is a fine fly-fishing river where better-than-average browns and rainbows are routinely brought to net on dry flies. The Tiny Blue-Winged Olive, Adams, Pass Lake, Sulphur, Trico, and Elk Hair Caddis should be in the fly box, or better yet on the end of a .005 (6X) tippet. Fishers for big fish should opt for meatier sinking flies. In any case, for reasons that are in dispute, the Rush produces better in the very early morning or under overcast skies. Now someone will refute that, too.

The Rush is subject to pesticide and herbicide runoff from farm fields and to scouring by flash floods, and yet year after year it produces trophies for those who will take the time to learn its secrets. Don't accept our word for it; go and find your big brown trout in your secret pool or riffle.

LOST CREEK
DeLorme 59

Lost Creek joins the Rush between WI 72 and US 10 and is crossed by Lost Creek Road. Several streamside easements also invite the attention of anglers. It is a tiny jewel of a stream worthy of an hour or two of precision casting with light lines and tiny flies for feisty brookies. There are two long, conjoined pools between the highways, but we choose not to pinpoint their location. They contain naturally reproducing brook trout that could be pounded to extinction in a matter of days.

Facilities for visitors to both the Rush River and Lost Creek at Ellsworth and River Falls.

TIFFANY CREEK
DeLorme 71

In memory of the Acerbic Angler, Richard John Frantes, 1922–1993, friend, companion, and fly-fisher extraordinaire.

Over a 5-year period, Dick Frantes, also known as Dry-Fly Dick, and I fished for trout together on more than 200 days in more than 50 Minnesota and Wisconsin streams. We outwitted big, rambunctious rainbow trout in a dozen trout lakes, too.

That most generous partner revealed all his secret fishing places to me, and I disclosed a few of mine. I gained on the exchange, because Dick had fished more midwestern streams than any other man, and by his own admission had been skunked more times on more streams than any other fly-fisher.

Our interests were complementary. He preferred a downstream drift through the riffles, while I spooked the trout in the upstream flats and pools. Dick outfished me at least three to one, but every trout fisher knows that flat water is more challenging. And if the Acerbic Angler were here, he'd have something acerbic to say about that! *Of course, Dick, you always used a dropper to double your chances.*

Dick was also an indefatigable note-taker. His monumental, detailed 35-year record reveals more than 8500 hours devoted to trout fishing on 271 different streams in the two states. Of the 10,576 trout he kept for the creel or released, 8136 were brown trout, 1855 were brook trout, and 574 were rainbows. There were also a handful of tiger trout and splake. If Dick were here, he'd remind me that until mid-1986 his record included only trout that he kept to eat, so the numbers are understated. By his calculations, Dick caught 1.4 trout per hour in Wisconsin and 0.8 per hour in Minnesota. Now, if you should denigrate those trout-per-hour numbers, we suggest that you begin to compile your own record.

On many days when I was too busy to fish, or when I thought I was too busy, Dick would scoot over to Tiffany Creek and annoy the brook trout for a couple of hours. Next day he'd report back faithfully, often understating the numbers, I'm sure, to make me feel better. For one reason or another, I never fished the Tiffany with him, and I'll regret it always. But after Dick was gone, I made a pilgrimage to that fine little brook trout stream.

The three spring feeders of the Tiffany converge near the town of Glenwood City in eastern St. Croix County at the junction of WI 128 and WI 170. Downstream from Glenwood City the main Tiffany is neither long nor wide, nor can you expect to catch a 15-inch brook trout there, but it will test your skill. Dick's comment on the occasion of our last conversation concerning the Tiffany was, "What a stream for hopper time!"

Dick fished the North Fork through Glenwood City only once. He recorded it in his notes: "Bad bottom, posted against trespass, and tiny." He didn't waste time on the tiny South Fork either, but he did devote 30 days to the conjoined Mid and South Forks, which he labeled the "Blues Fork." I never asked him why he labeled it that way, but I can guess. Most of his time was spent on the main Tiffany downstream from Glenwood City and around Downing in western Dunn County. Altogether, he totaled (1975 through 1992) 56 days, 180 hours, 559 brook trout, and 1 splake on the Tiffany.

You'll find the Middle Fork of the Tiffany on WI 128 about 8 miles north of I-94 on the south edge of Glenwood City. At the bridge, I'd call it small, brushy, and slow. I wouldn't recommend it there, either.

Just north of the bridge is a blacktop road going due east to Downing. That may appear on some of your maps as the old South Boundary Road, but the intersection is now signposted as 130th Avenue. I have inveighed against those mindless changes from descriptive name to numbing numbers before, so I shouldn't do it again. Proceed east to the first bridge, where Dick's Blues Fork begins. I like the looks of it here. Not necessarily easy going but it's open, wadable, with tall hopper grass at the margins and an upstream path on the left.

Farther east, past the blackened concrete foundation of a barn, there's some open pasture. You may have to ask permission there. Beyond that is another bridge a couple of hundred yards north of 130th Avenue. Upstream is open going; downstream is delightful, but short, ending in the sewage disposal settling pond. Both ways are worth a shot.

Continue east to the WI 170 bridge in Downing, where upstream there's old riprap through fairly open country and evidence of foot traffic along the banks. My friend preferred the upstream course. Downstream, Tiffany winds through cornfields.

When I was last there it was a glorious day—blue sky and fleece clouds, temperature in the mid-50s, bucolic farms, green-fringed hills and ridges. Even if the brook trout are recalcitrant on your visit, take time to breathe the pure air of peaceful, pastoral Wisconsin.

Proceed through Downing on Main Street, also WI 170, to the intersection opposite Sander's Service Shop. Angle northeast on South Boundary Road, which is signposted 1010 Avenue(!) to Anderson Road (130th Street). This is a narrow concrete dead end that leads to Anderson Farm. Park on the verge south of the humped bridge where other trout fishers have parked. The stream here is pretty, but brushy and wader deep.

There are two more bridges downstream where the river is wider, sandy down the middle, and wadable, with evidence of old riprap, typical of the places that Dick enjoyed. His last comment to me concerning that lower stretch was, "Tough going." Dick's advice was to fish between the two towns, but not too far below Downing.

The day passes, the wind sighs in the trees, roadside grasses bend like gentle riffle water, birds pipe far and wee in the tops of trees. Oak in the pasture lift in the wind to show the dull undersides of their still-green leaves. Aspen are trembling, as usual. It's a wonderful day to be out in the green and gentle land of my home state, Wisconsin. To me, there's no place like it.

So, Dick, old friend I'll finish here, smoke a cigarette just for you, and eat a pear for me, and watch the water for sign of rising trout. If I had Polish blackberry brandy I'd add it to my coffee—enough for both of us. If you can communicate, tell me how to fish that dark pool above the bridge.

Facilities at Glenwood City and at Menominee on I-94.

SEVEN PINES LODGE

DeLorme 83

We should not leave west central Wisconsin without mentioning Seven Pines Lodge (phone: 715-653-2323), a unique hideaway for year-round fly-fishers near Lewis on WI 35 and less than 2 hours' driving time from the Twin Cities. The graceful cedar lodge and outlying guest quarters have turned a darker silver over the years since *The Way of the Trout* was filmed here. Knapp Creek sighs silken-soft at twilight around the Stream House, and naturally reproducing brook trout and rainbows rise to a dry fly.

This is one of two Wisconsin lodges that cater to fly-fishers. It was built in 1903, and is now on the National Register of Historic Places. President and Mrs. Coolidge found a second-floor double with bath to be charming and comfortable in 1928.

Visiting anglers will find more than ½ mile of Knapp Creek that is rich, cold, clear, and improved with dozens of bank structures. Wisconsin fishing licenses are not required because this is private water.

7

Northwestern Wisconsin:
Indianhead Country

If you view an outline of the state and let your imagination run, you may see the stylized head of an Indian chief in the northwest quadrant, complete with feathers represented by the Chequamegon Peninsula and the Apostle Islands. Hence the name Indianhead Country to lure and charm tourists, though perhaps it is not politically correct.

By any name, mundane or imaginative, this area will be attractive to fly-fishers and their families—with its rushing rivers, ice-blue inland lakes, waterfalls, state parks, national forests, the glorious Apostles and their sailing ships, and the spectacular southern coast of Lake Superior. It is an area rich in the history of the early exploration of the continent and the later exploitation of copper and tall pines.

Some trout streams are tributary to the St. Croix, which empties into the Mississippi; more flow north into Lake Superior and contain runs of anadromous trout and salmon. We profile two creeks and three widely different, or wildly different, rivers.

THE NAMEKAGON RIVER
DeLorme 94

"Hurley, Hayward, and Hell." That's an old saying from the days of the river drivers, who knew they were the three toughest towns in the world, or out of it. A brash man could get an ear bitten off on a Saturday night in Hayward as easily as he could find a trollop in Hurley.

Hayward is now a neat, clean, welcoming, and conservative tourist town. But the historic Namekagon is still there, not much changed since the burly, bearded men in blanket coats came out of the woods on Saturday nights to get mean drunk and kick each other bloody in the streets. The lean and stringy men went into the woods by donkey engine, shank's mare, and flatboats poled upstream. They came out with spring, whooping the log rafts through white water to the mills at Hayward.

Most of the iron men have gone, but the storied Namekagon flows smoothly, tamed not too much since the peak of the logging at the turn of the century. It is still big water, riffling through narrows, gliding through pine plantations, spreading through the meadows of abandoned farms. The trout are there, too, awaiting the delicate fall of the fly. Only the species have changed. The native brook trout have retreated to the cooler waters of feeder creeks. In the few fast-water reaches one may strike an eager and acrobatic rainbow, hatchery raised, but the golden dark, crimson-spotted brown trout has adapted and now owns the waters.

From County Road M 4 miles east of Cable and downstream from Namekagon Lake Dam in Bayfield County, to the Sawyer County line at the north end of Pacwawong Flowage, the river is Category 3. From Pacwawong Dam down to the lower US 63 bridge, a distance of approximately 9 river miles, the Nam is Category 5, with Special Regulations designed to maintain a stock of better-than-average trout. From Phipps Dam down to Airport Road it reverts to Category 3; then below Hayward Lake there is another stretch of Category 5 to the Washburn County line. Because of this mix of categories, anglers will have to pay attention to the many signs posted along the river.

Prior to the institution of the category system in 1990, the Department of Natural Resources had rated the Namekagon as a Class II river: "Streams in this classification may have some natural reproduction but not enough to utilize available food and space. Therefore, stocking sometimes is required to maintain a desirable sport fishery. These streams show good survival and carryover of adult trout, often producing fish of better than average size." The application of Category 5 to a prime section of the Namekagon above Hayward was designed to enhance the carryover and growth of larger trout. In all, the Nam offers more than 30 miles of unparalleled wading water, with the possibility of catching and releasing a spectacular trout.

If time is of the essence, confine your activities between Philippi Landing on Randysek Road in Cable to the lower WI 63 bridge. In the riffle below the landing you ought to find some rainbow trout. In the village of Seeley on US 63, go west to the village hall and the private bridge (now removed). We prefer the upstream reach.

A quarter mile south of the village the Nam sidles up to US 63. Park at the roadside and fish up or down. We've had excellent fly-fishing in that most beautiful spot. Below Seeley there are numerous marked, fishermen's parking areas within sight of the highway.

About 1.5 miles south of Seeley you'll find Larsen (aka Larson) Road. Go west a stone's throw and then north to Larsen Bridge. Cross the river and park in a grove of trees on the riverbank. Fish upstream into classic dry-fly water.

A quarter mile north of Larsen Bridge take the River Road east to roadside parking at the elbow. Fish up among the old manmade islands or down through a long run that ends in a huge pool. We have had some of our best fly-fishing through the run, including success at matching a tremendous hatch of tiny blue-winged olives on the last day of the season.

Which reminds us of an experience. It was a hot day and the run hadn't produced as it should have. We waded up to the head of the run, where we met an angler from Duluth. He wasn't feeling too optimistic either, although he allowed that he'd caught a couple, and the evening before he'd caught and released browns to 14 inches while fishing a Sulphur dry.

While we were chewing the fat, a frog came skipping across the run like a Jetski, squeaking all the way and chased by an 18-inch brown. Honest. Minutes later a different frog gave us a repeat per-

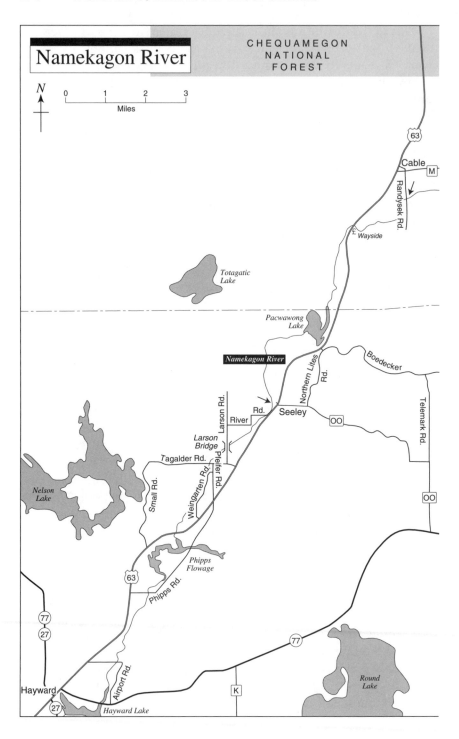

Namekagon River

CHEQUAMEGON
NATIONAL
FOREST

N

0   1   2   3
Miles

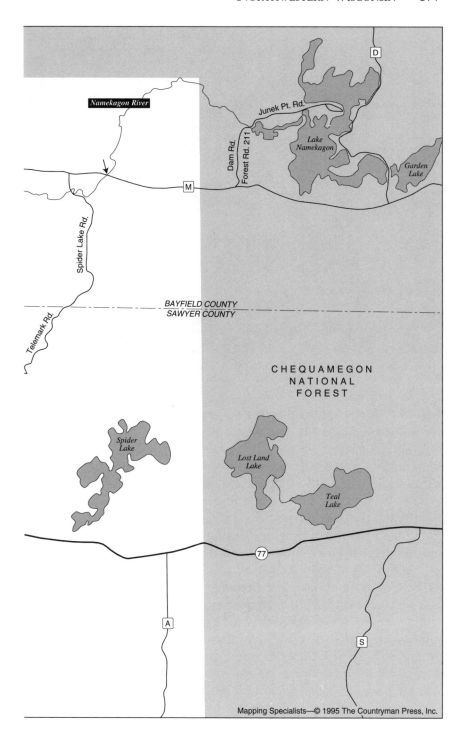

Namekagon River

Junek Pt. Rd.

Dam Rd.

Forest Rd. 211

Lake Namekagon

Garden Lake

D

M

Spider Lake Rd.

Telemark Rd.

BAYFIELD COUNTY
SAWYER COUNTY

CHEQUAMEGON
NATIONAL
FOREST

Spider Lake

Lost Land Lake

Teal Lake

77

A

S

Mapping Specialists—© 1995 The Countryman Press, Inc.

Ron Erlandson works his Black-Nosed Dace Streamer in the deep runs around the islands in the Namekagon.

formance. We pounded that run for the brown with everything we had in the boxes, but he disdained our offerings.

Bright in our memory is a day when our pal Eino Tutt, a master at swimming a lip-hooked minnow into the maw of an outsize brown, demonstrated his skill along McNaught Road at Cable. The auto trail ran between the house and the barn of a farm. Now the trail is bermed and the land is controlled by Telemark, a ski resort, and farther down by a gun club with warnings not to get in the way of the guns. Perhaps if you rent a condo at Telemark, you may be able to roll big browns as Eino did for us.

There is more good water between County Road M and US 63 than you can handle. We have our favorite places; you will discover yours, perhaps at the red cabin on Tagalder Road, at the end of the trail from the termination of Weingarten Road, behind the KOA campground, or back of Turk's Inn, an extraordinary supper club a couple of miles north of Hayward on US 63.

In his book *Remembrances of Rivers Past*, Ernest Schwiebert tells of his arrival in Hayward during the peak of the muskie fishing, when the men and boys of the town decamped to the lakes and flowages to throw dead suckers or hardware at that largest of freshwater fighting fish. Mr. Schwiebert began his unharried exploration of the river at the old railroad trestle on the north end of the town along Airport Road. When last we were there the trestle was still rusting away and the tracks had been taken up, but the river ran dark and secret between the abutments. It's cleaner now than it was then. We have made some progress since the Clean Water Act of 1972.

During an evening of superlative fishing, Schwiebert records in his catch three browns, the smallest of which was 21 inches, and the largest at almost 7 pounds, all taken on an artificial representation of *Isonychia sadleri,* a large mayfly commonly known as mahogany dun or maroon drake. This hatch may appear about the middle of June and again during the later part of August. The best fly-fishing is usually during the late-evening spinner fall.

As on most northerly streams, the notable hatches occur between opening day and the third week of June. Our local experts cite hatches of the Hendrickson, March brown, light Cahill, mahogany dun, and the pale evening dun or sulphur. All season long, tiny blue-winged olives will be present, in early mornings during the early days of the season, and late afternoons in September. Tricos may show themselves late June or early July mornings in the flats below the weedbeds. The brown drake, *Ephemera simulans,* #12, a Midwest superhatch, appears about the middle of June, or sometimes a week earlier. Late June or early July brings on the *Hexagenia limbata,* the largest midwestern mayfly.

Some of the hatches may peak before opening day. If so, hard luck. On the other hand, you may count your blessings. An earlier opener could put you into the middle of a northern Wisconsin spring blizzard. As Gus Kizer of the DNR at Hayward once said, "Fishing the Namekagon can be tough."

Our experience confirms that this large, semiwarm river can be difficult, particularly during the hot months. We recall all too vividly wading through more than a mile of entrancing water one day in late June without seeing a rise or enticing a somnolent trout to our searching Royal Coachman. Exhausted, we arrived finally at dusk at the private bridge at Seeley, where we sat to commiserate. And then, the spinners appeared—three different species of mayflies. Curious, how they could sort themselves out!

The spinners were a #12 gray drake, *Siphlonurus quebecensis—*

also a major hatch on the Wolf River—a #14 species of *Stenonema/
Stenacron* (blue-winged olive, brown body), and a #16 *Ephemerella*,
which was probably the fabled sulphur. After the adults had mated
and the females had dropped yellow egg packets and died, the trout
turned on, taking the spentwings in sips and swirls.

Water temperatures may rise to 76 degrees in quick, knee-deep
water at midafternoon during a hot spell. The same water will read
10 degrees cooler by 7 AM the following day. So fish the early hours in
summer and hope for a hatch of Tricos or tiny blue-winged olives.
But the confirmed fly-fisher will fish the pools of the Namekagon just
before dark, and after, with a large Light Cahill for heavy-shouldered
browns. If the trout aren't thumping the surface, dead-drift a big
brown Woolly Worm or a weighted Muddler through the pool and
along the surface coming back to the reel. John Goplin of the Twin
Cities Chapter of Trout Unlimited recommends a crayfish pattern
drifted deep. On Shogren's last trip in the special regulations section,
Bill saw a 6-pound brown chase a chub, so you might experiment
with streamer flies.

If you insist on fishing the daylight hours during warm weather
because the river is so beautiful, flowing like tawny port around your
knees, don't linger long in any one place. The water may be cooler in
another location, or a thin hatch of caddisflies or mayflies may be
localized.

The Nam is one of the easiest rivers to wade that we know, so
some of us forgo blind casting entirely and simply wade upstream in
search of one rising trout. Almost certainly it will be a good one. If
you get in among the islands, you can slow down there and drop a
terrestrial under the overhanging branches.

The Namekagon is part of the St. Croix Riverway. Much of the
riverbank has been acquired by the National Park Service; therefore
access is easy from County Road M for as far downstream as you
wish to hunt. Although there are large brown trout taken below
Hayward, you are more likely to find smallmouth bass. And yet,
and yet, that gigantic pool below the old iron bridge at Stinnett
Landing demands some dark-of-the-moon fly-casting for monster
brown trout. Frank Pratt, area fish manager for the DNR, said that
the growth rate for browns below Hayward is twice that of the growth
rate above the city. Browns to 13 pounds have been taken, but they
won't come easily. You're more likely to run into them accidentally
while you are fishing for smallmouth. Mr. Pratt advised that the lower

river performs best during cold weather, which means early season or late.

More than 30 years ago, before the need for special regulations, the accepted technique on the Namekagon was to fly-fish downstream in the middle, casting a trio of large and gaudy wet flies on a short, stout leader for big trout. Maybe that's not a bad idea even today.

We can't say that the Namekagon is a superb trout fishery—some who count numbers of trout as important would even call it marginal, because of the lack of natural reproduction. But still, when Frank Pratt goes for trout he chooses the Namekagon. It is so beautiful, and a fly-fisher's Utopia.

The Nam is also a favorite run for the "aluminum hatch." Fishers will have to share that scenic thread of tawny water with canoeists. But they are usually off the water when the evening rise begins.

Because the Namekagon is part of the National Wild and Scenic Rivers system, it is protected. Development along its banks is restricted. Riverside residences are being purchased as they come on the market, and are eventually removed.

In the Ojibway (Chippewa) tongue, Namekagon means "the place for sturgeon." That antediluvian fish has been speared and netted from the river. The long canoes of the voyageurs and the log rafts of the lumberjacks are only memories. But the Namekagon is a constant, golden tinsel through the forest-green fabric of Wisconsin. It is both promise and challenge to the peripatetic angler.

A wide range of overnight and dining accommodations are available in Hayward and Cable, at many lake resorts, and at numerous primitive campsites along the Riverway. Children will enjoy Hayward's Fishing Hall of Fame, where they can overlook the countryside from the gaping jaws of 144-foot muskie. Al Capone's hideout museum is located on the Lac Courte Oreilles Reservation near Couderay southeast of Hayward, close to the junctions of County Roads N and CC. The largest living white pine in Wisconsin will help to visualize this country as it was when the Frenchmen Radisson and Groseilliers first dipped paddles into its unmapped waters in 1659. The 300-year-old pine is 130 feet tall and 13 feet in circumference. It is located in the Flambeau River State Forest, 11 miles east of Winter on County Road W. The Park Service headquarters for the Riverway, on US 63 northeast of Trego, offers a fine selection of maps and pamphlets.

THE WHITE RIVER
DeLorme 94

The main stem of the White River flows for some 45 miles from the canoe access and park on Pike River Road near the village of Delta in Bayfield County to Lake Superior in Ashland County. It is Category 5 all the way. Our profiled section runs from the park down to the village of Mason close to US 63, a river distance of more than 20 miles.

At the park on Pike River Road it is quite small and clear, the haunt of naturally reproducing brook trout. There's a second canoe access at Kern Creek along White Road, then a foot trail from the end of the road. The river here is cold and deep, and can be difficult to wade during high water.

The real action for monster brown trout is that tortuous and torturous stretch through Bibon Swamp, almost invariably from a canoe, although there may be one or two trails to the river, the locations of which are secrets jealously guarded. The canoes put in at Sutherland Bridge close to the intersection of Town Line Road and Sutherland Road.

Some anglers claim that the swamp can be negotiated in a float of 5 to 6 hours, but recent experience suggests that is far too little time to fly-fish, either from the canoe or occasionally by standing chest-deep on hard bottom.

An additional complication is that the yearly heavy action is usually confined to a few weeks in late June and early July when the *Hexagenia limbata* is on the wing. On a recent trip into the upper end of Bibon Swamp, Bill Shogren was dropped off bankside during the early evening and picked up by canoe at 11 PM. Bill caught and released two brown trout of 16 and 17 inches; his partner, Pete Mitchell, connected with two 18-inch browns. On another occasion, Bill walked the bank around Sutherland Bridge and picked up four browns while other anglers who walked deeper into the swamp came out with fewer.

If that whets your appetite for a most unusual experience, don't let us deter you, except to warn that the swamp water is exceedingly cold and very deep, the current swift, and the mosquitoes ferocious on midsummer evenings. Many fly-fishers have tested Bibon Swamp but once!

We should add something about the *H. limbata*. This burrowing

*This brown fell to a big Hex nymph pattern on the White River,
just before the evening hatch.*

species of mayfly has a life cycle, from egg to adult, of somewhere
between 8 to 12 months, depending on the temperature of the water.
During the nymphal period it must leave its U-shaped burrow in clay
to molt—shedding its exoskeleton to allow for growth. The literature does not give us the number of molts, but each time it crawls out
of its burrow it is vulnerable to predation. Therefore there should be
weeks, or perhaps several months, prior to emergence when a large
yellowish nymph laid over the silt should produce action. One major
study of the Hex reported that trout get 60 to 70 percent of their
annual food requirements from that mayfly. The browns grow quickly
on their diet of Hex but do not reproduce, probably because of the
lack of spawning gravel.

In some respects, Bibon Swamp may be the most unusual, difficult,
and challenging 20 miles of water in Wisconsin. It may be only a
once-in-a-lifetime trip, and we wish you joy of it.

For approximately 10 miles, from Mason downstream to the White
River impoundment at the Ashland County border, the river flows faster
through a succession of riffles and pools. We have it on good advice
that this section contains cased caddis, in local parlance "stick caddis," sculpins, and, during May and June, is "crawling with 1-inch-

long green crayfish." The planted brown trout are reputed to run larger than average. Anadromous trout and salmon are the main quarry below the impoundment.

Modest facilities and canoe liveries at Mason; complete accommodations at the city of Ashland on Chequamegon Bay, at Cable to the south, and Iron River to the northwest.

The Iron River Trout Haus in Iron River is a little out of the ordinary. This is one of two bed & breakfast retreats in Wisconsin that are wholly devoted to fly-fishing for trout. It offers fly-fishing schools, fly-tying sessions, and casting for rainbow trout in three ponds on the premises.

THE BOIS BRULE
DeLorme 93 & 101

Here, where the magnificent Bois Brule joins mighty Lake Superior, is a dramatic meeting of moving water and sand and sky and inland sea. It must have been so when Daniel Greysolon, the Sieur du Lhut, came to it one summer evening in 1680 when the sun was a band of bronze on the silver surface of the great blue lake.

The river was called the Misakota in the tongue of the Ojibway, Nemetsakouat in the language of the Dakota. Later it was known as the Burntwood by the British and Bois Brûlé by the French. Today it is printed as Bois Brule on the official maps of northwestern Wisconsin in Douglas County, but it is familiarly and affectionately known as the Brule to legions of trout and steelhead fishermen.

In those ancient days it was No-Man's-Land between the formidable Chippewa (Ojibway) out of the east and the indomitable Dakota, also called Sioux. Du Lhut's mission was to make peace between the tribes so that the fur trade could resume for the greater glory of the King of France and for the enrichment of the merchants. Du Lhut, a representative of the Governor-General of New France, did not make poetry of the wild waters and rock ledges of the lower Brule or the meanders of the middle river between high green banks, nor of the dark slow upper third through bog country under lofty pines, where even now the eagles scream and brook trout rush to a gaudy fly.

In his terse, military report, du Lhut, or Duluth, said only that he entered the river, "where after having cut down some trees and broken through about one hundred beaver dams, I went up said river, and

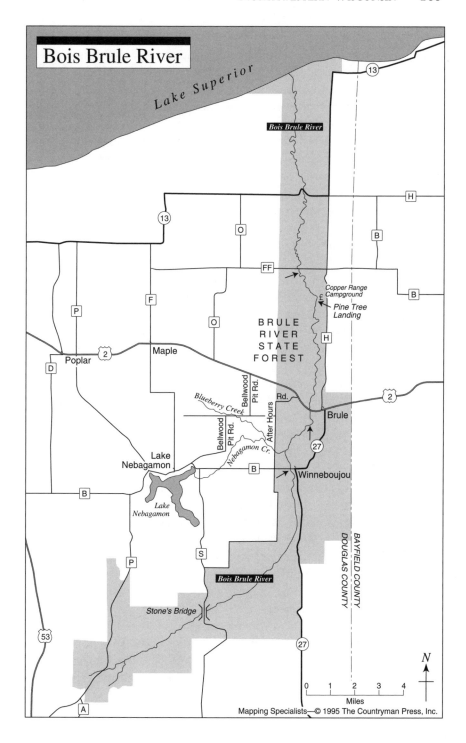

Bois Brule River

Lake Superior

Bois Brule River

BRULE
RIVER
STATE
FOREST

Copper Range
Campground

Pine Tree
Landing

Poplar

Maple

Blueberry Creek

Bellwood Pit Rd.

After Hours Rd.

Brule

Nebagamon Cr.

Lake
Nebagamon

Winneboujou

Lake
Nebagamon

BAYFIELD COUNTY
DOUGLAS COUNTY

Stone's Bridge

Bois Brule River

N

0   1   2   3   4
Miles

Mapping Specialists—© 1995 The Countryman Press, Inc.

then made a carry half a league to reach a lake, which emptied into a fine river [the St. Croix], which brought me to the Mississippi."

Since 1680, the Brule has been a warrior's path, an explorer's track into the interior, and a trade route. It has been logged, stolen, sold, and resold. Several miles of it have been tastefully embellished by summer homes and lodges of rustic elegance. In the 1870s commercial fishermen extracted brook trout by the ton from its spring ponds, packed the fish in barrels, and shipped them to Chicago. One of the ponds was appropriately named Fulton Market, after New York City's famous market. In 1907 the state of Wisconsin recognized its unique historic, scenic, and environmental qualities by establishing the Brule River State Forest, encompassing 52,000 acres. For all of this time it has offered superb fishing for the artful angler.

The northward-flowing Brule is a river for three seasons. South (upstream) of US 2, fishing is restricted to the regular trout season, from the first Saturday in May through September. That 15 miles of the upper Brule is rated as Category 1, allowing for a bag of 10 trout, but not more than 5 of either rainbows or browns. Thirty miles of river downstream (north of the village of Brule) are open from April 3 through November 15, Category 5, with special bag and size limits applying to several species of trout and salmon.

In addition to the split categories and variety of salmonids, the Brule offers three faces to the angler. The upper third is slow water over sand and silt, wandering through many spring ponds, rich in waterweeds and insect life. A shorter middle section has the characteristics of a meadow stream—deep pools at many crooked corners and overshaded runs that are sometimes too deep to wade.

The lower river is most like a freestone mountain stream—long glides, ledges, and rocky runs that will snick the bottom out of a canoe. Though the riverbed is hard, the banks are thickly forested over slopes of red clay that are subject to erosion, frequently leaving the water turbid. Around the Oxbow, a couple of miles from the mouth, we have seen long, deep fissures where the slope, trees and all, was sliding into the river.

To further enhance, or maybe to complicate, the angling opportunities, there are five distinct types of trout and char that have graced the river for so long that they are thought of as natives: brook trout, resident rainbows and browns, and migratory rainbows (steelhead) and browns.

In addition, three species of Pacific salmon have established spawning rights in the river in recent years. Coho and chinook salmon were introduced into Lake Superior in 1966 and 1967, and have since spawned in the Brule. Pink salmon were introduced into the lake in 1956, but it was not till the late 1970s that they appeared in the lower Brule.

With all of these populations and species milling around and competing for spawning gravel, space, and food, naturally there is concern that some favored species will be hurt. A DNR Fish Management Report from 1984 is inconclusive: "The Pacific salmons, to date, have not demonstrated any obvious adverse effects on trout populations in the Brule River, since migratory brown and rainbow populations (numbers) were similar to those reported in past studies. Their effects, however, may remain to be seen if numbers of salmon spawning successfully were to increase significantly. Coho and especially chinook salmon have the potential to outcompete brown trout, spawning during fall, for available or preferred spawning sites, because of their larger size. Young salmon could potentially compete with juvenile trout for available food and habitat." The report goes on to state that pink salmon "may not compete to a great extent with trout while in the river because of life history differences." Anecdotal evidence since 1984 does not suggest that the fishery for browns and rainbows has deteriorated to any marked degree, although the winter season for steelhead has been eliminated to protect the stock.

The movements of the various species in and out of the river are complicated and are worth a few paragraphs of explanation.

We quote from a Wisconsin DNR fisheries report: "[migratory] Brown trout begin to enter the river in July with the peak of the run usually in September. Some return to the lake after they spawn in the fall but others return rapidly as the ice goes out in the spring. These fish are wary and prefer deep, calm water. The best fishing is when the water is murky, on cloudy days, early morning, late evening, and at night.

"There are two steelhead (anadromous rainbow trout) runs each year. The fall run starts in September and these fish return to the lake after they spawn the following spring. The spring run starts in March and these fish return to the lake in May and June. Steelhead prefer faster water than browns."

Coho and chinook salmon spawn in the fall and have found their way into at least one of the feeders where the young may compete with the natives. Young chinooks have been found in Blueberry Creek,

John Rowell fishes the Bois Brule.

a tributary of Nebagamon Creek that joins the Brule from the west about ¾ mile north of County Road B.

The hunt for migratory steelhead and chinooks in the Brule is a separate story, and most of the action takes place north of Highway 2 during the spring and fall extended seasons. The techniques are different, as is the equipment—fluorescent yarn and micro eggs; or spawn sacks, heavy rods, and reels loaded with monofilament rather than fly line. A few diehard fly-fishers stick to sinking fly lines and large stonefly nymphs.

The brook trout, which were the only trout (read char) indigenous to the river in historic times, are now found primarily in the upper third.

From the headwaters to Winneboujou Landing on County Road B, some 15 miles, the Brule is almost impossible to get to on foot because of private land, although there is one long foot trail in from the west side, partly through private land. In the headwaters section, most fly-fishers take to the canoe. The canoes go into the water at Stone's Bridge Landing on County Road S. The 12 miles from Stone's to Winneboujou will consume about 5 hours, alternately paddling and drifting. If one wants to take his limit of 10 brook trout, the trip may involve an hour or two more. A #5 line is preferred with a .005 leader, the butt end greased for surface fishing the pockets.

Approximately 5 miles downstream from Stone's, below Cedar Island, there are a few short, sharp rapids, none of which is rated worse than Class 2 difficulty for canoeists. Above Cedar Island there is a short section of unrated fast water. The novice may want to reverse direction at that point and return to Stone's against an easy current. Such an excursion would include the very best of the brook trout water, but one would miss some of the scenery through Cedar Island and the mirror waters of Big and Lucius Lakes, where the huge resident browns hang out. The ponds at Cedar Island look very like the water of the River Test at Whitchurch, England—green fronds of grass and clear runnels among them where the brown trout lie finning. A wise choice for the visiting fly-fisher is to hire a guide and canoe in Brule, see the whole show, and let someone else do the work.

Cedar Island is an extensive, gracious estate of some 4500 acres, its buildings fashioned of cedar logs and shakes. Built in the 1890s and meticulously maintained since, it was visited and fly-fished by those distinguished Presidents-fishermen Coolidge, Hoover, and Eisenhower. The Brule was also fished by Presidents Grant and Cleveland in the 1870s and 1880s.

Fishing the Brule should be at least a once-in-a-lifetime experience for every dedicated fly-fisher. The quiet fisherman will come upon the great blue heron stock still within a tangle of deadfall; he will see the eagles and hear them shout a raucous warning. He may see the soft-footed mink hunting along the bank. It is said that on some drowsy evening one may startle the rare Wisconsin moose feeding knee-deep in a spring pond, but that, we believe, is more poetic fancy than reality. Certainly you will watch the graceful white-tailed deer watching you.

The resident brown trout that inhabit the upper reaches of the river are like stream trout anywhere. In the spring they will rise readily to a fly; on summer days they will sulk in cool and darkened places until they are teased out with repeated casts over their lies. In the evenings the browns will feed in the long flats, at the lips of pools, and on the placid surfaces of the upper lakes when the hatch is on. If you are so fortunate as to fish the Lucius or Big Lake section at sundown, remember that big flies take big brown trout. The resident rainbows are found in faster water and can be taken with the Brown Bivisible, Spiders, and attractors.

And that brings us to the exploration of a conundrum. We have never encountered good brown trout fishing below Pine Tree Landing (which is north of Copper Range Campground) during the summer months, although the water is as promising as any you have ever seen. One theory holds that the lower river is so well known to steelheaders (every pool is marked on a map available from Brule River Sportsmen's Club) that resident browns don't have a chance to grow to respectable size. Another theory posits that the residents are displaced from the best lies by the movement of migratory rainbows and browns.

We have had our best summertime wade fishing for resident browns and rainbows from County Road B down to the first rapids, around Copper Range Campground, and upstream and down from Pine Tree Landing. An evening fly-fisher will enjoy easier wading upstream from Winneboujou Landing at County Road B into the summer home section.

According to a former fish manager at Brule DNR headquarters, the best summer fly-fishing is in that stretch from 2 miles above and below the ranger station and Brule River Campground at Brule. Upstream is fast water to Little Joe and Long Nebagamon Rapids. Downstream there are softer meanders to US 2. Access to the river is at the parking lot at Winneboujou, in the campground area next to the ranger station (park entrance fee required), and on the west side of the river from a fire trail exactly 1½ miles north of County Road B off After Hours Road. The fisheries expert also noted that migratory browns spawn near the ranger station, around the mouth of Nebagamon Creek, and below Cedar Island. Many of those fish will hold station in the Meadows section downstream from US 2 until the onset of spawning in October. So, one could recommend the Meadows in August and September, but without any guarantees. Although the migrating browns, which average 22 inches and 4½ pounds, are not active feeders, they may be provoked or teased with attractors.

A hatful of small rainbows may be taken most days in the rapids and particularly through the Brule River Campground, but they seldom exceed 9 inches. Most of them are migratory, so by the time they reach that length they are usually on their way to the lake.

The Brule is a cool river, fed by dozens of springs in the brook trout waters and by several cold-water creeks. In midsummer the water will read a steady 55 degrees between Stone's Bridge and Winneboujou. Two miles from the mouth the water temperature may reach 65 degrees on a bright summer day. A DNR study states that the water is medium hard.

In a multifaceted stream like the Brule, the predominant mayfly hatches will vary among sections. Brown drakes, *Ephemera simulans,* and Hex, *Hexagenia* genus, will be found in the slow water from Stone's Bridge through the lakes and the summer-home section. *Callibaetis,* or speckled wing, a slow-water dweller, will be limited to the lakes and ponds. March browns, *Stenonema* genus, are reported to emerge late afternoons and early evenings June through early July in the rapids between Cedar Island and WI 2. Tricos should show early mornings beginning toward the end of July through September in the slower flats below fast water wherever there are sufficient weedbeds. *Baetis,* tiny blue-winged olives, are present all season long. In the early months they'll appear in the morning; in September they'll often appear in late afternoon. Caddis will be intermittently present up and down the river all season long, as will the midges and stoneflies. The Hendrickson, *Ephemerella subvaria,* has been reported on opening day of the regular season, afternoon emergence, with sporadic hatches until the end of May. Sulphurs of the Ephemerellidae family appear occasionally afternoons through late evening from May through June.

On a river as complex as the Brule, with its diverse habitat, the various hatches are difficult to pin down. In general, the largest species, Hex and brown drake, are found in slower water where there is an accumulation of silt. Tricos and *Baetis* will inhabit the weedbeds in the upper two-thirds; stoneflies are found among the rocks in well-aerated water. Caddis, depending on the species, will be found everywhere. It is best to be prepared to match the hatch with an artificial that reasonably approximates the natural.

There are numerous developed entry points to the river on the east side from Winneboujou to the mouth, but as mentioned before the lower third of the river will be tough going for traditional fly-fishers: The wading is difficult and the classic mayfly hatches scant and unpredictable.

The Bois Brule is a river of extraordinary beauty and historic interest. Since 1907 the State of Wisconsin has attempted to preserve its unique qualities through careful management, and to expand public ownership of its corridor by acquisitions and gifts. Today the devoted fly-fisherman must share this resource with canoeists during the lazy summer days. But when shadows form and peepers come out of hiding, when the quick water speaks in tongues, then the river belongs to the one who casts a fly. It is yours. Treat it well.

BLUEBERRY CREEK
DeLorme 101

Blueberry, a nursery for brooks, browns, and rainbows, is a tortuous stream, open in some places, densely overgrown in others, but a marvelous place to spend a couple of summer daytime hours wading upstream and casting a small hopper to the edges. Access is at a bridge on a gravel road 2 miles north of County Road B on After Hours Road, then approximately 1.5 miles west on Bellwood Pit Road.

Immediately upstream of the bridge is a fine pool; beyond that is bog and brush wilderness. Access to the open stretch downstream is through Humphrey's private 40. You'll have to ask him about that.

NEBAGAMON CREEK
DeLorme 101

Nebagamon Creek also contains all three species of trout. It drains Nebagamon Lake and is consequently somewhat warmer. Find it on County Road B west of Winneboujou and from After Hours Road ¾ mile north of County Road B. Following a downpour, Nebagamon can double the volume of the water in the Brule, thus playing havoc with aquatic life downstream.

Overnight accommodations in the Brule area are not extensive. There is a motel with restaurant, and a fly shop with modern log cabins in Brule. The Lumbermen's Inn at Iron River is a favorite stopover. Farther away there are facilities for sleeping and eating at Superior, and at Herbster and Cornucopia on the Lake Superior shore along WI 13. Canoe liveries are at Brule. Excellent maps are available at Brule River Canoe Rental and from the Brule River State Forest Headquarters, Brule, WI 54820.

MINNESOTA

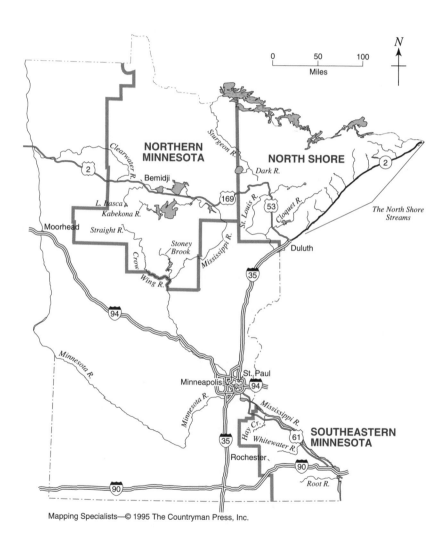

N

0   50   100
Miles

NORTHERN
MINNESOTA

NORTH SHORE

Clearwater R.

Sturgeon R.

2

Bemidji

Dark R.

169

L. Itasca
Kabekona R.

St. Louis R.

53

Cloquet R.

Moorhead

Straight R.

Stoney
Brook

Mississippi R.

Duluth

The North Shore
Streams

2

Crow

Wing R.

35

94

Minnesota R.

Minneapolis

St. Paul

94

Minnesota R.

Mississippi R.

35

Hay Cr.

Whitewater R.

61

SOUTHEASTERN
MINNESOTA

Rochester

90

90

Root R.

Mapping Specialists—© 1995 The Countryman Press, Inc.

8

Secret Streams of
Southeastern Minnesota

Through brooding hardwood forests, ancient watercourses have worn
their way down to the Mississippi, exposing weathered limestone cliffs
and crenellated towers. Clear, cold springs rush from rock caverns,
and watercress blankets a thousand seeps. Brook trout flit in crystal
cups of tiny tributaries, and saffron-bellied brown trout prowl the
pools as darkness falls. In some fast-water sections, even the irides-
cent rainbow will clear the water in mighty leaps.

Each year, fishing for wild trout in southeastern Minnesota im-
proves. Since 1984, 17 streams have been identified or improved and
included on the map as designated trout waters. Several hundred miles
of trout habitat have been added to pre-1984 streams. Under the
ministrations of the Minnesota Department of Natural Resources,
streambanks are riprapped, lunker structures are inserted, easements
acquired. Fences and cattle crossings are installed. On a few streams,

too few in our opinion, special regulations have been applied, sometimes over the fierce objections of a cadre of anglers and a couple of
legislators from the southeast. The larger, long-term battle for improved water quality has yet to be won, but the energies of the state
are being applied aggressively.

That huge, shaggy right triangle of the southeast encloses more
than 600 miles of trout waters in more than 90 named rivers and
creeks, from Red Wing on the north to the Iowa border. Three major
stream complexes are protected by state parks. Other streams meander through patches of the 42,000-acre Richard J. Dorer Memorial
Hardwood Forest. Wildlife management areas, totaling an additional
31,000 acres, adjoin or enclose segments of 10 streams. County parks
and city parks are also thoughtfully located on the banks of several
first-class streams.

Access to the streams of the southeast is easy at 100 bridges and
across public lands. Where easements are not marked, a visiting angler should ask permission to cross the fields. Most Minnesota farmers are unusually generous with fishers who are polite, who close the
gates, and who leave no trash behind. Many of those farmers also
employ enlightened farming practices—not plowing or grazing close
to the streambanks, installing cattle watering systems away from the
streams, or leasing easements to the DNR. More than a few are active in local sportsmen's clubs and in chapters of Trout Unlimited.
Cooperating farmers may also benefit financially from the lease or
sale of easements and from the habitat improvements that enhance
the esthetic and economic value of their properties.

Fishing for the three species of trout is very, very good—on many
days, spectacular. Anglers who dare to brave the rigors of a Minnesota winter may even raise browns and rainbows in 12.7 miles on
sections of Hay Creek, the Middle and South Branches of the Whitewater, and on Beaver Creek, a tributary of the Main Branch of the
Whitewater. Special regulations during the special season, January 1
through March 31, require catch and release and barbless hooks.

Special regulations are also applied to sections of Hay Creek, and
the Main, Middle, and South Branches of the Whitewater during the
regular season, from the Saturday closest to April 15 through September 30.

The Section of Fisheries of the DNR grades its trout streams as
"Good," "Fair," or "Poor." The DNR is unduly modest. Many Good
streams might appropriately be labeled "First Class" or "Blue Ribbon." Many Fair sections are changing to Good, often with the hands-

on help of local chapters of Trout Unlimited. Of the 600 miles, more than 250 are classified as Good or Fair—enough to exhaust the energy of even the most devout fly-fisher.

The DNR's Long Range Plan For Fisheries Management (1987) states, "Brown trout are the major species present, although many streams contain brook trout and a few contain stocked rainbow trout. Trout standing crops are 100 pounds per acre on high quality streams and can be over 300 pounds on excellent streams. Thirty-four percent of the stream miles have wild trout . . . Fishing pressure is characterized as heavy on 23 percent, moderate on 25 percent, and light on 43 percent."

Water temperatures range from 32 degrees in winter to a summer high of 75 degrees in some sections, but the normal range encountered by fly-fishers is from the low 40s to the high 60s. Alkalinity ranges from 200 to 300 parts per million, a range desirable for the growth of aquatic life; and pH is typically close to the neutral 7.0.

The mayfly and caddis emergences of southeastern Minnesota vary from year to year in onset, duration, and intensity. Some species of aquatic insects will blanket the water of a favorite stream one year and be only a remnant presence the next. Spring floods may scour aquatic invertebrates from a watershed, while just over the hill, another watershed, having been treated to normal precipitation, will witness the timely arrival of predicted hatches. Other variations in natural phenomena, such as drought or prolonged cold spells, may also affect emergences.

Where you find massed waterweeds and cress you'll find scuds. In the warmer sections, usually downstream, there will be leeches, forage fish, crayfish perhaps, and always a smorgasbord of terrestrials. Stoneflies are not common in the southeast.

Few of the streams profiled are wide and deep by western standards. None is swift like the Brule and Wolf of Wisconsin, and mayfly sizes generally range from small to minuscule. A 3- to 5-weight rod with a double taper or weight-forward floating line will serve. A favorite working tool is an 8-foot rod with a 9- to 10-foot leader tapering to .005 (6X) and .006 (5X) for #12 hoppers, and .007 (4X) for occasional forays after trophy browns with Woolly Buggers, Muddlers, or streamers.

Chest-high waders are useful in the spring; hip boots are usually sufficient after the water levels recede. Wading staffs help to negotiate slippery banks, and are mandatory during the winter season, when ice shelves form along the margins. Felt-bottomed waders or hippers must not be used during the winter; they're deadly on ice. One added warning: Be on the lookout for barbed wire. The old fences from abandoned farms have fallen and the wires are snares for the too-eager angler.

The peculiar topography and geology of the southeast pose dangers for the future of trout fishing. In the middle sections many streams are cold, hard, spring-fed, and perfect for trout. In their extreme upper reaches they may collect silt and multitudinous forms of pollutants from fence-to-fence farming, expanding communities, highway and bridge construction, and other ills.

Although the streams are buffered against acid precipitation by their passage through limestone, they nevertheless are fragile. A pulse of pesticides or herbicides could kill all aquatic life. A malfunction of a city or village disposal system could write finis to wild trout spawn. Occasional fish kills have been recorded as a result of the accidental or deliberate introduction of toxic substances.

Extensive cavity systems and subterranean channels have developed near the upper reaches of the major drainage basins. Sinkholes, common in the *karst* topography of southeastern Minnesota, collect runoff and funnel it into the aquifers.

Fortunately, these potential disasters are being addressed by various agencies of the state and counties of Minnesota. Volunteer environmental organizations have formed powerful coalitions to protect clean air and clean water. Even farm organizations are concerned with the long-range effects of commercial agriculture on the purity of drinking water and the quality of life.

In the past 20 years the dedicated professionals of the Department of Natural Resources, often unsung, frequently underfunded, and probably underpaid, have improved the quality of trout fishing in the area. Each year, a few more miles of streams show up as trout habitat on the map. The unpaid workers of the Hiawatha, Wa-Hue, and Win-Cres Chapters of Trout Unlimited have donated thousands of hours and tens of thousands of dollars toward improvements.

Bill's comment on one of the streams profiled below should set the stage for your venture into the southeast: "It's just another one of these wonderful trout streams . . . so many of these streams are so similar. They all have their open meadows, brushy areas, wooded slopes, and pastureland. There's so much good, clear water; you see little pods of trout, clouds of midges, so it's difficult to individualize them." But we'll try.

THE NORTHERN TRIO

These three streams are accessible from US 61, which parallels the west bank of the Mississippi. Hay and East Indian drain directly into the Mississippi; West Indian joins the Zumbro, a warm-water river.

HAY CREEK

DeLorme 34

Hay Creek in Goodhue County joins the Mississippi River at Red Wing, which is less than 60 miles from St. Paul and Minneapolis. The trout-fishing stretch may be reached from MN 58 or County Road 1 out of Red Wing.

The upper 7½ miles, down from the gigantic fenced spring in Section 33, are rated Good. For any of you who sometimes feel that your individual action can't amount to much in the long and sometimes lonely battle to save your favorite stream, know this: It was through the single-minded action of Al Farmes, whom we gratefully

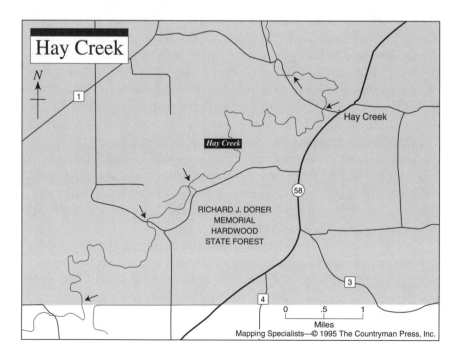

Dave Fass, a dedicated trout conservationist, is into a hefty brown on the North Branch of the Whitewater during a blue-wing olive hatch.

acknowledge in the front of this book, that the spring was fenced to keep out cattle, an act that may well have saved all of the stream for trout. To find the trail to the spring, take MN 58 south from Red Wing for 6 miles through the crossroads village of Haycreek. Continue on this road for a bit more than 3 miles to a west-running dead end in Section 35. This is the first gravel road south of the junction with County Road 4. Park at the dead-end barrier and take the trail down to the spring.

Below the great spring the stream wanders through silent and mossy glades and under the remains of abandoned railroad trestles. At evening, the setting reminds us of Edgar Allan Poe's "ghoul-haunted woodland of Weir"—dead, bone-white cottonwoods, dark and mysterious pools, the sour smell of decaying oak, the crazy, leaning trestle pilings like prehistoric dolmens.

Two river miles downstream from the spring is the first bridge. Between the first and second bridges, almost a mile through pasture has been improved by extensive riprapping and fencing. Two years ago, Trout Unlimited chapters put up the funds for a watering tank and cattle fence about midway between the two bridges. The cattle no longer trample the banks or laze in the stream.

The pasture pools are a favorite winter haunt, especially in the area completely boxed in by DNR fence. We've been there as early as the first week of January under blue skies and bright sun, with air temperature in the 20s, casting a #20 Griffith's Gnat to trout rising in the pools. One recent March 3, finding tiny black stoneflies swarming on fenceposts, we promptly switched to a #18 Black Ant and took trout. The pasture lies within a 3.9-mile section posted to special regulations both winter and summer.

To find the pasture and the bridges take the west-running road a mile south of Haycreek from MN 58. Or take County Road 1 on the north edge of Red Wing for 5.4 miles south to the schoolhouse; turn left and go about 3 miles to the first bridge below the great spring.

Stream improvement projects like fencing, riprapping, and special regulations are designed to increase the numbers of trout, or the biomass (pounds of trout per acre), or to produce trout of larger size. Biomass has increased on Hay Creek over the past several years, but size of trout has not increased significantly.

Hay Creek is the most heavily fished of the streams of the southeast, and yet, on the second afternoon of a recent season I met only two fishers spin-fishing down from the big spring. By dusk, I had it all to myself—and I wondered what was creeping up behind me from the shadows!

On a more recent occasion Al Farmes and I fished Hay between the hours of 11 AM and 5 PM. Oddly, there were more trout fishers on that Tuesday than there had been on the previous Sunday, which is an indication that not all fly-fishers storm the streams on weekends.

I fished up from the upper bridge in Section 27, starting at the huge pool under the decaying trestle, which is usually good for at least one brown trout. Later, after I'd skipped a number of runs and pools because absolutely nothing was happening, I came up behind a pair of fishermen trampling the banks ahead of me. They walked boldly to the edges of every pool to peer in—surely no way to sneak up on a trout. I surmise that all of the water I explored fruitlessly had been "fished" in like manner.

Al, meanwhile, had hiked upstream a long way along the old railroad grade. Way up there he discovered a pool where trout were feeding actively on midges. Al crawled on hands and knees to the head of the pool, where, he says, he sat on his butt and with great care succeeded in catching and releasing 18 trout on a #18 soft-hackle, fished in the film. Al's theory is that the wind gusts were drowning midges before they could become airborne and that the trout were picking them off.

The morals of this story are two. Be prepared to walk away from the access points to find a section that hasn't already been pounded to death, and approach the stream with infinite caution—on hands and knees if necessary. Or slide your way into casting range on the seat of your pants.

Downstream from the village of Haycreek there are a couple of bridges, some deep pools, and about 3 miles of marginal trout water through public lands.

Nearest city with overnight and dining facilities is Red Wing on US 61.

WEST INDIAN CREEK
DeLorme 35

West Indian Creek joins the Zumbro River at Theilman in Wabasha County. County Road 4 parallels it upstream and joins MN 42 near Plainview. West Indian includes 1½ miles of stream rehabilitated with funds from the state's Reinvest in Minnesota program. Biomass of trout has increased by more than 300 percent due to improved over-winter survival. That section fishes easiest in the spring; by summer the bankside weeds are head high. A visitor could begin at the abandoned bridge about 100 yards east of the new bridge and wade upstream to a delightful pool and beyond through waist-deep water between cornfields. Most of the 6-plus miles of West Indian run through bottomlands of corn and soybeans, but at the upper end there are crystal pockets in DNR lands.

It was once one of our all-time favorites, but one year spring floods killed it for the first few months. It's back on our list. West Indian is known for its robust browns—broad-shouldered, deep-bodied, and energetic. Near the Minnesota Sportsman's clubhouse there is a succession of deep, slow-moving runs and emerald pools. Sometimes you can snake two trout from a pool before you put them down. Although the weeds are thick, particularly by late summer, a devious fisherman ought to do well with a nicely tied #16 or #18 Adams.

Excellent overnight and dining facilities at Wabasha on US 61. Outstanding country cuisine at the Anderson House since 1856.

EAST INDIAN CREEK
DeLorme 35

East Indian, which is appropriately a few miles east of West Indian, in Wabasha County, with access from County Road 14 off US 61, is a small stream containing naturally reproducing brook trout. Short rods, light lines, and small flies are recommended. Its upper reaches are being improved by the DNR with the aid of the Wa-Hue Chapter of TU. *Nearest city with facilities: Wabasha on US 61.*

THE WHITEWATER RIVER COMPLEX
DeLorme 26 & 35

By the end of the second decade of this century the valley of the Whitewater had become the wreckage of a dream. Shortly after the 1851 treaty with the Dakotas, which opened the land to settlement, land-hungry pioneers advanced up the floodplain of the Mississippi. They wanted free land. The Whitewater River and the folds of lush green hills seemed to be the end of the long journey north and the beginning of independence and wealth. Black-soil bottomlands and the alluvial shelves below high bluffs were there to be seized and ripped open to seed. The massed ranks of black walnut, hickory, and juniper were to be cut and burned. Life in the late 19th century would go on forever, it seemed—peaceful, fruitful, and profitable.

The pioneers hacked the trees without thought, planted the slopes, and burned deep-rooted grasses. Prosperity seemed just around the corner, but in 1900 the floods began. Heavy rains fell year after year, washing away the topsoil and filling the valleys with debris. Towns vanished in spring floods. Fields yielded less and less. The long dying of the valley had begun.

As farms were abandoned or foreclosed, the pioneers moved once more—north or west toward other promised lands. The clear trout waters of the Whitewater and dozens of other streams ran thick with mud. A handful of farmers who survived the ravages of ignorance and nature were finally finished off by the Depression of the 1930s.

As early as 1919, the state purchased its first parcel of exhausted land to be included in the projected Whitewater State Park. Fifteen miles of the Whitewater and many miles of tributaries are now included in the park.

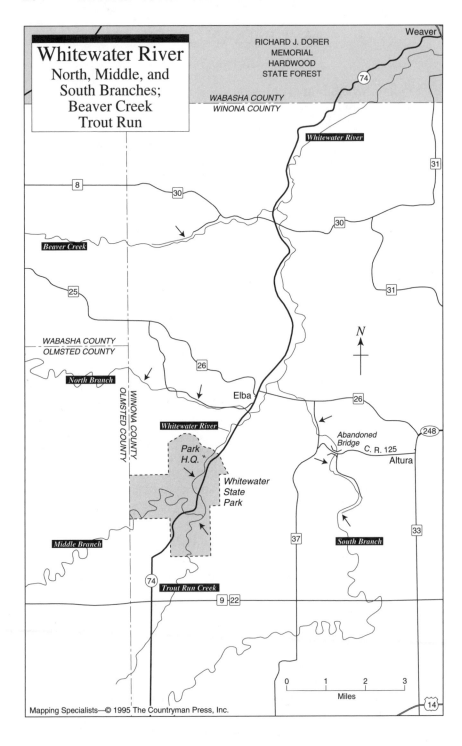

Whitewater River
North, Middle, and
South Branches;
Beaver Creek
Trout Run

RICHARD J. DORER
MEMORIAL
HARDWOOD
STATE FOREST

Weaver

WABASHA COUNTY
WINONA COUNTY

Whitewater River

Beaver Creek

WABASHA COUNTY
OLMSTED COUNTY

North Branch

WINONA COUNTY
OLMSTED COUNTY

Whitewater River

Elba

Park
H.Q.

Whitewater
State
Park

Abandoned
Bridge   C. R. 125

Altura

Middle Branch

South Branch

Trout Run Creek

N

0   1   2   3
Miles

Mapping Specialists—© 1995 The Countryman Press, Inc.

In 1938, Richard J. Dorer joined the Minnesota Department of Conservation, now the Department of Natural Resources, and began the visionary and painstaking work of rebuilding the battered valleys of the Whitewater. Gullies were blocked and filled, slopes were replanted, and grazing was halted in the watershed. Land was taken for back taxes or purchased for inclusion in the Whitewater Wildlife Management Area. The Whitewater River complex of three branches and two feeders embraces more than 50 miles of classic fly-fishing water.

THE NORTH BRANCH OF THE WHITEWATER
DeLorme 26

The North Branch on Fairwater Road, west of the village of Elba in Winona County, offers roadside access to 3 miles of respectable fly-fishing in the spring, but becomes less productive after the middle of May due to marginal water quality. This 8-mile branch, which is always a few degrees warmer than the others, originates in farmland on the savannas where fence-to-fence farming is practiced. It muddies quickly, clears slowly, receives less recharge from springs, and is subject to pesticide and herbicide runoff. Its middle reaches, through a heavily wooded and narrow valley, are not accessible to heavy equipment, so the DNR has not been able to reconstruct habitat. Most brown trout are stocked. Nevertheless, a fisherman who is willing to pick his way into the jungle above the last DNR parking lot will find solitary and picturesque pools.

One May day up there we autopsied a brown and found its stomach stuffed, sausagelike, with green, segmented midge larvae. We switched to midge nymphs and emergers. While we enjoyed a catch of small trout delicately inveigled from smooth runs, worm fishers were taking browns to 14 inches from the holes.

Dining at Elba on MN 74, and public and private campgrounds on the middle branch of the river.

THE MIDDLE BRANCH OF THE WHITEWATER
DeLorme 26

Six miles of the Middle Branch snake through Whitewater State Park. This is labeled the Middle Fork on DeLorme. It is as fine a reach of

*Al Farmes on the cliff pool on the Middle Branch of the Whitewater
in Whitewater State Park during the winter season*

open water as we know. Browns are both wild and hatchery stock;
sizable rainbows are planted annually to amaze the campers. Four-
and 5-pound browns are taken every year and often displayed proudly
at Mauer Brothers Tavern in Elba.

Approximately 3 miles, from the confluence with Trout Run near
the South Picnic Grounds, downstream to the MN 74 bridge in Section 9, are open January 1 through March 31 to catch and release,
with barbless hooks only.

Midges will be on the wing on most winter days. *Baetis* mayflies,
blue-winged olives #18, may show as early as late February. Tiny
early black stoneflies should be trit-trotting across the snowbanks.

On February 17 and 18, we found orange scuds among the weeds,
and almost every decent run or pool was occupied by an angler. Surprising to find so many fly-fishers outside on a winter day, but it was
a long, dreary winter and a 48-degree air temperature on a Minnesota February weekend was evidently enough to pry them away from
their vises—or vices.

Drift your weighted orange scud in the emerald green pools and
under the bridges.

There is also a 3.3-mile section posted to no-kill during the regular
season. If you fish within park boundaries you'll need a park sticker,
winter as well as summer, but this is excellent fly-fishing water, so it's

worth the price. Buy the sticker at park headquarters on MN 74 about 2 miles south of Elba.

In the summer you'll likely find campers flinging spinners into the pools, but during the winter season you'll usually find peace and quiet, except in the Cliff Pool in the Cedar Hill Campground. Not to fret; if the pool is occupied, go down about 50 yards to a second, insignificant pool. It doesn't look like much but we've had our best success there. Still farther downstream, not far beyond where the Dakota Trail crosses the river on a series of cast concrete blocks, is a long run. You might see it as a long narrow pool. No matter: It'll drive you crazy. There's another favorite long, curving pool outside the park downstream of the County Road 39 bridge.

Upstream, outside of the park boundaries, the Hiawatha Chapter of TU has devoted years of extravagant care to improve habitat, with excellent results in the production of larger trout.

And last, don't miss the live trout and stream display, partly funded by several chapters of TU, in the headquarters building at the north edge of the park.

TROUT RUN
DeLorme 26

The tributary to the Middle Branch of the Whitewater, Trout Run in the park, is a classic small spring creek—glass-clear, weedy, cold, with a mix of wild browns and brookies. Exceedingly light tackle may capture a minor masterpiece. But not all the residents are small. Mike Schad, of the Wa-Hue Chapter of TU, had been soft-footing along Trout Run for a couple of hours without notable success. He finally planted himself on the bank with boots in the water to take five. A very large trout swam out from under the bank between his feet and moved away leisurely, no doubt thumbing a fin in disdain. That's trout fishing for you, at least in southeastern Minnesota.

THE SOUTH BRANCH OF THE WHITEWATER
DeLorme 26

The 10 miles of the South Branch are a favorite haunt of fly-fishers. A mile of it, upstream from the abandoned bridge near Crystal Springs Hatchery, is under special regulations during the summer season—

trout over 10 inches must be released. Take County Road 26 east from Elba to County Road 37, then south to County Road 112 east to the broken bridge. Watch for the hatchery sign.

This wild section, which averages 25 feet in width, offers an optimum mix of habitats—a few deep, jade pools, swift runs over gravel, classy flats over limestone rubble, and even some grass verges where one can splat a grasshopper during the dog days. In April of 1986 the South Branch surrendered a 5-pound, 2-ounce brown to an artificial grasshopper, a bit early for hoppers but who knows what goes on in the brain of an opportunistic trout?

Late one evening in April, after the big pool ½ mile above the broken bridge had been pounded all day by spin-casters and fly-rodders, I created a fake hatch by drifting a Light Cahill among the branches of a sunken tree. On the 30th cast, or more, a brown surprised me. Three more browns to 13 inches and a chunky rainbow clued in on the "hatch" in short order. I'd read about creating a false hatch in the literature, but this was the first time I really worked at it. I've tried it again since; you should too when you've got time to pound up trout.

About 2 miles of the South Branch are open January 1 through March 31, from the bridge on County Road 37 downstream to the junction with the Main Branch at Elba. There's a complex pool that we dearly love about ½ mile below the bridge. Take the trail alongside a cornfield. You'll love it, too, if you can outwit a brown there on a gorgeous February day.

At the end of January, with the air temperature in the 40s under a blue sky, Mike Dziki of the Kiap-TU-Wish Chapter of TU released a 21-inch brown "log." A DNR census taker was hidden behind some bushes. He said, "You are going to release that trout, aren't you?" Mike finagled the brown with a #18 all-purpose brown nymph. Yes, it is possible to experience fine fly-fishing in winter, even in the North Star State.

During the summer you might like to try the upper pastures of the South Branch. Take County Road 112, a dirt road going west out of Altura, which is east of the river, to find the abandoned bridge previously referred to, then go south along the east bank. Paul Krogvold came all the way from Norway to fish it with us. Paul had no complaints, kneeling and casting to scores of visible, rising browns.

THE MAIN BRANCH
DeLorme 26 & 35

Downstream from Elba, the Main Branch flattens and slows for 13 miles, partly through a wildlife refuge, to the Mississippi. A 1978 flash flood dumped enormous quantities of silt in this stem. The natural process has been slow, but the 10 miles below Elba produce some large trout in huge pools. It won't be easy, and the action may be like watching a big-league pitcher go through his motions, but big-fish fishers may want to give it a shot. A 3.1-mile section is posted for special regulations in summer.

We cherish three places on the Whitewater complex: the snag pool on the South Branch on a warm summer evening when the bats begin to fly; a split pool at the end of a walk through cornfield stubble to the South Branch on a shining day in February when the temperature is in the 20s and the air is still; not least, we find a challenge in those complex pools and runs that rub up against the cliffs where swallows dart.

BEAVER CREEK
DeLorme 35

Beaver Creek, which enters the Main Branch of the Whitewater 5 miles downstream from Elba, parallels County Road 30. Go west on County Road 30 from the junction with MN 74 for perhaps a mile. Beaver is a small stream that in the past has harbored some very large trout, including the one-time state-record brown. There's a winter season on a 3.9-mile posted section, for barbless hooks and catch and release. Look for a set of steel-gray barns just east of a signposted "WW 10 TWP" low-maintenance road. In the winter it's better to walk in than to chance getting stuck. About 1½ miles upstream you'll find DNR parking at a barrier.

We met a young fly-fisher there in February who admitted to having released eight browns on a Black Gnat. We suspect the Black Gnat was seen by the trout as a midge or winter stonefly. There are tons of small brown trout between County Road 30 and the barrier; farther upstream is brook trout water.

Beaver is a terrific stream for a novice who wants to learn how to fish small water and tight corners, and keep his fly out of streamside vegetation and trees.

Bill described our fall trip lyrically: "If you perfect your skills, the native browns will cooperate. I caught two 9-inch browns, then two 10-inchers, on a #16 Hare's Ear. Intermittent showers enhanced the powerful aroma of the autumn hardwood forest. Butternuts were strewn across the gravel road; and to cap the memory, 27 wild turkeys crossed ahead of us. What a sight; what a day!"

Nearest city with overnight and dining facilities: St. Charles on I-90. Cosmopolitan facilities at Rochester, about 25 miles west on County Road 9.

THREE STREAMS OF THE ACUTE ANGLE

These three lie in the acute angle between I-90 and the Mississippi and flow directly into the great river.

ROLLINGSTONE (RUPPRECHT) CREEK
DeLorme 26 & 27

Rollingstone, or Rupprecht Creek on the DNR trout map, is about 4 miles southwest of Rollingstone on MN 248. Take County Road 27 south about 1½ miles west of the village of Rollingstone, then bear to the left on the first gravel road to the bridge and stile in Section 13.

We recommend the upstream reach from the bridge, at first through slow, deep water. Then the stream opens into meadow where the fishing can be extremely good, particularly in deep water in September, when a Pass Lake streamer is the fly of choice. Look down into a pool at the trout. They stare up at you, but they ignore your offering. Big trout lie under the deadfalls; you may have to sneak up on them at evening or during a rain. Upstream of the valley, the stream narrows and brush closes in.

GARVIN BROOK
DeLorme 26 & 27

The Garvin Brook Fishery Area lies about 10 miles west of Winona and southwest of Stockton in Winona County on US 14. To quote a fly-fishing authority, "It is a blue-ribbon stream with high standing crops of wild trout." "Crops?" That's the parlance of farm country. Forgive us. Trout aren't crops; never have been, never will be. That description, though, was made before the 1989 flood that hit Garvin and the town of Stockton and wiped out much of the stream structure and a good share of the town. But Trout Unlimited and the DNR have been hard at work. Since the flood, numerous bank structures have been replaced and the trout "crop" is improving. By the time you read this, Garvin may have been restored to its former glory.

Above and through Farmers Community Park at the Arches, a railroad overpass west of Stockton on US 14, the stream is narrow through woodland. For more than a mile below the Arches it lazes through a meadow protected by DNR easement.

Which reminds us of our first experience on Garvin with Dick Frantes. (See our commemoration of Dick in the profile of Tiffany Creek.) Not far downstream of the Arches there's a beautiful pool where we got some fine pictures of Dick getting skunked again. Below the pool is a chute that opens into another long pool. Dick went to the tail and began to drop his fly close to the margin. Suddenly his fly disappeared. Then, to our amazement, so did his leader and a portion of the front of his line. A trout had taken it under a bank cover that none of us had realized was there. The picture will remain bright in memory. Let that be a lesson to you who fish the streams of southeastern Minnesota. Look carefully for bank covers and lunker structures. They are not always visible. Not long ago, Bill Shogren stepped off a bank, expecting to wade out into the pool, and promptly went in over his waders. He also dunked his new microcassette recorder.

Bank covers that have been in for a season or two are not easy to spot. Look for a grass bank with a clean straight edge and the suspicion of deep water at the edge. Those caves harbor trout, often the largest in the stream. We've had success by dropping a fly exactly at the edge of the cover as the evening sun goes down.

Facilities: Some at Stockton; everything at Winona on US 61.

PICKWICK AND LITTLE PICKWICK CREEKS
DeLorme 27

These two creeks lie in the point of the angle and about midway between Winona and LaCrescent/La Crosse on US 61. Take County

Road 7 west from US 61 to Pickwick. Fish upstream along County Road 7 or along Little Trout Valley Road. On some maps the streams are labeled Big Trout Creek and Little Trout Creek, but Pickwick is a more romantic name. No doubt the village of Pickwick was named in the 19th century by an admirer of Dickens; at least we like to think so.

These two are true success stories. For more than 10 years the Win-Cres Chapter of Trout Unlimited has improved them, adding structures, de-brushing, narrowing, and deepening the streams. Sometimes spring floods have torn out the works but TU has persevered. Two once-degraded streams through precipitous country are now great fisheries, monuments to the work of dedicated volunteers, which should be encouragement to all of us.

Facilities at Winona and LaCrescent.

TRIBUTARIES OF THE ROOT RIVER

The Root River is a mighty complex of forks and branches that drains much of four counties and includes more than 100 miles of trout streams. Trout Run Creek and Torkelson Creek are tributaries of the main stem; another group that follows swells the waters of the Main and South Branches of the Root. The four streams of Winona County drain into the main stem; and two other groups either cluster around the South Fork or enter the main stem. We have grouped them for the convenience of traveling fly-fishers.

TROUT RUN CREEK
DeLorme 26

Trout Run Creek, in southwestern Winona County and northern Fillmore County, a cold-water tributary to the main stem of the Root River, from the village of Saratoga on MN 74 downstream, includes 12½ miles classed as Good. It may be in a class by itself. Begin at the bridge about 1 mile south of Troy on County Road 43, where through pastureland it reminds us of dew-diamonded, emerald-green Ireland in spring. Not more than 1½ river miles downstream you'll find the fabled round red barn, if you want to wade it all the way. To reach the red barn by road, take the first gravel road going east, approximately ½ mile south of the bridge.

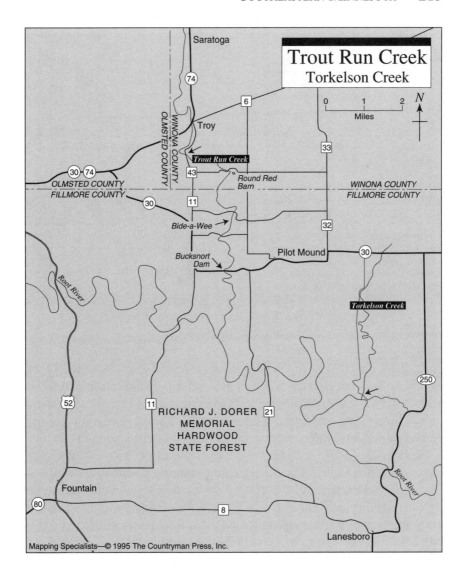

Upstream from the round red barn is tough going for a ways under heavy overhang but with great potential for careful fly-fishers. We know the lie of an 18-inch brown. There are downstream paths on both sides from the barn bridge. Better yet, look for a trail on the west that climbs a ridge, then drops into an area that appears to be an abandoned campground flanked by shallow pools that will reward your skill.

If you keep going downstream, you'll arrive at a stretch of deep,

*Fly-fishers on Trout Run Creek, between the Bide-a-Wee
and the slab bridge*

dark, slow water. We take station on the forested west bank, where we watch big browns surface lazily to pick off an unsuspecting mayfly or midge. We must sharpshoot for individual trout and often we put them down, but it's the kind of challenge that we like. It reminds us of the technique necessary on some of the famous western spring creeks.

Next bridge down is Bide-a-Wee, in olden days a cabin and camping community, with a few remaining cabins upstream and superb fly-fishing down through ¾ mile to the slab bridge, mostly through pasture. About midway between Bide-a-Wee bridge and the slab is a long, deep pool with steep banks and a quick drop-off. Reserve this one for evening fishing, when substantial browns should feed on top. You may have to slide boots into water and lean back against the slope to hold position. Don't be impatient, and keep your backcast high.

Next down from the slab bridge is Bucksnort Dam on MN 30. Above the dam is a long pool and Humphrey's "Devil's Seat," where he often sits at ease and waits for a bruiser brown to rise. Meanwhile, his pals fish downstream through riprapped pastures and riffles, where on one memorable day Dick Frantes raised 39 browns on a hopper while Humphrey got zilch. He did see, though, upstream and around the corner from the Devil's Seat, in the depths and protected by a snaggle tree, an 8-inch brown crosswise in the mouth of some great shadowy, fishy form. There are no northern pike in these icy waters; draw your own conclusions.

We recall vividly, and still with a shiver, an April opener above the slab bridge with Ken Hanson of the Kiap-TU-Wish Chapter, Dick Frantes, and a flotilla of dark Hendricksons struggling to rise through a sleet storm. Why they chose to emerge, and why we chose that bitter day to fish Trout Run, we do not know. To add insult to injury, Ken must have caught and released 20 browns to our somewhat fewer.

In three consecutive years of electro-shocking surveys, standing stocks of naturally reproducing brown trout varied from 2500 per mile to a high close to 5000—superior numbers for any stream, anywhere. Among them will be a few busters that exceed 18 inches. Look for them in impossible places. We can't guarantee the numbers on your visit, but we can guarantee a quality experience on Trout Run, if you take pains to maintain a low profile and cast the longest leader you can handle.

Accommodations at St. Charles on I-90 and at Lanesboro and Preston to the south.

TORKELSON CREEK
DeLorme 26

Torkelson, a tributary of the main stem of the Root, a bit south and east of Trout Run and a few miles due north of Lanesboro on MN 250, is a little jewel. Some places you can jump across, but follow it upstream on the unmarked gravel town road that angles northwest off MN 250 at the green mile marker #5. Use the stiles and watch for rising trout. About the third meadow up it gets really good, and the valley scenery is spectacular. The DNR invested $30,000 in habitat improvement, so it must be something special.

Exceptional accommodations at Lanesboro to the south.

THE SOUTH BRANCH OF THE ROOT RIVER COMPLEX

The South Branch of the Root and its feeders are about as good as it gets in southeastern Minnesota for fly-fishers who want to explore and experience a variety of waters. These seven streams include more than 35 miles of Good water. According to a former fish manager for the DNR, 25,000 adult browns, ranging from 9 inches to 12 pounds, inhabit the Root complex. A few rainbows are added each year, together with several hundred thousand brown trout fry. Naturally reproducing brook trout are in the tributaries. DNR surveys commonly find 2000 to 3000 trout per mile.

SOUTH BRANCH OF THE ROOT RIVER
DeLorme 26

A visitor can go west, upstream from Lanesboro in Fillmore County or from the city of Preston at the junction of US 52 and MN 12, or begin in and around Forestville State Park on the west. County Road 12 connects Preston and the park. Conveniently, 3 of the most productive miles lie within the park, a short stroll from fishermen's parking, from either of two campgrounds and a picnic ground. The park stretch is preferred by most fly-fishers, but that's not to denigrate many days of superior fishing downstream from the park boundary, where the Root widens and deepens, all the way into a beautiful riffle and pool right in Preston.

In August, the Root through the park draws the Trico crowd from far distances. Be prepared for some crowding early mornings. Trico fishers, however, aren't heavy-booted bank runners; they usually confine their downstream puddle or S-casts to relatively small areas of the stream.

John Schorn, a skillful fly-fisher from the Twin Cities who fishes the Root early and often, maintains that the trout there are peculiarly oriented to the surface. He says this is probably because the river through the park, and particularly along the picnic grounds near the Meighen Store, is shallow and shaded by mature oaks, so the fish are not driven deep by sunlight. We, too, have enjoyed excellent dry-fly fishing at the picnic grounds.

Along County Road 118 between the east boundary of Forestville State Park and the bridge south of Carimona, look for roadside parking at a stile. A fenced easement about 300 yards long leads to the river, where there are huge pools and sparkling runs.

One memorable day there comes to mind. As a spectator armed only with a camera on a May morning, I followed Jay Paulson, who released more than 20 browns, fishing upstream with a small dark

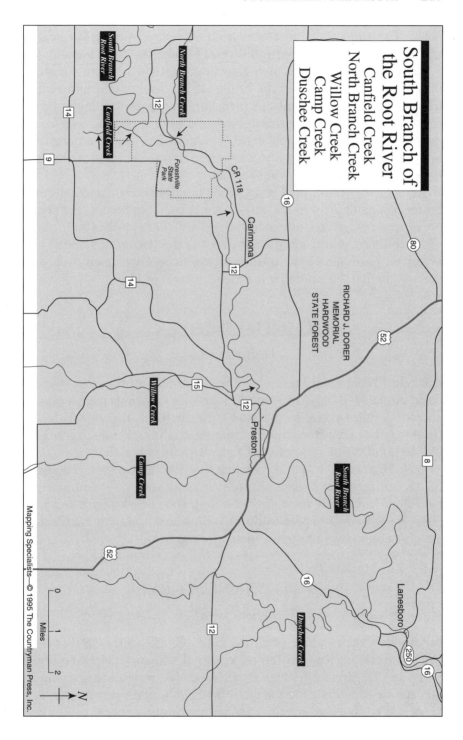

South Branch of
the Root River
Canfield Creek
North Branch Creek
Willow Creek
Camp Creek
Duschee Creek

Hare's Ear and a tiny fluorescent strike indicator. Among Jay's catch were a 16-incher, two 15s, and several I eyeballed at 14 inches.

Returning to Preston: Coming up County Road 12 from the south into Preston and just over the bridge, if you look you'll find on the left a rough road to a bankside picnic area with a spool table. Just a few hundred feet upstream is a jewel of a pool spreading over boulders, broken limestone, and sand. The pool has given us delightful hours over selective brown trout there. On one occasion Al Farmes took a dozen without moving his feet.

Above the Preston pool is a ½-mile-long horseshoe and a second bridge. We can't say that the horseshoe has been productive, but above the second bridge on a dirt road is fly-fisher's heaven. Roadside parking is up there, with a steep bank down to the stream. It's one of our favorites, particularly the upstream pool where we've enjoyed several mayfly hatches, notably the Hendrickson in May.

CANFIELD CREEK
DeLorme 26

Canfield Creek, a tributary of the South Branch of the Root and labeled on the DNR map as South Branch Creek, springs from a cavern about 1½ miles above its junction with the Root in the park. Small trout may be taken from that fascinating small creek, which contains untold numbers and varieties of Ephemerellidae mayflies.

Dick Hanousek, a world-traveling fly-fisher and writer, may hold the record for trout caught and released in Canfield—65 in a single day. But Dick's an expert with the long rod, fine leaders, and tiny flies. We wouldn't expect to do as well, but you might. Caddisflies are also abundant in both Canfield and the Root.

NORTH BRANCH CREEK
DeLorme 26

Forestville Creek (labeled North Branch Creek on the DNR map), which enters the Root in the park near the historic Meighen Store (circa 1858), offers 2.6 miles rated Good. It's worth the investment of a couple of hours since the DNR has rehabilitated a mile of it. Bill avers it is really excellent since the habitat improvement.

WILLOW AND CAMP CREEKS
DeLorme 26

Willow and Camp Creeks are two feeders that enter the Root at Preston. Although neither creek is anything to write home about, Camp Creek is marginally better. If a visitor stays overnight in Preston, he could try either creek after dinner.

Bill often stays overnight at Mrs. B's Bed & Breakfast in that charming old town of Lanesboro. He notes there are four or five B&Bs in and around town, first-class eating for gourmets and, not least, a beautiful riffle and deep pools on the main Root that produce some big browns at evening. His advice is to fill up on good food, then take a leisurely stroll down to the river, booted and armed with a stout rod and an outsize fly.

Another day on the Root complex is retrieved from my storage system to share with you. On a miserably cold day in late April, when the water temperature was only 44 degrees, I watched John Rowell, the "Master on the Brule of Wisconsin," take a half dozen browns just below Canfield Creek on a "flymph," which could be described as a hybrid nymph/soft-hackle. Later, I burned up a couple of hours casting and spooking a pod of trout stacked up in a diversion channel where the water was warmer. I took a couple to prove that it could be done while Rowell went downstream and filled out his dozen.

Overnight and dining facilities for all of the South Branch of the Root at Preston and Lanesboro. Mrs. B's Bed & Breakfast (phone: 507-467-2154) at Lanesboro is renowned for quality accommodations and cuisine. Also try Birch Knoll Ranch B & B at Box 11, Route 2, Lanesboro, MN 55949 (phone: 507-467-2418 or 612-475-2054).

DUSCHEE CREEK
DeLorme 26

Duschee Creek joins the South Branch of the Root at Lanesboro. It's mostly a small, clear stream with habitat improved by the DNR and sweet pools at the upstream bridges along County Road 21 about a mile southwest of town off MN 16, but below the fish hatchery the water runs murky. We've caught fish at the hatchery outlet and down toward the highway, but the small pools upstream are preferred. The creek contains brown and brook trout.

GRIBBEN CREEK
DeLorme 26

A few miles east of Duschee you'll find Gribben Creek, crossed several times by County Road 23 going south from MN 16. Some folks would call Gribben tiny. Its 3 miles of Good water have been improved by the DNR, but during normal water levels the riffles are too shallow for practical nymphing and there are only a handful of pools. A friend has labeled it an "intimate" stream. But Gribben has been one of the most productive for wild brook trout. An older electro-survey indicated more than 8000 trout per mile and 350 pounds per acre—astronomical numbers that we can't promise now. Small streams are most likely to incur year-to-year changes.

One fly-fisher recalls with awe when five mayfly hatches appeared in succession over the course of a single day, and he matched all five. We agree that Gribben is an intimate stream. A visitor should work slowly into the state forest unit to find his pool. Gribben yields its secrets most readily when the banks are full and there's a touch of color in the water.

DIAMOND CREEK
DeLorme 26

A couple of miles east is Diamond Creek, south of MN 16. Take the gravel road off County Road 107 in Section 11 to the site of the old schoolhouse; start fishing. Hit this two-branched stream early in the year, because the weed growth is amazing as the summer wears on. Early mornings are more likely to bring the naturally reproducing brook trout out of hiding.

FOUR STREAMS OF WINONA COUNTY

These four streams lie immediately south of I-90 in lower Winona County and add to the main stem of the Root.

RUSH CREEK
DeLorme 26 & 27

Rush Creek includes more than 7 miles of Good and Fair water. It comes highly recommended by Bill Haugen, an expert fly-fisher and guide from Rushford. In the abnormally low waters of one recent dry year, dozens of trout were stressed and pooled above the bridges on County Road 25, but we didn't harass them. Sometimes it's better to observe and to preserve. Between the County Road 25 bridges north of Rushford, on a giant pool, a family with picnic baskets and coolers were enjoying a day out. The kids were drowning worms and keeping a few trout, but that's O.K.; those kids will become the leaders of our next generation of volunteer conservationists.

My partner and I did take a few feisty browns upstream in pastureland after asking permission of a friendly farmer to walk down his lane to the spring creek. Up there, the fishing was not at all like shooting fish in a barrel; nevertheless, we put them back.

Bill Shogren records a phenomenal rise of light Cahills one early June afternoon: "Every 6 feet a Cahill came down, but many would complete the run successfully." It was a puzzle to him why they weren't all picked off by the numerous trout.

There have been extensive improvements behind the Miller farm on the east side of the river, but Bill prefers to "billy-goat" down into the valley from the west, where at night one can hear the coyotes howl. On the west you may have to ask permission to take the long hike down.

On June 21, 1991, the accidental or deliberate discharge of some kind of chemical wiped out aquatic life on 2½ miles of stream, but by now even that section should have bounced back.

PINE AND HEMMINGWAY CREEKS
DeLorme 26

Pine Creek is a tributary of Rush Creek from the west and is reached from County Roads 2 and 25. Town roads also cross the stream. It runs through hills, hardwood forests, and turkey country, and provides good brown trout fishing. Hemmingway, which is crossed by County Road 29, is a tributary of the Pine and one of the southeast's premier brook trout fisheries. To gain access to the interior reaches of Hemmingway, you may have to ask permission.

Both streams show terrific caddis hatches that render great numbers of trout. Pray for heavy overcast or slight drizzle. You'll appreciate it.

MONEY CREEK
DeLorme 27

Money Creek is a little junky, without much water movement, but it contains bigger trout. Bill kicked out an 18-inch brown from under a stump, and later broke off a 19-incher. In one pool, the Pass Lake streamer was followed by three browns in the 14- to 15-inch range. Amazing! The two branches of Money Creek can be reached from County Road 19 in Winona County, a few miles south of Wilson on I-90.

Complete facilities for the four streams of Winona County at Rushford in upper Fillmore County.

SOUTH FORK OF THE ROOT RIVER COMPLEX

Six named streams are included in this complex. Feel free to explore several of them on your own. We profile two.

SOUTH FORK OF THE ROOT
DeLorme 26 & 27

Go south out of Rushford or north out of Mabel in Fillmore County on MN 43 to County Road 12, which is just north of Tawney and south of Choice. Take County Road 12 west to cross a new concrete bridge; follow County Road 12 west about 1½ miles to a gravel road on the left near a rise in the road. Take the gravel road south to the South Fork of the Root; fish upstream. You can spend all day in this beautiful area. Pack your lunch and walk in. You know that you're dealing with deeper water and therefore bigger trout. It's our number-one stream to return to next spring. Bill advises, "Lunkers have been taken out of this stretch, so I'm going to lose myself in this river."

Facilities at Lanesboro and Rushford.

WISEL CREEK
DeLorme 26

Wisel Creek, a tributary of the South Fork of the Root, is one of the quality streams of the southeast. Enchanting! There are both browns and brookies north and south of County Road 18 east of Henrytown and about a mile west of MN 43. South of County Road 18, which is upstream, you'll pass through a variety of landscapes—hardwood forest, pastureland, and open fields. There are several good-looking runs and dark pools. In the pools, you must be patient. Drift your Pheasant Tail or Hare's Ear through them and you will catch trout, along with an occasional sucker. If you persevere, you'll hook up with a lunker brown, a reel screamer—that fish for a photo.

Facilities at Lanesboro, Harmony, Spring Grove, and Caledonia.

THE BEAVER CREEK COMPLEX

The Beaver Creek complex, 5 miles west of Caledonia in Houston County, includes East, West, and the Main Beaver.

EAST BEAVER CREEK
DeLorme 27

East Beaver, a gem of a spring creek, lies wholly within Beaver Creek Valley State Park on County Road 1. Foot trails follow the stream from the parking lot near the east entrance for 2½ miles of Good water down to the junction with West Beaver. There is a second DNR parking lot within a couple of minutes' walk from the junction, which is close to the bridge on County Road 10. From the junction at the footbridge the main stream widens to 40 feet and deepens to the dam at historic Schech's Mill. Along this slow, clear, deep stretch, wading is difficult; trout are visible but not usually responsive.

Going upstream from the footbridge by manicured trail along East Beaver, the fishing is primarily to pockets and pools. Several narrow, chest-deep runs are the result of older streamworks. Although the creek is narrow, the trout are of good size. They stack up along the bank, angling toward center stream, alert for drifting morsels.

East Beaver continues to receive the tender attention of fisheries

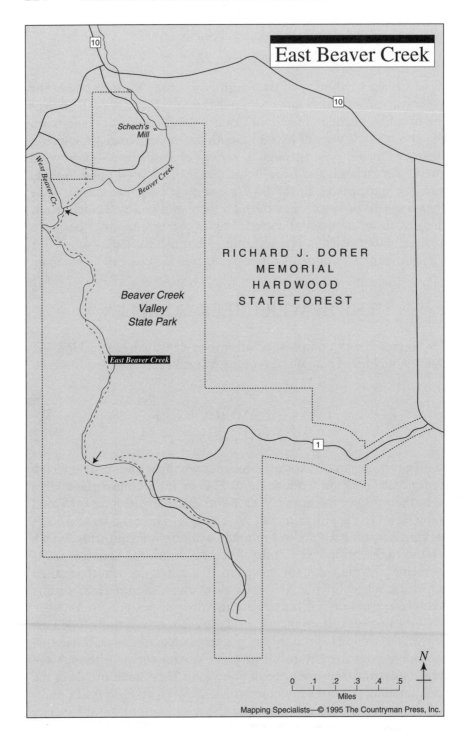

East Beaver Creek

biologists and park employees. Even if the fishing should be slow on the day of your visit, the surroundings are breathtaking—if you appreciate a crystal stream flowing softly through a rugged back of beyond.

WEST BEAVER
DeLorme 27

West Beaver may be a tough one. The last time we were there it was choked with fallen snags and pinched between thickets. An easement through a farm field and a bridge upstream provide access. West Beaver is not rated more than Fair, although it may have improved as a result of DNR habitat work on 2 miles. Bill's assessment is that it is really pretty good, especially far upstream, where he's run into a ton of brookies around the County Road 12 bridge.

THE MAIN BEAVER
DeLorme 27

Certain anglers of our acquaintance, among them Jay Paulson, whom we followed one fine day on the South Branch of the Root, sing the praises of the main stem below Schech's Mill at the County Road 10 bridge. They claim that the trout are large, even if not so plentiful. We've enjoyed the pasture and meadow fly-fishing within sight of that romantic old mill on several occasions, when we could attest to the fact that the trout were not plentiful. You should fly-fish upstream from the bridge and imagine that you're wading a pristine stream in the middle of the 19th century—or before. As we have said, there's more to fly-fishing than catching fish.

Facilities at Caledonia on MN 76.

THREE STREAMS OF
THE SOUTHEAST CORNER

Some folks might characterize these three as minor streams, but they have the virtue of lying closest to travelers from outside the state.

Sandy Rolstad on the South Branch of the Root River in Forestville State Park. This area is known for prolific trico hatches.

PHOTO BY JOE MICHL

THE NORTH FORK OF CROOKED CREEK
DeLorme 27

The North Fork of Crooked Creek in southeastern Houston County lies west of Freeburg on MN 249 and offers fine trout fishing. This creek can be susceptible to a swift spring runoff from melting snow or early thunderstorms. The fish may disappear for a while, probably downstream to deeper holes in the main creek, but they soon return.

There is extensive pastureland fishing, and you should see some scary-sized submarines cruising. Be careful in your approach and delicate with your cast. For big trout, nighttime is by far the best time.

Below Freeburg the main creek is all sand; not recommended.

Facilities at Caledonia on MN 249.

WINNEBAGO CREEK
DeLorme 27

Winnebago, in the extreme southeast corner of the state in Houston County, is paralleled by County Road 5. It includes a bit more than 8 miles of Fair water in the upper reaches. Access is limited, and the Winnebago doesn't get as much play as several more popular streams, but on at least one opening week it produced the best fly-fishing for brown and brook trout of any stream in the state. One disconsolate angler, Mark Beilke of the Twin Cities, had a 22-inch brown (eyeballed) break off on a black ant. I've seen dozens of trout stacked up in the pool between the buttresses of the abandoned bridge along County Road 5. I couldn't raise a trout, but that was before I had learned more about midge fishing with a Brassie or Griffith's Gnat (or a black ant). Below the bridge, in the riffles through a beef cattle pasture, I improved my average using the old reliable Gold-Ribbed Hare's Ear #16.

Facilities for visitors at Caledonia, and at La Crescent, Minnesota, and La Crosse, Wisconsin, on US 61 and I-90.

BEE CREEK
DeLorme 27

Bee Creek on County Road 27 in lower Houston County can be fun! (The DNR trout map labels it Bee; the DeLorme labels it Waterloo

Creek.) Go upstream from the quaint village of Bee or southeast from Spring Grove on MN 44. This is a nifty little stream that's not fished too much, but every year local fishers take some exceptional browns out of this minor treasure.

South of Bee village is the state of Iowa, where the creek is known as the Waterloo. Iowa also produces some excellent trout fishing, put-and-grow or put-and-take, in a small section of the northeast, but that requires an Iowa license and is a story for some other book.

Facilities at Spring Grove and Caledonia.

Southeastern Minnesota streams are user friendly, not dangerous, but watch for bulls and barbed wire. The streams are suitable for all ages, and you won't get lost. You are never too far from a road, field, farm, or other mark of civilization. There is a softness in the air, and the vistas are idyllic.

We never venture into that coulee country without fishing at least one new stream. We know where we can always catch trout, and will fish those familiar spots, but we always seek a new stream to explore. Put a sandwich, apple, and water flask in your vest and go pioneering. You'll never be disappointed. Explore! You may find your Shangri-la.

It is twilight on one of our favorite rivers of the southeast. Shadows stretch and fireflies wink on. Dark water from the chute slows on the pool and spreads, forming a conundrum of shining currents. I kneel, prayerfully, on the shingle beach and begin to cast a white-winged, cocky Cahill. A wild turkey gobbles in the fastness of the woods. Bats dance in that peculiar stuttering two-step. The last other angler has gone to home and hearth. Then the silvered surface blisters beneath the fly. The hook is lightly set, and there's a brown, palely gleaming green and gold in the last light. Will there ever again be such a night as this?

N.B. At this writing, we expect that the special winter season on a few streams profiled in this section will continue into 1996 and beyond, perhaps with additional stream sections, but nothing is guaranteed. Regulations change and politics exert influence on the fish managers. Check with the DNR before you travel into southeastern Minnesota on your winter foray.

9

The North Shore:
Arrowhead Country

A gyre of gulls over the Knife River sounds like a basket of kittens mewling. An insubstantial mist drifts in from Lake Superior. This is the North Shore of Lake Superior, known also as the Arrowhead Country. With a bit of imagination you could swear that you are on the Atlantic Coast somewhere north of Boston. Nearly 150 miles of Minnesota shoreline fringe this gigantic lake, in area the largest body of fresh water in the world. Twenty-eight major streams and many smaller ones pitch down along this rugged shore from the Canadian Shield between Duluth and Grand Portage near the border with Canada. Up and over the crest of the escarpment, sometimes called the Laurentian Divide or the height-of-land, hundreds of remote, interior streams await the exploring fly-fisher. The three Arrowhead counties, St. Louis, Lake, and Cook, contain 272 designated trout streams, most flowing toward the big lake from the height-of-

229

land; others flow north into the Boundary Waters.

As a bonus, or more than that, brook trout, rainbows, splake, or brown trout are stocked in more than 100 lakes, which remain open through October 30. The splake is a cross between a female lake trout and a male brook trout. A *Guide to Lakes Managed for Stream Trout* is available from the Minnesota Department of Natural Resources.

Much of the fly-fishing action along the shore is for trout and salmon during their spawning runs from the lake to the first barrier falls or impassable rapids.

For those interested in fly-fishing for huge trout and salmon, the season is continuous for most species in Lake Superior and its tributaries downstream of the posted boundaries. The regulations for the several species of *Salmonidae* are complex and may change from year to year. A careful reading of the current year's Minnesota Fishing Regulations is necessary.

This area is so vast, so wild, and so productive of quality fly-fishing over a dozen varieties of trout and salmon that it's difficult to know where to begin—or where to end.

So let us begin with a look at a chart, the "Lake Superior Fishing Calendar," from the Minnesota DNR's "North Shore Fishing Guide." It lists lake trout, brook trout, brown trout in streams, steelhead, steelhead in streams, Kamloops rainbows, Kamloops in streams, chinook salmon, chinook in streams, Atlantic salmon in streams, coho salmon, and pink salmon in streams. The "Coasters" may even be making a recovery. That would be remarkable! The Coasters were (are?) a subspecies or population of huge brook trout that fatten in Lake Superior and spawn in the rivers. I remember boating a 5-pounder in the upper reaches of Lake Nipigon in Canada in the 1950s. Strictly speaking, that may not have been a Coaster, but one of a unique population of brook trout indigenous to Nipigon, but it foreshadows superb fly-fishing if the Coasters return. Even smelt wiggle onto the beaches at the mouths of rivers in their spawning ecstasy, but they won't come to a fly. They're more often taken in dip nets, or even in golf bags!

Some of these species of trout and salmon are taken in deep water offshore, others in the first few hundred yards or first few miles of river below the barriers. But brook trout and brown trout in streams (and rainbows, too, in some sections) are the legitimate targets of this book.

Fishing for resident brown and rainbows in the upper reaches of the streams is rated Good by the DNR, although the brook trout run small.

Our experience has been that there are plenty of brook and brown trout. Thirteen- and 14-inch brook trout are possible, even larger ones on occasion. There are few professional guides who'll take you into the backcountry specifically for stream trout, but at least one of them said that he'll take you to 14-inch brook trout "if I can blindfold you."

North Shore streams depend on runoff rather than on springs and seepage, so their flows are unstable, surging after a rain or snowmelt and dwindling to a trickle during a prolonged drought. On these spate streams a case can be made that beaver dams have some utility, holding water for a slower, later discharge. In slow, broad, middle sections of streams, a canoe or float tube may be useful. Shawn Perich, an author and fly-fisherman who lives on the Shore, tells us to look for wide, slow-moving water over a silty bottom. He adds that many of the best streams arise in lakes.

The streams of the North Shore and those over the height-of-land are deficient in the amount and variety of food for trout. The bedrock over which these streams flow has few of the water-soluble minerals necessary to maintain the alkalinity required for the development of a wide variety of aquatic insects. However, there are plenty of caddisflies, Tricos in weedy sections, and emergences of *Hexagenia* in slower, silty reaches. Also, the streams remain cool throughout the year, and there are many deep and shaded runs where trout can hide.

In streams that provide only marginal habitat, the DNR stocks brown trout, which tolerate warmer water than do brook trout.

As you travel northeast from Duluth along US 61, previously described as "one of the 10 most beautiful drives in the country," you'd be hard-pressed to deny it. The forested slopes in summer show every variation on the palette of green. In late September and early October, the view is a romance of Impressionist color. In all seasons, dozens of waterfalls plunge precipitously, and rapids braid around boulders. County and state parks and waysides invite the photographer to record the view of lake and cliff and cascading water. The itinerant fly-angler may pause and study his maps.

If Duluth is your headquarters for initial forays into the interior, you might want to try your luck and skill on the broad waters of the St. Louis River in Jay Cooke State Park, in Carlton County, southwest of Duluth along MN 210.

Prior to World War II a few experts took sizable brown trout in the park and brook trout from a number of feeder creeks, including

Big and Little Otter Creeks and Silver Creek, which meets the St. Louis in the park.

Then the St. Louis River fell on hard times from various nefarious forms of pollution and from the uncontrolled flow below a power dam. In 1979, a cleanup of the river began, but the problem of what constitutes sufficient water flow below a dam to support a trout fishery is still being argued.

The truth is that not many fly-fishers catch and release brown trout in the park today, so few that the St. Louis is not a designated trout stream. However, on one day in late May, Jay Paulson, whose exploits we have recorded elsewhere, and his wife were picnicking in the park behind the park office. Noticing an interesting eddy flecked with foam, Jay tied on a #12 Humpy and promptly landed two 19-inch browns. This is not a profile of a famous stream, merely an admonition to keep your rod handy and be prepared to experiment. Bill and Jim's fly-fishing lives are replete with such serendipitous adventures.

Going northeast along US 61 from Duluth, highway milepost markers can be used as guides for locating river mouths, state parks, and other points of interest. Every mile is marked with a green-and-white milepost marker. Gooseberry Falls State Park is at milepost 39; Split Rock Lighthouse at 46; Tettegouche State Park at 58.5; Crosby Manitou at 59; Temperance River State Park at 80.5; and Cascade River State Park at 100 miles.

As you head up from Duluth the rivers change in character. Close to the city the rivers are short and lack substantial headwaters systems. Therefore, in the spring they flood, then drain rapidly. In the summer the flow is slow and shallow. Farther up the North Shore, the streams are more complex, extending deeper into the interior. The watersheds are extensive and include lakes and marshes. Beavers have added thousands of small impoundments.

THE KNIFE RIVER
DeLorme 66 & 67

Without attempting to draw with too fine a point, we'd say that the Knife River, which empties into the lake at the junction of St. Louis and Lake Counties, is the first major complex with excellent fishing for brook, brown, and rainbow trout in its upper reaches. The Knife is also the Shore's most popular steelhead stream. It is one of the few where the barriers are not imposing enough to prevent migratory rainbows from working their way up into the headwaters. The Knife is said to contain about 70 percent of the Shore's steelhead spawning water. Because of the quality of the steelhead habitat, special regulations apply. The river and its tributaries, from County Road 9 upstream, are open only from May 15 (the date may vary), rather than on the traditional Saturday closest to April 15. The closing date is September 30, as usual.

The Knife is crossed by County Roads 9 and 11 west of Two Harbors, and by several county roads upstream. Upstream from County Road 11 is as good a place to start as any.

Lodging and dining facilities at Two Harbors, milepost 26.

THE GOOSEBERRY COMPLEX
DeLorme 67

The next major complex is the Gooseberry River at Gooseberry State Park, milepost 39, where the river rushes over three spectacular falls. This river is deceiving. In late summer the volume of water reaching the lake may seem too meager to support good fishing in the upper reaches. But go up and inland to find excellent fly-fishing for brook trout. According to Dr. Thomas F. Waters in his comprehensive work *The Streams and Rivers of Minnesota,* and in his lovingly written *The Superior North Shore,* water is lost downstream through seepage into fractured rock.

The barrier to anadromous penetration into the interior is 7.3 miles up from the lake; the main stem extends for another 25 miles and contains brooks, browns, and rainbows.

Your opportunities for stream trout lie upstream of County Road 3 and east of County Road 2, straight north out of Two Harbors.

Travelers' accommodations at Two Harbors and at Silver Bay.

THE BAPTISM RIVER COMPLEX
DeLorme 77

Past Split Rock Lighthouse at milepost 46, which is worth a stop to see the historic lighthouse and a brilliant panorama over the lake, and the town of Silver Bay at milepost 54, you'll reach the mouth of

the Baptism in Tettegouche State Park at milepost 58.5. The first
boundary is 5 miles upstream and the main stem extends for only 3.4
miles above the barrier. Beyond that, the Baptism splits into the East
and West Branches, some 14 miles on each leg, where you'll find brook
trout, browns, and some rainbows.

MN 1 parallels the West Branch upstream toward Finland for 4 or
5 miles, then crosses it upstream. At Finland, the East Branch of the
Baptism, which contains more naturally reproducing browns than
the West Branch, parallels County Road 7, also known as Cramer
Road. This is where we suggest that you test the river, as far upstream as Blesner Creek in Crosby Manitou State Park. There are
wide, slow places on the East Branch where a canoe or float tube may
be advantageous. This long stretch is easy to fly-fish and will produce
better-than-average brown trout in the slow pools. Woolly Worms
and Muddlers are suggested if trout aren't feeding on insects at the
surface.

Downstream from Finland the Baptism is rocky and steep, dropping some 700 feet in 10 miles to the lake.

Facilities at Silver Bay and all along US 61.

Bill Shogren with a brown from the East Branch of the Baptism River.
The Pass Lake Streamer is a favorite pattern.

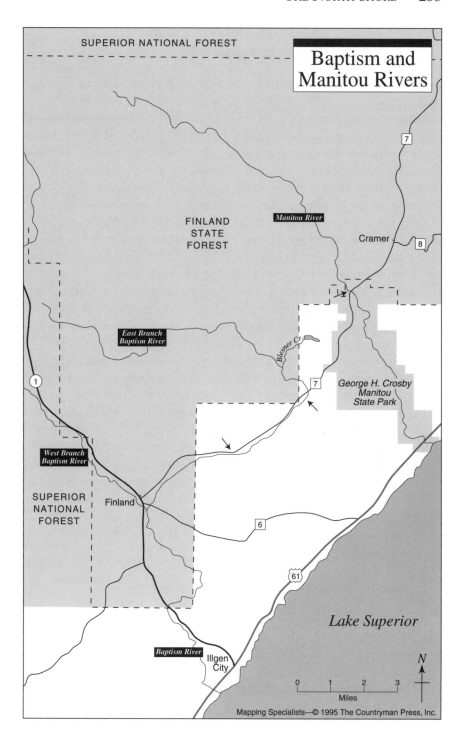

Baptism and Manitou Rivers

SUPERIOR NATIONAL FOREST

FINLAND STATE FOREST

Manitou River

Cramer

7

8

East Branch Baptism River

Blesner Cr.

7

George H. Crosby Manitou State Park

West Branch Baptism River

SUPERIOR NATIONAL FOREST

Finland

1

6

61

Lake Superior

Baptism River

Illgen City

N

0   1   2   3
Miles

Mapping Specialists—© 1995 The Countryman Press, Inc.

THE BEAVER RIVER
DeLorme 77

If you enjoy long walks into the interior wilderness and can follow a trail without getting lost, this Beaver River is for you. Follow the directions closely and carry overnight survival gear—compass, matches, bug dope, a tested flashlight or two, food and water, and a stout knife, just in case. Always let someone know where you are going, in the event of a fall and a breakage of bone. Humphrey always recommends a wading staff to prevent falls in the wrong places. Shogren, being younger, relies on strength and common sense.

Take Heffelfinger Road, Forest Road 397, out of Finland (on MN 1) for 14.8 miles west to Forest Road 399. Go left for 4 miles to the orange steel gate. Walk in on the trail; keep to the main trail. In a half hour you'll find a bridge that crosses Little Big 39 Creek. Another 20 minutes should take you to the Beaver. There's a fine pool below the bridge and others above the bridge where there has been some habitat improvement. Appreciate the fly-fishing over brooks, browns, and maybe rainbows, but give yourself time to walk out before darkness settles in.

Which reminds us of Bill's tale of woe. When obtaining directions from DNR personnel, Bill was told, "It's about 15 minutes in to a good section of stream." What they forgot to mention was that they were on an ATV, which moves faster than walking pace. It took Bill almost an hour to cover the same ground! Interrogate your sources and record their directions. DNR and national forest personnel are eager to help, and they always want to know how you fared on their recommended section. Report back, as we do. A postcard from your home will suffice.

You should also be able to find Forest Road 397 by going east from Jordan, which is on County Road 204, just off County Road 2.

Facilities at Silver Bay and at Tofte.

THE MANITOU RIVER COMPLEX
DeLorme 67 & 77

The Manitou River reaches the lake at milepost 59, just south of the border between Lake and Cook Counties. The first fish barrier is practically at the mouth of the river. The George H. Crosby Manitou State Park headquarters is located east of County Road 7 about 5 miles upstream from Lake Superior.

For those of you who prefer to mix camping with your fly-fishing, headquarter in Crosby Manitou and fish along the West Manitou River Trail as it drops 600 feet through the park. Both rainbow and brook trout inhabit the river through those 4 or 5 miles of flashing water. Campsites are located at a dozen locations close to the river.

Upstream, you should fish the river at the County Road 7 bridge, primarily for brook trout. We have cast a Pass Lake at dusk to enthusiastic, dark, and beautiful brookies.

A third location is farther up in the Finland State Forest. Fish the North Branch of the Manitou downstream from the trail on Forest Road 361, via Forest Road 172 from Isabella (on MN 1) east to 362 and 361.

Facilities at Two Harbors and at Schroeder.

ARROWHEAD CREEK
DeLorme 77

Arrowhead Creek, northeast of Isabella on MN 1 north of Finland in the Superior National Forest, is a premier brook trout stream. Go east from Isabella on Forest Road 172 for 0.75 mile, then north on

A beautiful cascade on the Manitou River.
Attractor flies catch the brookies here.

Forest Road 369 for 5 miles to a crossroads where Forest Road 173 comes in from the west. Take the east branch. Proceed less than a mile to the river, where the habitat has been improved. It's a little better downstream than up, through narrow and deep water around boulders, past plunge pools and lunker structures in a wild setting.

Dining and lodging at Silver Bay on US 61, and camping in the Finland State Forest and at campgrounds in the Superior National Forest.

THE TEMPERANCE RIVER COMPLEX
DeLorme 67 & 78

From here on up the coast every stream lies wholly within the boundaries of the Superior National Forest, within the Grand Portage State Forest, or within the Grand Portage Indian Reservation at the Canadian border. Consequently, there are few highways, but many unimproved roads and trails. A Superior National Forest map (see "Maps" in chapter 1) will be useful in this backcountry, as will the recommended survival gear and stout hiking boots. We pack our waders and survival gear in a knapsack and hike in to the streams.

There are many campgrounds in the Superior National Forest and superb facilities all along the coast highway, but towns and villages with overnight accommodations are sparse in the interior.

We might as well get the mossy old joke out of the way. The Temperance was, probably apocryphally, so named because it had "no bar at the mouth." Most North Shore rivers, but not all, form a sandbar at the mouth during the winter. In the spring, the snowmelt washes the bars away and the anadromous species begin their migratory runs.

The Temperance fish barrier is at the lake. The main stem extends for 21 miles into the interior.

The Temperance River joins the lake at milepost 80.5. The Sawbill Trail, County Road 2 at Tofte on US 61, parallels the river upstream. As with the other river complexes, your targets are the sites where the river is wide and rocky, in this case around the Temperance River Campground, and upstream via County Road 2 and several forest roads and trails. Any of the tributaries that cross County Road 2 is worth a cast for brook trout.

At one time the Temperance, a favorite with Jim Humphrey, was a first-class brook trout stream. In recent years the river has warmed,

Sandy Rolstad fishes the fast water on the Temperance River.

for reasons that are in dispute. It may be that the many headwaters lakes and ponds have warmed due to logging and the consequent removal of shade; logging debris may also have drifted into the river. In any case, the brook trout have retreated to the feeders. To compensate, the DNR has planted browns in the main river.

The Temperance is one of the North Shore's longest rivers, having its headwaters in the Boundary Waters Canoe Area. In the middle sections it is a wide and rocky stream, the kind we love to fly-fish. And we admit to a prejudice: If browns become the dominant species of trout and char, we'll not be unduly distressed.

This may be a proper place to insert a word of warning. The last few miles of many of these North Shore rivers pitch down dangerously. The last 4 miles of the Temperance, for example, speed through an exceedingly narrow canyon. Anglers pursuing their quarry downstream into the canyons should be aware of the possibility of a sudden rise in the water level; it may be impossible to climb the rock face.

Travelers' accommodations at Tofte and all along the shore.

THE CASCADE RIVER COMPLEX
DeLorme 78

The Cascade, which drains an area of 120 square miles, begins in a complex of warm-water lakes and ponds in the Boundary Waters Canoe Area. The middle section is productive of brown trout; the tributaries contain brookies. County Road 45 crosses it about 4 miles above Cascade River State Park at milepost 100. We've fished it upstream at the Forest Road 157 crossing and farther up near the junction of County Road 57 and Forest Road 158.

The sections we waded are perfect for fly-fishing. The river is wide, with room to shoot the long casts so beloved of fly-fishers. The pools are big and the runs are deep and long, even during the low water of September. We filled out our self-imposed quotas of dark and chunky brook trout on streamers, Hare's Ears, Hornbergs, and Adamses.

The canyon downstream, above and through the park, provides spectacular scenery but difficult access; and if you find a trail down into the canyon you'll probably have to come out the way you went in. It's a unique experience for hardy souls.

Facilities at Tofte and Schroeder and camping in the park.

FOUR STREAMS OF THE GRAND MARAIS AREA

There are many wonderful rivers and creeks farther up the shore. The city of Grand Marais, milepost 110, at the beginning of the Gunflint Trail, County Road 12, is an excellent staging point for sorties into the interior.

Grand Marais is currently the northern end of the North Shore State Trail, also called the Superior Hiking Trail, a story in itself. *Backpacker* magazine has named the trail one of the nation's greatest, and one of the world's top 25. It begins in Duluth on County Road 10 and runs for 153 miles to Grand Marais. The trail is serviced by seven parking areas, 14 shelters and campsites, and 40 bridges. It crosses 60 creeks and rivers where fishermen will gain access to many interior trout streams.

Ninety-five percent of the trail traverses public lands, and because it lies away from the lake inland, it crosses the middle sections of many streams where you'll find the best fly-fishing for trout.

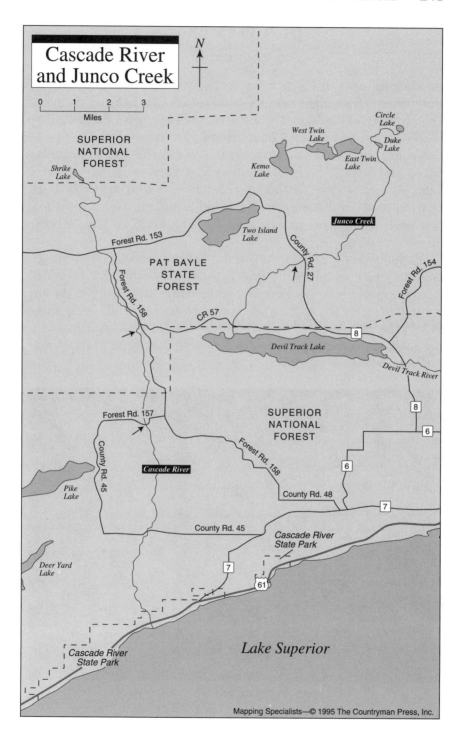

Cascade River
and Junco Creek

N

0   1   2   3
Miles

SUPERIOR
NATIONAL
FOREST

Shrike
Lake

Circle
Lake

West Twin
Lake

Duke
Lake

Kemo
Lake

East Twin
Lake

Forest Rd. 153

Two Island
Lake

Junco Creek

County Rd. 27

Forest Rd. 154

PAT BAYLE
STATE
FOREST

Forest Rd. 158

CR 57

8

Devil Track Lake

Devil Track River

8

Forest Rd. 157

6

Cascade River

SUPERIOR
NATIONAL
FOREST

Forest Rd. 158

6

County Rd. 45

Pike
Lake

County Rd. 48

7

Deer Yard
Lake

County Rd. 45

Cascade River
State Park

7

61

Cascade River
State Park

Lake Superior

Mapping Specialists—© 1995 The Countryman Press, Inc.

JUNCO CREEK
DeLorme 79

Junco Creek rises in Circle Lake north of Grand Marais and flows southwest for 18 miles to empty into Devil Track Lake on the western extremity of the lake. There are two bridge crossings, at County Road 27 upstream and at County Road 57 close to the lake.

Our recommended adventure on this wonderful stream begins at the County Road 27 bridge. Fish up- or downstream. Bill says, "There is one good spot after another. You can fly-fish with ease over much of it, but roll-casting is necessary in other places. You'll use all of your skills, going from one great spot to another. This stream beckons you onward."

The Junco has been improved with bank structures, deflector logs, half-logs, and even a Hewitt ramp. A path follows the left bank—Ah! and there goes a yearling bear across the path! Midges are in the air, but any attractor fly, such as our favorite Pass Lake, will bring these dark brook trout out of hiding.

A complete range of facilities for travelers, history enthusiasts, and fly-fishers at Grand Marais.

*The canyon section of the Devil Track River
offers long, deep, clear pools.*

DEVIL TRACK RIVER
DeLorme 79

The Devil Track is close to Grand Marais. Take US 61 north to County Road 58; then go 8 blocks to a parking area on the Superior Hiking Trail. Approximately 2 blocks on the trail takes you to the canyon section of the Devil Track. The climb down to the river is not easy; coming up is worse, but you'll be rewarded with complex pools and stocked rainbow trout. It's gorgeous here—the pools are 20 to 40 feet long and 4 feet deep. You might even encounter a moose at the Moose Crossing sign, and that may be the most awe-inspiring memory of your trip.

Comprehensive accommodations at Grand Marais.

KADUNCE CREEK
DeLorme 79

Go north on US 61 to County Road 14; follow it north and east to the stream. Fish downstream or up at several Forest Road 140 crossings. The fish barrier on Kadunce is close to the lake; the river length is a bit more than 7 miles. This is a scenic brook trout stream with beaver dams and sparkling riffles upstream and a state wayside at the mouth. We like this one a lot, as does Sandy Rolstad, of the Twin Cities Chapter of TU. We three like it for its prolific brook trout and its manageable size, more probably because it is not so famous as the river complexes and attracts fewer fly-fishers. There is a fish sanctuary for 0.2 mile close to the mouth, where fishing is permitted from June 1 through August 31 only.

Facilities and amenities at Grand Marais.

IRISH CREEK
DeLorme 79

Irish Creek is as far as we go up the North Shore on this trip, but it is one stream that you may want to reach for. Take US 61 along the coast toward Hovland. Go north on County Road 16 for 8.5 miles to Irish Creek Timber Road, then left for 1 mile to the bridge. We had a ball there, casting an Adams and a Royal Coachman streamer to 6- to 8-

inch brook trout. There is a series of pools below the bridge where the brook trout collect at the surface. Beavers have taken over much of the stream; we're not sure whether their constructions will improve or degrade the stream, but for now it's great.

Facilities at Grand Marais and Hovland.

After our bouncing around all over the North Shore Arrowhead Country, our admonition to you is to confine your exploration to one watershed. Invest a week and get to know the main stem and its many feeders. Don't overlook the backcountry lakes that are managed for stream trout. Bring your float tube and canoe.

If you must fly-fish for anadromous species below the barriers, bring your heavy-duty rods and reels and yarn flies.

You might even cast for a triple play: anadromous rainbows and chinooks at the mouth of a river, brook trout, browns, and rainbows in the middle sections, and stream trout in a hundred lakes. This may be one of the best areas for fly-fishers in the Lower 48—if you search for its secrets. It may be the wildest experience outside of Canada. Come and explore.

Maps of these wonders are available at many commercial establishments along the shore, in the coastal towns, at state parks, and in the Superior National Forest.

10

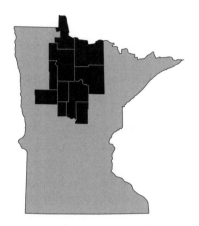

Northern Minnesota:
Paul Bunyan Country

This immense area was the domain of the legendary Paul Bunyan, the mightiest lumberjack of them all, and Babe the blue ox. Today, representations of that pair can be seen in the environs of Brainerd in Crow Wing County, a gateway to the northern playgrounds of Minnesota. At the Paul Bunyan Center, junction of MN 210 and MN 371, the world's largest animated talking Paul tells stories from the lumbering days. Your children will love talking to Paul.

This is the land of 10,000 lakes, thousands of miles of rivers and creeks, hundreds of resorts, state and national forests, Native American reservations, the sprawling, empty Koochiching State Forest, and the wilderness of the Voyageurs National Park and the Boundary Waters Canoe Area. Many species of wild mammals inhabit the forests and graze in the glades. White-tailed deer are omnipresent; those ubiquitous beaver, which maintain a near-symbiotic relationship with humans, constitute a pest on many trout streams. You may encounter a bear foraging for grubs or berries; if so, keep your distance. There are moose in the Boundary Waters and north of the Iron Range, and coyotes, bobcats, and lynx.

You may hear wolves ululate under a gibbous moon not far north of the city of Bemidji. Two thousand gray wolves range the northern forests; there is even a pack in the Mille Lacs National Wildlife Area, just 70 miles north of the Twin Cities. There has been no recorded incident of a wolf attacking a human but you shouldn't let toddlers or young children wander far. Wolves are territorial; they particularly don't welcome dogs in their living room.

You will probably not see the secretive cougar, known variously as puma, panther, and mountain lion, but a few of them range down from Canada into the northern reaches. We count our blessings that some small part of the original America has been saved for future generations.

Anglers come primarily to seek the tasty walleye, the elusive muskie, the deepwater lake trout, or the smallmouth bass in the primal waters of the canoe country. Other visitors come from around the world so they can brag that they jumped across the Mississippi. Well, that's not quite true, but you can walk across the Mississippi on a series of stepping-stones at the outlet of Lake Itasca in Clearwater County north of Park Rapids off US 71.

The search for the source of the Mississippi is a fascinating tale of challenge, defeat, and ultimate success. As early as 1700, DuCharleville, a Frenchman out of New Orleans, turned back discouraged at St. Anthony's Falls in what is now Minneapolis. In 1805, Lieutenant Zebulon Pike, of Pike's Peak fame, reached Cass Lake. Close, but no cigar. In 1823, Count Beltrami, an Italian adventurer, declared a small lake north of Bemidji as the true source. Not quite. In 1832, Henry Rowe Schoolcraft, a geologist who hoped to help make peace between the Ojibway (Chippewa) and the Dakota (Sioux) tribes, arrived at Lake LaBiche, where he concocted the name Itasca by dropping the first and last syllables from the Latin, *veritas caput,* meaning true head. And you thought that Itasca was a Native American name.

Fly-fishers who tire of boats, roaring outboards, and racing Jetskis on the flat water of the lakes can don boots to wade more than 100 secluded trout streams in Paul Bunyan country, far from the madding crowd. Crow Wing County alone has 13 trout streams, Cass County to the north encloses 17, and Hubbard to the northwest includes 15.

Farther north, Beltrami County has seven streams, including the long Clearwater River, which harbors both brown and rainbow trout. Even Clearwater County, the site of Lake Itasca, has seven streams. St. Louis County, which is partly in the Arrowhead region of the state, contains 85 designated trout streams.

Although they are widely dispersed, there is a trout stream for every taste, from brook trout rivulet to wide-bodied water for better-than-average brown trout. We showcase four streams of differing aspects in this north central section. You can search out more trout streams on your voyage of discovery into the wilds of northern Minnesota.

STONEY BROOK
DeLorme 54

Stoney Brook rises in Cass County and flows for 19 miles to empty into Upper Gull Lake west of Nisswa. Although it is a long brook, only the last 2 miles through public land or leased easements have been extensively improved during the past decade. Much of the bull work on the stream has been performed, and partly paid for, by a handful of dedicated trout fishers from the Paul Bunyan Chapter of Trout Unlimited. Other Minnesota chapters have contributed funds for the annual projects.

To summarize the work projects: Hewitt ramps were repaired, banks stabilized, a log bridge constructed, runs deepened, bank covers and lunker structures installed, and riprap and brush bundles added. The list goes on, and the fishing for naturally reproducing brook and respectable browns is an example of the improvement possible through the cooperation of the Minnesota Department of Natural Resources and volunteers.

Stoney Brook is not a wide stream. Fly-fishers will need to move carefully, utilizing the utmost skill with short rods, light lines, and short, fine leaders under a dense canopy of trees. Although we usually recommend the longest leader you can handle, in brush you'll have to go short and fine if you want to keep your leader out of the trees. A poet might describe the experience as fly-fishing under the nave of a cathedral.

We suggest that you begin your exploration of the brook at the Fritz Loven County Park close to the shore of Upper Gull Lake. Take

*Minnesota's DNR and Trout Unlimited (led by Mickey Johnson)
revived Stoney Brook with habitat improvements.*

MN 371 north from Brainerd toward Nisswa past Round Lake on
the east, then proceed west on County Road 77 to County Road 78.
Cross Upper Gull and take the first road north to the park. There is
additional DNR parking upstream where County Road 78, having
turned north, parallels the stream. The park section is quite open; the
upstream section, where much of the improvement work is visible, is
the stretch that might be likened to the nave of a cathedral.

We have participated in similar grunt work on the Kinnickinnic,
the Willow, and the Rush Rivers of Wisconsin and Trout Brook in
Minnesota, so it is always a special thrill for us to reap the rewards
of the work of our fellow anglers on their cherished streams. Therefore, we always release our trout on Stoney Brook in deference to
their labors; we hope that you will, too, out of the goodness of your
heart.

Cass County has 16 additional trout streams, all brooks or creeks,
except for the Shingobee River, which lies partly in Hubbard County.
Inquire locally for information on their current potential.

*All possible facilities at Brainerd, Nisswa, and dozens of lake re-
sorts.*

THE STRAIGHT RIVER
DeLorme 61

The Straight River, which for many years was considered to be the best brown trout stream in the state, with 4- to 6-pound browns being common, lies west of the city of Park Rapids, which is at the junction of US 71 and MN 34. The Straight flows from Straight Lake in Becker County at Osage on MN 34 southeast into Hubbard County.

The Straight had fallen on hard times for more than a decade, but now we believe it is coming back, due to the efforts of the DNR. We don't know if it will ever again attain that exalted title of the best trout stream, because there are too many other streams that have been improved in the last few years, but it is a good one now.

Local anglers identify a location on the river by referring to distance from Park Rapids, that is "Two Mile Bridge," "Five Mile," and so on. Visiting anglers should take a leaf from their books. County Road 117, the division between Becker and Hubbard Counties, is "Five Mile." County Road 123 at Osage is "Nine Mile."

Although this river flows from a lake, with all the potential that implies for warming water downstream, there are many springs to cool the water sufficiently for trout. Douglas Herman, an angler who has fished the river for years, notes that within ½ mile or so of the lake outlet the Straight's volume has already doubled as a result of spring flow.

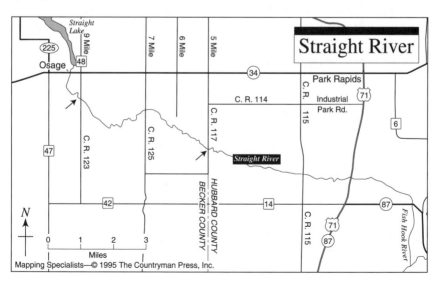

This river reminds us of the upper Kinnickinnic of Wisconsin. The banks are brushy and there's silt at the margins, but there is also a narrow wading path of sand and gravel down the middle. Anglers can enter the river at any of the bridges or culverts and from a number of paths that lead to the river between the bridges. The state owns blocks of land on the river, particularly upstream of Five and Six Mile entries, and has acquired easements above Nine Mile, and for most of the section between Three and Four Mile, downstream of Two Mile, and on the north side of the river between One Mile and US 71.

We can recommend the public lands above Five Mile where brown trout are known to reproduce (more than 1000 trout per mile) and the ½ mile or more upstream of Six Mile where Humphrey's fly-fishing pal Dick Frantes sold easements on 80 acres to the DNR. You can hike to the river from the dead end of Six Mile Road on the north. This is where Humphrey would fish if he were going out to-morrow. Bill Shogren has had excellent brown trout fishing upstream of Five Mile, very late evenings in June. Even though the Hex hatch did not appear on this latest June trip, due no doubt to a week of cold weather, his Muddler was good for a 16-inch brown. On his way out around 11 PM, Bill exchanged notes with two young enthusiasts, Chad Hanson and Dan Grabow from the city of Detroit Lakes, who had released one 17-inch brown. They told Bill that the Hex hatch was just building.

The large and juicy *Hexagenia limbata,* which has appeared on the river as early as June 10, probably accounts for the fact that the browns here can grow large. Look for the Hex during the latter weeks of June and the first two weeks of July. Try streamers fished deep in and around the logjams if there is no surface activity. Ed Atcas, a skilled fly-fisher from the Twin Cities, swims tarpon flies for outsize brown trout! We know big-fish fishers who throw black and silver Rapalas for huge brown trout, so why not tarpon flies?

An angler is more likely to find the Hex in the upper 3 miles of the river, which are slower and more silted; lower down there's more swift water and gravel. Huge browns are taken below Straight Lake, where there are easements above and below Nine Mile crossing.

Although, as noted above, there is good natural reproduction in only one section, browns have not been planted in recent years. The DNR's goal is to improve trout habitat to allow for natural repro-duction, which makes sense to us.

The Kabekona River in Hubbard County produces some nice brookies.

Becker County has 6 additional designated trout streams; Hubbard has a total of 15, including the Kabekona River, our next stop on this modest sample of northern Minnesota.

All facilities for travelers at Park Rapids and at many lake resorts.

THE KABEKONA RIVER
DeLorme 61 & 71

The Kabekona River rises in the Paul Bunyan State Forest in Hubbard County and flows southeast into Kabekona Lake near MN 64. US 71 and MN 200 intersect at the crossroads village of Kabekona, about two-thirds of the way up the river from the lake.

We recommend that you begin at the culvert on County Road 36, 0.5 mile north of MN 200 and 3 miles west of the town of Laporte. Fish upstream, taking the middle, and cast to every likely spot. Wear chest-high waders, move slowly while casting an attractor like the Pass Lake, and you may have a fabulous day, as we did. Bill took the day's prize with a chunky, superbly painted 10-inch brookie taken on a Mickey Finn. "A phenomenal day!" said Bill.

A walking and snowmobile trail bridge over the Dark River

As noted elsewhere, Bill can become ecstatic when wading up cold, deep, difficult, and demanding brook trout streams; Jim prefers brown trout taken from complex pools. Pulled in two directions, they cover the country and a spectrum of streams.

There is a second entry at the gravel road west of County Road 36. This section, which is 7 miles from the mouth of the river, according to a DNR report, " . . . has mostly hard sand bottom, undercut banks, with brush and vegetation overhanging the stream." In a recent electro-shocking survey the brook trout ranged from 3.0 to 11.4 inches. Surveys on other sections recorded "quality-size" brookies, 8 to 10 inches, at all locations; "preferred size," 10 to 12 inches, at four of five locations, and "memorable size," 12 to 14 inches, at two of five stations. These are not large fish by the standards of some anglers, but then, an 11-inch brook trout is a rarity throughout its range, in spite of all the stories one hears about 12- and 14-inchers creeled routinely. In short, Kabekona is an excellent brook trout stream with a satisfactory mix of riffles and pools, and with the high probability of creeling a breakfast of sweet brook trout. If a solution is found to the overly energetic work of Paddy the Beaver, Kabekona will improve.

Other access points are at County Road 44 in the headwaters, at

US 71, on MN 200, and southwest of Laporte on County Road 93. This lower section broadens, flattens, and slows.

Much of the land surrounding the stream is publicly owned, and easements have been leased through most of the remainder.

Some facilities at Laporte; everything at Bemidji to the north and Walker to the south.

THE DARK RIVER
DeLorme 75

The Dark River, appropriately named for its root beer coloration, rises in St. Louis County north and west of Virginia on the Mesabi Iron Range. It may be easier to get to the choice section of the Dark by going north out of Chisholm on MN 73. It flows for more than 20 miles to join the Sturgeon River, which in turn flows north into the Rainy River and some of the most remote country of the continent. After that, trace its ultimate destination, if you can.

According to a report by the Waybinahbe Chapter of Trout Unlimited: The Dark River is the premier trout stream north of Chisholm.

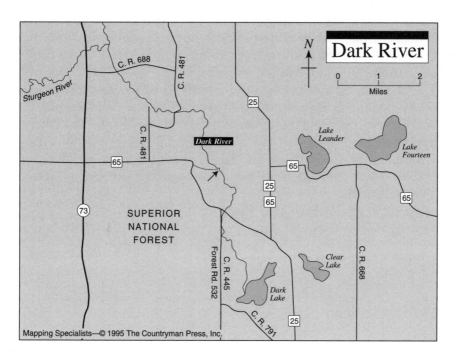

In recent years, the DNR and the Forest Service have worked jointly to enhance the fishery through extensive habitat improvement. Access has also been improved, by clearing a walking trail and creating casting room along the stream.

Most of the river lies within the boundaries of the Superior National Forest or within the Sturgeon River State Forest. It is wilderness fishing, but accessible. Because the headwaters are close to iron mine settling ponds, which warm the water, we do not recommend the river upstream of Dark Lake. Below the lake the river may be reached from MN 73 (north of Chisholm) via Forest Road 272, County Road 65, and County Road 688 above the Sturgeon River. You will find other roads and trails to the river if you consult your DeLorme or St. Louis County maps.

The 10½ miles from Dark Lake to the junction with the Sturgeon River are described in a DNR report: "The river flows from flat terrain covered with ash, aspen, birch, alder, willow, and grasses through a steep rolling forested area covered predominantly with jack pine, Norway pine, aspen, and birch. The soil is composed mainly of sand and rock." Ownership is 90 percent federal and 10 percent private.

The Dark River contains a thriving population of brook trout, with some brown trout reproduction. In an unusual turn of events that puzzles fisheries managers, the brook trout are taking over from the browns. Usually the brown trout drive out the brookies in water that is suitable for both. Large brown trout are more likely to be found close to the junction with the Sturgeon River.

Our preferred entries are at the County Road 65 crossing and secondly downstream, from the trail where County Road 65 takes a southward turn. On a recent occasion we released browns of 15, 12, and 10 inches.

Beavers are a problem on the Dark, but a trapper has been hired to remove some dams so trout can move upstream to their preferred spawning areas.

Facilities at Chisholm and Virginia.

Appendix A

Fly-Fishing Shops and Guides

FLY-FISHING SHOPS

Wisconsin

The FlyFishers
8601 W. Greenfield Ave.
Milwaukee, WI 53214
414-259-8100

Lunde's Fly Fishing Chalet
2491 Highway 92
Mt. Horeb, WI 53572
608-437-5465

Laacke and Joys
1433 N. Water St.
Milwaukee, WI 53202
414-271-7878

Brule River Classics
Highway 27, PO Box 306
Brule, WI 54820
715-372-8153

Spring Creek Angler
PO Box 283
Coon Valley, WI 54623
608-452-3430

Fontana Sports
6678 Odana Road
Madison, WI 53701
608-833-0678

Bob's Fly Shop
1504 Velp Ave.
Green Bay, WI 54303
414-499-4737

Anglers All
2803 Lake Shore Drive
Ashland, WI 54802
715-682-5754

Ace Hardware
500 E. Northland Ave.
Appleton, WI 54911
414-731-0500

Mike's Mobil Service
Junction Hwys. 55 & 64, Langlade
White Lake, WI 54491
715-882-8901

Wolf River Fly Shop
Rocky Rips Road, Langlade
White Lake, WI 54491
715-882-5941

The Sporting Goods & Fly Shop
118 S. Broadway
De Pere, Wl 54115
414-336-4427

Minnesota

Burger Brothers
"5 Metro Locations," St. Paul/
  Minneapolis
9801 Lyndale Ave. (Bloomington)
Minneapolis, MN 55420
612-884-8842

Burger Brothers
1201 S. Broadway
Rochester, MN 55902
507-289-4224

The Fly Angler
7500 University Ave. N.E.
Minneapolis, MN 55432
612-572-0717

Bob Mitchell's Fly Shop
3394 Lake Elmo Ave. N.
Lake Elmo, MN 55042
612-770-5854

Rodcraft
6445 Lyndale Ave. S.
Richfield, MN 55423
612-869-7151

Joe's Sporting Goods/Ski Shop
935 N. Dale at Como
St. Paul, MN 55103
612-488-5511

NEIGHBORING STATES

Iowa

Second Avenue Bait House (Orvis)
133 Franklin
Des Moines, IA 50314
515-282-4217

Illinois

Fly & Field, Inc.
560 Crescent Blvd.

Glen Ellyn, IL 60137
708-858-7844

Wildlife Refuge, Inc.
1130 E. Main
Carbondale, IL 62901
618-529-2524

Trout & Grouse
300 Happ Road
Northfield, IL 60093
708-501-3111

Saturday Morning Company
126 W. Main St.
Barrington, IL 60010
708-382-3010

Orvis Chicago
142 E. Ontario at Michigan
Chicago, IL 60611
312-440-0662

STREAM GUIDES

WISCONSIN

Southeast

Trout Bum, C.A.
John Langhout/Bill Rishel
PO Box 182
Plymouth, WI 53073
414-892-4909

Southwest

Rocking Trout Spring Creek
  Fishing Service
Clay Riness
PO Box 166, 400 Anderson St.
Coon Valley, WI 54623
608-452-3433

Spring Creek Angler
Dennis Graupe

PO Box 283
Coon Valley, WI 54623
608-452-3430

Northeast

Tom Urban's Fishin' Pole Guide
  Service
Tom Urban
916 Margaret St.
Rhinelander, WI 54501
715-362-3618

John Ramsay
N15414 Black River Road
Ironwood, MI 49938
906-932-1093 or 932-4038

Northwest

Brule River Classics
Chloe Manz
Highway 27, PO Box 306
Brule, WI 54820 715-372-8153

Brule River Guide
Roger Lindelof
PO Box 164
Glenwood City, WI 54013
715-372-8719

Lorn D. Bown
2500 Spruce Road
Webster, WI 54893
715-635-7989

Rick Mosse Guide Service
Rick Mosse
2017 Lackawanna Ave.
Superior, WI 54880
715-392-5293

Iron River Trout Haus
Ron Johnson
PO Box 662, 205 W. Drummond
  Road
Iron River, WI 54847
715-372-4219 or 1-800-262-1453

Steve Therrien
1708 N. 21st St.
Superior, WI 54880
715-392-4685

Central

Springwater Guide Service
Ron Manz
11710 S. 64th St.
Wisconsin Rapids, WI 54494
Call after 3 PM: 715-325-5412
After 5 PM: 608-635-4700

MINNESOTA

Southeast

Wayne Bartz
328 18½ Ave. S.W.
Rochester, MN 55902
507-289-7312

Bill Haugen
PO Box 221
Rushford, MN 55971
507-864-2867

North Shore

Black Bear Outfitters
Dick Krech
332 Highway 1
Silver Bay, MN 55614
218-353-7315

Appendix B

Resource Texts and Equipment for the Study of Aquatic Insects

There's a jungle of information (misinformation, too) to plunge through before you can identify common mayflies and other aquatic insects, but don't lose hope yet. A handful of introductory texts will point the way. Number one on our short list is the *Instant Mayfly Identification Guide* by Caucci & Nastasi (Comparahatch Ltd., 1984), cheap and available at your fly shop. Two: *Naturals, A Guide to Food Organisms of the Trout* by Gary A. Borger (Stackpole Books, 1980). Three: *Aquatic Entomology* by W. Patrick McCafferty (Science Books International, 1981), available in softcover: a wealth of general information, including superb illustrations. Four: *Selective Trout*, in softcover, by Doug Swisher and Carl Richards (New Century Publishers, Inc., 1971). Appendix A of this one is a gold mine. Five: *Hatches, A Complete Guide to Fishing the Hatches of North American Trout Streams* by Al Caucci and Bob Nastasi (Comparahatch, Ltd., 1975). Six: *Nymphs, A Complete Guide to Naturals and Imitations* by Ernest Schwiebert (Winchester Press, 1973).

For those more technically inclined, we recommend the monograph by W.L. Hilsenhoff of the University of Wisconsin Department of Entomology, entitled "Aquatic Insects of Wisconsin." It may be found in your library under the call letters QL 468.W62 or W595 7H, or purchased from the Geological and Natural History Survey, 1815 University Ave., Madison WI 53706. Among other things, it lists those aquatic insects that are indigenous to Wisconsin and contiguous states. (Understand, though, that Lake Michigan represents a barrier that some mayfly species cannot cross.)

If you decide to go whole hog you'll want *The Mayflies of North and Central America,* the definitive work, by Edmunds, Jensen, and Berner. The first edition, University of Minnesota Press, is out of print, but it may since have been reprinted by a publisher that specializes in reprints. Or consult your used-book dealer.

In our opinion, identification of nymphs is more difficult than identification of duns or spinners, so in recent years we've equipped ourselves with a butterfly net, a small aquarium net hooked to the belt, and a couple of small plastic bottles. Sweep at least five specimens of the duns or adults out of the air or off the surface and transfer them to a bottle. They will be easy to examine at home under a bright light with an 8- or 10-power magnifier. Once you gain experience, specimens can frequently be identified on-stream with a 3-power loupe.

If you prefer to begin your studies by picking nymphs from stones or waterweeds, carry the white cover of a pillbox. Pop the nymph and a little water into the cover and you can count its gills and watch the sequential action of its breathing. A 2- or 3-power glass will be adequate for that examination. Nymphs must be returned to the stream unless you have a collector's license from the Wisconsin Department of Natural Resources at Madison, WI 53702.

Specimens may be preserved for a year or two in a 50/50 mix of alcohol* and water. The positive identification of a handful of aquatic insects will add one more dimension to your art of fishing for trout.

*Ethyl alcohol is preferred but not generally available. Isopropyl alcohol works O.K.

About the Authors

Jim Humphrey, a native of Milwaukee and an intermittent resident of Minnesota, is active in the Twin Cities Chapter of Trout Unlimited. Before he quit his job to write novels, he was operations vice-president for a group of insurance companies. Twice he was the Minnesota state fencing champion; and he plays chess. He has lived in 6 states and fly-fished for trout in 14. Jim lectures, occasionally guides, and has published more than 100 articles about trout fishing under the name J.R. Humphrey.

Bill Shogren has lived all his life in Wisconsin and Minnesota, except for short stays in Cincinnati, Ohio, and Chicago, Illinois. He has been active in Trout Unlimited, holding the positions of president of the Twin Cities Chapter, president of the Minnesota State Council, and board member of both organizations. Bill fly-fishes for all the freshwater species and has fished for trout in the Midwest, the West, and South America. Recent years have brought Bill and his fly rod to the salt flats of Florida and the Caribbean for bonefish, permit, and tarpon.

Index of Streams

Also from The Countryman Press and Backcountry Publications

The Countryman Press and Backcountry Publications, long known for their fine books on the outdoors, offer a range of practical and readable manuals on fishing and fly-tying.

Bass Flies, Dick Stewart
Building Classic Salmon Flies, Ron Alcott
Fishing Small Streams with a Fly Rod, Charles Meck
Fishing Vermont's Streams and Lakes, Peter F. Cammann
Flies in the Water, Fish in the Air, Jim Arnosky
Fly-Fishing with Children: A Guide for Parents, Philip Brunquell,
Fly-Tying Tips, Second Edition (revised), Dick Stewart
Good Fishing in the Adirondacks, Edited by Dennis Aprill
Good Fishing in the Catskills, Second Edition (revised) Jim Capossela, with others
Good Fishing in Lake Ontario and Its Tributaries, Second Edition (revised) Rich Giessuebel
Good Fishing in Western New York, Edited by C. Scott Sampson
Great Lakes Steelhead: A Guided Tour for Fly-Anglers, Bob Linsenman and Steve Nevala
Ice Fishing: A Complete Guide...Basic to Advanced, Jim Capossela
Michigan Trout Streams: A Fly-Angler's Guide, Bob Linsenman and Steve Nevala
Pennsylvania Trout Streams and Their Hatches, Charles Meck
Trout Streams of Southern Appalachia: Fly-Casting in Georgia, Kentucky, North Carolina, South Carolina and Tennessee, Jimmy Jacobs
Ultralight Spin-Fishing: A Practical Guide for Freshwater and Saltwater Anglers, Peter F. Cammann
Universal Fly Tying Guide, Second Edition (revised), Dick Stewart
Virginia Trout Streams, Second Edition (revised) Harry Slone

We publish many guides to canoeing, hiking, walking, bicycling, and ski touring in New England, the Mid-Atlantic states, and the Midwest.

Our books are available through bookstores, or they may be ordered directly from the publisher. For ordering information, or for a complete catalog, please contact:

The Countryman Press
W.W. Norton & Company, Inc.
800 Keystone Industrial Park
Scranton, PA 18512
http://web.wwnorton.com